P9-BBU-492

Keep Your Brain Sharp

This book is dedicated to Carolyn Horne. Carolyn's life is testimony to the way personal choices can produce eminence and expertise at work, and closeness and intimacy in relationships at 50+.

As a tomboy teenager, Carolyn did not consider herself good at books, or good at boys. She studied pottery and drama and became an accomplished actress and, eventually, an inspiring teacher. Ever curious about what went on in the heads of her children, Carolyn took time out to study for a degree in psychology at Bedford College, London. Later she switched from educational psychology to teacher training. Again, she took time out to study for a Masters in Education, producing seminal research on 'the match' in early years' development.

At 50+, as Director of Education at the now University of Cumbria, Carolyn built the UK's largest single campus programme of primary education in the UK. Her innovative programmes were characterized by creative thinking on early years' child development, novel forms of in-service training and new, accelerated forms of full-time study.

At 50+, Carolyn agreed to take on a UK college that was faced with imminent closure by inspectors. She and her team turned the college around in less than six months. The day after she got the good news about her college, Carolyn was hit by a car and killed, while training for her second London marathon.

At 50+, Carolyn's death was a tragic loss for her husband, her family and her many close friends. Her death also deprived the world of the burgeoning benefits of her 50+ brain, which would have continued to add life to all our years for at least another 30 years!

Teach Yourself®

Keep Your Brain Sharp

Terry Horne and
Simon Wootton

For UK order enquiries: please contact Bookpoint Ltd,
130 Milton Park, Abingdon, Oxon OX14 4SB.
Telephone: +44 (0) 1235 827720. Fax: +44 (0) 1235 400454.
Lines are open 09.00–17.00, Monday to Saturday, with a 24-hour
message answering service. Details about our titles and how to
order are available at www.teachyourself.com

For USA order enquiries: please contact McGraw-Hill Customer
Services, PO Box 545, Blacklick, OH 43004-0545, USA.
Telephone: 1-800-722-4726. Fax: 1-614-755-5645.

For Canada order enquiries: please contact McGraw-Hill Ryerson Ltd,
300 Water St, Whitby, Ontario L1N 9B6, Canada.
Telephone: 905 430 5000. Fax: 905 430 5020.

Long renowned as the authoritative source for self-guided learning –
with more than 50 million copies sold worldwide – the **Teach Yourself**
series includes over 500 titles in the fields of languages, crafts, hobbies,
business, computing and education.

British Library Cataloguing in Publication Data: a catalogue record
for this title is available from the British Library.

Library of Congress Catalog Card Number: on file.

First published in UK 2008 by Hodder Education, part of
Hachette UK, 338 Euston Road, London NW1 3BH.

First published in US 2010 by The McGraw-Hill Companies, Inc.

This edition published 2011.

Previously published as *Teach Yourself Training Your Brain for
the Over 50s*.

The **Teach Yourself** name is a registered trademark of
Hodder Headline.

Copyright © 2008, 2010 Simon Wootton and Terry Horne

In UK: All rights reserved. Apart from any permitted use under UK
copyright law, no part of this publication may be reproduced or
transmitted in any form or by any means, electronic or mechanical,
including photocopy, recording, or any information, storage and
retrieval system, without permission in writing from the publisher
or under licence from the Copyright Licensing Agency Limited.
Further details of such licences (for reprographic reproduction)
may be obtained from the Copyright Licensing Agency Limited,
of Saffron House, 6–10 Kirby Street, London EC1N 8TS.

In US: All rights reserved. Except as permitted under the United
States Copyright Act of 1976, no part of this publication may be
reproduced or distributed in any form or by any means, or stored in
a database or retrieval system, without the prior written permission
of the publisher.

Typeset by MPS Limited, a Macmillan Company.

Printed in Great Britain for Hodder Education, an Hachette UK
Company, 338 Euston Road, London NW1 3BH, by CPI Group
(UK) Ltd, Croydon, CR0 4YY.

The publisher has used its best endeavours to ensure that the URLs
for external websites referred to in this book are correct and active
at the time of going to press. However, the publisher and the author
have no responsibility for the websites and can make no guarantee
that a site will remain live or that the content will remain relevant,
decent or appropriate.

Hachette UK's policy is to use papers that are natural, renewable
and recyclable products and made from wood grown in sustainable
forests. The logging and manufacturing processes are expected to
conform to the environmental regulations of the country of origin.

Impression number   10 9 8 7 6 5
Year   2015 2014 2013 2012

Acknowledgements

We are indebted to so many brain researchers (biologists, biochemists, neurologists, neuroscientists, dieticians, social workers and cognitive psychologists), and so many brain research centres specializing in ageing, that it is iniquitous to name only five individuals and three centres.

That said, we especially acknowledge that much of our material was first researched with Roger Armstrong at LBS, University of Central Lancashire; Peter Checkland, Department of Systems Thinking and Practice, University of Lancaster; Tony Doherty, at the Centre for Social Enterprise, University of London; P. J. Howard at the Centre for Cognitive Studies in Carolina, USA; Sayaka Mitsuhashi of the Okinawa Centenarian Centre; and David Gamon, Allen Bragdon, Ian Robertson, Guy Brown, Susan Greenfield, Jeff Victoroff, James Fixx, Rosemarie Janski, Zak Tan, Pam Ayres, Felix Dennis, Ian Deary, David Snowdon, Paul McKenna, Richard Templar, Sally Moon and Nathan Haselbayer of the International High IQ Society. We are grateful to their publishers, where they have given help with tracing sources or have given permissions to reproduce diagrams or tables. We are especially indebted to the Saunders Brown Centre for Ageing in Kentucky, USA, Members of the Noetic Institute, UK, and the Institute of Brain and Ageing at the University of California, Irvine. This book is part of a long journey with many companions, usually for only part of the way. Part-way companions have included many research students, too many to mention. We thank them for their legacy of findings and good questions.

Frances, of Age Concern, stands out. As a part-time student on an MBA programme, many years ago, it was Frances who first challenged our view of the elderly as needing help. She said the elderly needed opportunity. She was right.

We thank our families finally: Fakhrun Nisa and Danya Horne; and Gillian, Ellis, James and Holly Wootton, for their sacrifices and support in this, our joint endeavour.

Contents

Meet the authors

We both started our adult lives as chemists: Terry specialized in the chemistry of complex organic molecules and Simon specialized in biochemistry. Later, while working for pharmaceutical companies like Pfizer and Eli Lilly, Simon was very involved with pharmaceutical drugs that effectively changed the chemistry of the brain, in order to help manage moods, or alleviate depression. At this point our career paths diverged. Simon moved into health services, both private and NHS, while Terry became interested in managers and how they thought about solving problems, taking decisions and making plans.

Happily, some years later, our career paths converged. Simon returned to university and, based on his research, together we wrote *Strategic Thinking*, one of Kogan Page's bestselling books on strategy. *Strategic Thinking* has been translated into Chinese, Spanish and Russian, and a third edition is due out this year. With another research student, Tony Doherty, there followed *Managing Public Services – Implementing Changes: A Thoughtful Approach to the Practice of Management*, a bestselling book for Routledge, which is also due out in a third edition.

In the meantime, the number of students going to university had risen from 1 in 10 school leavers, to 4 in 10 school leavers. Many of these additional students had neither the thinking skills, nor the cognitive capacity to study properly for a degree. How could thinking skills and cognitive capacity be developed?

We put our heads together – literally – and began to think about the brain as if it were a chemical factory. In this we had support from Professor Susan Greenfield, one of the world's leading neuroscientists. Together, we produced what Susan Greenfield has since described as 'the world's most advanced models of the way the brain thinks'.

There are two important implications of our models of the way the brain thinks. Firstly, Simon knew that the chemical reactions which carry your thoughts through your brain can be made to go faster and further by changing the general chemical conditions in your brain; he also knew that you can learn to control those chemical conditions by choosing what you eat, what you do and how you feel. We had discovered that your effective intelligence was determined by your choices, and not just by your genes.

Secondly, Terry was fascinated by Susan Greenfield's idea of neuromodulation. This was the realization that once one of your thoughts had caused a particular neural pathway to be run, this changed the residual chemicals left along the neural pathway. Those chemicals then made it easier for that neural pathway to be run again. We had discovered that the very act of thinking strengthens your ability to think. It is now possible to design thinking activities which connect up different parts of your brain and which can then strengthen those connections.

The brain training books which we have written for managers, students, adults and the 50+, are the result of a happy convergence of biochemistry and cognitive science. In her foreword to our 2010 book *Train Your Brain*, Professor Susan Greenfield says:

> *Not only is the book an up-to-date review of the latest thinking in science ... but, exceptionally, this is the first book to the best of my knowledge that gives practical advice on how to exploit those findings and apply them to your own life... There are exercises and helpful appendices, all making for an enjoyable and comprehensive read.*

Professor Susan Greenfield, Director of the Royal Institute

Only got a minute?

The physical state of your brain is not determined by your genes – it is a lifestyle choice. If earlier lifestyle choices have damaged your brain, the advice and exercises in this book can reverse the damage – whatever your age.

This book will help you to do three things:

1 Exploit the advantages of your brain over younger brains. As long as you are not under time pressure, your experiential learning and your creative problem solving will improve as you get older. Your IQ at 50+ can be 10–25 per cent higher than when you were a child. The only way to acquire more experience and broader general knowledge is to get older.

2 Maintain and enhance advantages in mental performance that you acquire as you get older, and defend these advantages against degenerative disease, by creating spare cognitive capacity. When you do things described in this book, your brain will develop better myelin insulation on its neural pathways – enabling it to think faster, with less error.

3 Add life to your years, and not just years to your life, knowing that the last ten years of your life can be the best ten years of your life. If you have survived to be 50 years old, you will need to reframe what you now think of as 'old'. For you, now, 60 is no longer old. One hundred is old. A pension at 65 is no longer an 'old age' pension. It is a supplementary income for which you have worked, saved or invested. You will be more, not less, able to work – as long as the work is mental not physical.

Preface

Adding years to life and life to later years

Rage, rage, against the dying of the light

Dylan Thomas

This book is for everyone. Which of us will not, one day, be older? If you have ever wondered what goes on in the head of a parent, a grandparent, an older friend or your own head as you get older, then this book is for you.

There are many other books on brain training, but few acknowledge that the brains they train are ageing. When ageing is acknowledged, it is usually as a problem to be lived with, like amnesia, or slower reactions. Yet the neuroscience research underpinning our first book shows that your brain gets better and better at thinking as you get older.

> *The research is up to date and very readable. It contains some of the world's most advanced models of the way the brain thinks.*
>
> Professor Susan Greenfield

Nine out of ten of the components of good applied thinking improve with age. The 50+ can exploit this advantage over younger brains. New memories form more slowly, but this can be overcome.

For example, verbal thinking, visual thinking, ethical thinking, critical thinking, predictive thinking, creativity, problem solving and learning from experience all improve with age. If these particular skills are exploited, the problems caused by a slower speed of new memory formation can be avoided or sidestepped.

Provided that you do not suffer from a degenerative brain disease (and you can minimize the chances that you will), the loss of speed can be delayed, diminished and reversed in later years. The ongoing development of intellectual power, until you are at least 90, is a realistic goal for readers of this book. Protecting that power from disease becomes a lifestyle choice and the book explains how to make that choice.

Other books will exhort you to 'use it or lose it'. We have researched and evaluated different possible uses of the brain, in order to discover which uses most enhance the power of the brain to think. In four earlier books on thinking skills for planners, strategists, managers and public service professionals, we isolated 12 components of thinking. By exercising each component separately, or in more advanced combinations, you can improve your ability to think clearly and to clearly express what you think. You can exploit the components of applied thinking which improve with age.

This will give you a choice about whether or not to carry on working. Sometimes people retire because they find the problems too complex or too confusing. But the confusion is not often caused by complex problems. Confusion is caused by trying to solve complex problems too quickly. You need to start earlier. Fortunately, in later years, enhanced skills in predictive thinking can help to anticipate some problems, avoid others, and to make an earlier start on solving the rest.

When you anticipate problems and refuse to be rushed, you will calm the panic of those around you. Your ability to keep your head, when younger ones around you are losing theirs, is characteristic of strong leaders.

Of all the improvements with age that we have uncovered, none are more dramatic than the way IQ and intelligence improve as you get older. The gains in IQ shown by the Scottish 70- and 80-year-olds returning to resit tests they sat when they were 11 years old astonished them, but did not surprise those of us who have experience of working with mature learners. Deeper analysis of the diets and lifestyles of the 50+ with high gains in IQ is revealing – your IQ is not determined by your genes or your age, but by things over which you have control. Even your risk of degenerative disease, or dementia, is now down to choices you can make (see Chapters 3 and 4). Perhaps not genius but eminence, or at least expertise, is a realistic goal for people who choose to carry on working well into their later years (Chapters 2 and 5).

In later years, we often prefer relationships characterized by reasonableness and thoughtfulness. But we cannot be reasonable if we cannot reason. We cannot be thoughtful if we cannot think reflectively (Chapter 6).

In earlier work with Tony Doherty, at the University of London, we established that an inability to work and an inability to form close relationships were two major obstacles to human health and happiness (Chapter 1). This book can help you to achieve both. It can help you continue to work and continue to form close relationships in later life.

With this book, you can 'add years to your life as well as life to your later years'.

American Society of Gerontologists

Introduction

The superior thinking skills of the 50+ brain

On 8 November 2007, the comedian Ken Dodd was 80 years old. The BBC programme *Songs of Praise* arranged a surprise party for him. His repartee was light and quick. His memory of his lines was faultless. 'I don't mind getting older,' he quipped, 'as long as I don't get to be old!' However old Ken's body will one day become, barring disease, his brain is likely to get better and better as he ages.

Mae West used to say that she was never too old to become younger. In a way she was right. Her older brain would have become better at critical thinking, creative thinking and reflective thinking and at making predictions. Her verbal and numerical IQ would already have been higher than when she was younger, and her long-term memory would also have been better. True, she would have been slower to process new information and form new memory, but her experience, street wisdom and powers of prediction would have taught her to start sooner and to make notes. As long as you are not under time pressure, your experiential learning and your creative problem solving will get better as you get older. This might help to explain why your IQ is 10–25 per cent higher than when you were 11 years old (see Chapter 2). Experiential learning and creative problem solving benefit from experience and broader general knowledge, and the only way to acquire experience and general knowledge is to become older! Your memory of what you already know will get better, not worse, because your recollection improves with the number of times you make a given recall. The older you are the more likely you are to have made a recall.

Einstein also resolved never to grow old, no matter how long he lived. Einstein resolved to remain a child – a curious child – in the face of the mysteries of the world in which he found himself. He bequeathed his brain to science. Einstein's brain looks much like yours or mine. What seems to matter is how you use your brain. When you do the kinds of things described in this book, your brain will develop better myelin insulation on its neural pathways – enabling it to think faster with less error. When you do the kinds of things described in this book, your brain can also develop more cognitive capacity than it currently needs. This can help you to preserve your mental performance even if you contract a disease that damages your brain. In Chapters 1 and 3 we will discover that nuns who had remained academically very able until they died were found, on autopsy, to have brains that were riddled with Alzheimer's plaques, but because they still had more than enough cognitive capacity left intact, no one, themselves included, ever knew that they had Alzheimer's disease.

The physical state of your brain as you age is not determined by your genes – it is a lifestyle choice (Chapters 1 and 4). If earlier lifestyle choices have damaged your brain, the advice and exercises in this book can reverse the damage – whatever your age.

Death is not what it used to be

Writing in the *Guardian* newspaper in November 2007, Dr Guy Brown, winner of the Wellcome Trust Prize, claimed that 'death is not what it used to be'. The nature of death is set to change markedly for the 50+. We think that the decline in acute deaths by, for example, infection, violence, stroke or heart disease (see Figure 0.1), will lead to a rise in slower deaths from neurodegenerative diseases like dementia, Parkinson's or Alzheimer's. The 50+ generation will be stalked by Three Deadly Ds – Disability, Dementia and Degenerative disease. Any of these could turn the last 20 years of your life into a living death. It must be a kind of living hell to wake up every morning, feeling afraid, in a place you do not recognize, to have things done to you, for no reason, by people you do not know (albeit they might be your own children). Yet this prospect is not inevitable. Barring physical illness, and in some cases in spite of physical illness, the 50+ should expect to remain mentally fit and sharp well into their nineties (Figure 0.2).

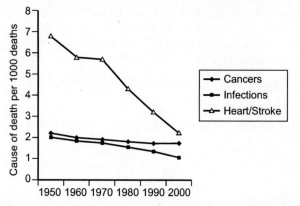

Figure 0.1 Early twentieth-century 'killer' diseases now account for only about 0.6% of deaths (based on England & Wales, ONS 2004).

Figure 0.2 Rising life expectancies of Western women, 1600–2000 (based on Deppan, H. (2002) Science, 296, p. 1030).

What matters is what you do in order to train and maintain the fitness of your brain. There are many exciting and enjoyable things that you can do, both to exploit the growing power of your brain and to defend it from disease. You can add life to your years, and not just years to your life.

You should resist the idea of retirement. (Unless it entitles you to a lump sum which you want to use to start your own business – see Chapter 5. Colonel Sanders started KFC when he was 67. Last year 40 per cent of successful new business start-ups in the UK were started by people over 50.)

What do you mean, old?

If you have survived to be 50 years old, you will now need to reframe what you think of as 'old'. For you, now, 60 is no longer old, 100 is old. You can no longer justify a pension at 65 on account of 'old age'. It is a supplementary income for which you have saved or invested. You will be more, not less, able to work than a younger person – as long as the work is mental not physical (Chapter 5).

At the moment, according to the UK Government Actuary, there are only about 10,000 old people in the UK, i.e. people who are more than 100 years old. By 2070, this number will probably have risen to about half a million people.

You need to make sure that your physical lifespan is matched by an extension in your healthy lifespan, otherwise you can expect to suffer from disability, dementia or degenerative disease – the 3Ds.

The dreaded DDDs

During the 1990s, the life expectancy of the 50+ increased by an extra 2.2 years, but 'healthy' life expectancy increased by only 7 months. Because the increase in your lifespan is linear, and the chance of brain disease is exponential, the baby boom generation is increasingly likely to die from degenerative brain disease, and unnecessarily so, given that there are relatively simple means of defending yourself against this (see Chapter 4). By 2008, 700,000 people in the UK had already succumbed to dementia. If the advice in this book goes unheeded, by the time you are 90 nearly 2 million people in the UK alone will be suffering from dementia. The suffering of the families of the demented will be pervasive. The social cost of caring for 2 million demented people will be hard to finance. National and local governments, and social and medical agencies, as well as the 50+ themselves, need to take this book seriously.

ARE YOU HEADING IN THAT DIRECTION?

In 2007, the Institute of Public Health in Cambridge (UK), reported on people's health in the year before death and they found that nearly half suffered from a moderate to severe cognitive deficit in the year before they died. Around 30 per cent had full-blown dementia. Yet there is no necessity for the present 50+ generation to become part of these statistics. Would your life be worth living if your head went in that direction? We are in danger of merging and confusing living and dying. In the UK, death is already preceded by 10 years of chronic ill health. At the moment, perhaps being out of your mind is the only way to escape a life not worth living. It does not have to be this way. It is not necessary for the years between 80 and 100 to be accompanied by loss of mood, loss of memory or loss of marbles.

THE ROAD TO HELL

Perhaps this road to hell has been paved with the good intentions of a health and safety executive that has devoted resources to preventing accidents. Accidents may have been a better way to die than from protracted brain disease. Perhaps we would not choose, if choose we could, to spend our last remaining year in a care home for the mentally impaired. At the moment, research resources are devoted primarily to preventing us from dying, instead of encouraging us to live livelier, even riskier lives. If we lived livelier, riskier lives we might be more likely to die suddenly and thereby have a better acute death, as well as live a better life. Unfortunately, acute death is often protracted into chronic death and disability: a heart attack becomes an ongoing heart condition to be managed; a stroke becomes vascular dementia for our families to live with; diabetes, AIDS and some cancers become qualifications for long-term disability and mobility allowances. It becomes more and more profitable to develop drugs that maintain us in chronic ill health, than to develop drugs that either cure us, or help us to die a good death!

Making the end a life worth living

The three goals of this book are to enable you:

1 to exploit, for economic gain for yourself and others, the superior powers of the 50+ brain

2 to maintain and enhance the advantages in mental performance which you acquire as you get older, and to defend them against degenerative diseases by creating spare cognitive capacity

3 to demonstrate how you can add life to your years and not just years to your life, knowing that the last ten years of your life can be the best ten years of your life.

The best is yet to come. Think on! Read on!

Don't retire!

Who decided it was a good idea to retire at 65? The answer is Bismarck – when he himself was over 70 and an extremely effective Chancellor of Germany! Why? Under pressure to introduce a state retirement pension, but not wanting it to cost too much, he asked: 'On average, when do people die?' On being told 65, he agreed, 'OK, then give them a pension at 65!' Such an arbitrary age for retirement mattered less in those days, when businesses were more likely to need your brawn than your brain. However, in a knowledge-based economy, when competitive advantage comes from how much better you think about what you know, we should be recruiting 65 year olds, not retiring them.

When it comes to problem solving, leadership, decision making, creative thinking or making money, an older brain is better. Because ageing was associated with loss of brain size, or brain weight, this was mistakenly assumed to be associated with irreversible loss of brain cells and with inevitable mental decline. Your cognitive capacity is, in fact, determined by the number of interconnections between your neurons, not the number of neurons in your brain. The number of neurons in your brain can increase, as well as decrease, depending on lifestyle choices you make. How you use your brain, and what you choose to use it for, can increase both the number and the quality of the connections in your brain. Consuming excessive alcohol, for example, can accelerate neuron losses to 60,000 cells a day. Unattended grief, unmanaged blood pressure, and the absence of thoughtful conversation, can all impair thinking (Chapters 1, 4 and 6).

Age does not cause brain disease

Mary Hamm studied 5,000 50+ citizens, over 10 years, in California. She found that age was not, of itself, a factor in brain deterioration, although physical illnesses and lack of physical and mental fitness sometimes had side effects on brain functioning. Although there is some slowing down of new memory formation and in the speed of new information processing as people get older, it is possible to work around this, as such processing is only one part of one of the ten components that make up effective applied thinking (Chapter 5). As Keith Simonton discovered, creative thinking actually improves with age. Edison, Monet, Picasso and Titian produced their best work in their seventies and eighties.

The more we train our brains, the higher our performance becomes and remains. A well-used brain has a higher ratio of synaptic connections to neurons. Neural nerve growth factor (NGF) is released by the process of thinking. This, in turn, promotes the thickening of the myelin insulation around the axons of connected neurons. The neurochemistry of this is described in 'First thoughts' (see page xxvii), for readers who like to know 'why' as well as 'how' the cognitive capacity of their 50+ brains can increase.

Willis and Schaie have shown than it is never too late to prevent, or reverse, cognitive deterioration and to boost mental performance, even if you have allowed it to decline significantly. Optimism and humour (Chapter 1) and thoughtful conversations (Chapter 6) are important in developing intelligence, as well as in deepening intimate relationships (Chapter 6). Better talking leads to better thinking, which leads to better writing, which leads to better action, which leads to feeling better, which leads to… etc. – it is a virtuous circle (see Figure 0.3).

Carl Cotman also found that certain types of physical and mental exercises can arrest and reverse mental degeneration and promote the growth of new brain cells (Chapter 1).

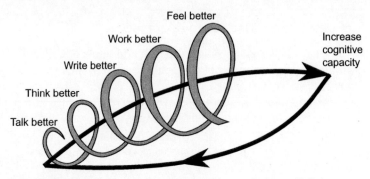

Figure 0.3 The virtuous circle of talking better, thinking better, writing better, working better and feeling better increases cognitive capacity.

Minding your own business

Far from considering retiring, you should be pursuing your interests and curiosity and promoting your career horizons. You should consider setting up your own business (Chapter 5). In a brain-based economy, at 50+ you may be only a third of the way through your potential working life! You will need to keep your brain fit, in the same way that you know you need to keep your body fit. This book teaches you the kind of lifestyle you need to lead and the kind of exercises you need to do. There is no need to threaten your brain with slogans like 'Use it or lose it'. Your brain will get better as you get older and, if you exploit your brain's maturing powers, it will get better still. Think about it!

10 THINGS TO REMEMBER

1 The 50+ have superior thinking skills to younger adults.

2 In the UK, at least half a million of the 50+ will live to be 100+.

3 You need to match your mental lifespan to your physical lifespan.

4 You can exploit, for economic gain, for yourself and others, the superior powers of the 50+ brain.

5 You can enhance the advantages in mental performance that you acquire as you get older, and defend them against degenerative diseases by creating spare cognitive capacity.

6 You can add life to your years and not just years to your life, knowing that the last ten years of your life can be the best ten years of your life.

7 Your brain will not automatically deteriorate as you get older.

8 Increased cognitive capacity is linked to talking more, thinking more, learning more, and writing more, and to working better and feeling better.

9 Do not stop working, paid or otherwise. Pursue your interests and curiosity and continue to broaden your career horizons.

10 Consider using your superior thinking skills to set up your own business. The mindset of the 50+ brain is well matched to the needs of entrepreneurs and senior managers.

Suggested further reading

Austad, S., *Why We Age* (Wiley, 1997).

Brown, G., *The Living End: The New Sciences of Death, Aging and Immortality* (Macmillan, 2008).

De Grey, A., 'Time to talk SENS', *Science*, 959 (2002), p. 451.

Dementia UK *Prevalence and Cost* (LSE/Alzheimer Society, 2007).

Deppen, J., 'Broken limits to life expectancy', *Science*, 296 (2002), p. 1028.

Hall, S., *Merchants of Immortality: Chasing the Dream of Human Life Extension* (Mariner Books, 2005).

Hayflick, L., *How and Why We Age* (Ballantine Books Inc, 1996).

Hayflick, L., 'The Future of Ageing', *Nature*, 408 (2000), p. 266.

Hughes, J., 'The Future of Death', *Journal of Evolution and Technology*, 6 (2001), p. 1.

Olshansky, S., *The Quest for Immortality: Science at the Frontiers of Aging* (W. W. Norton & Co, 2005).

Robine, J. and Romieu, I., 'Healthy Active Ageing' (REVES, http://reves.site.ined.fr/en/resources/reves_papers, 1998).

Thane, P., *History of Old Age* (J. Paul Getty Trust Publications, 2005).

Vaupel, J., 'Biodemographic trajectories of longevity', *Science*, 280 (1998), p. 854.

Yesavage, J., 'Incidence of Alzheimer's and cognitive impairment', *Journal of Psychiatric Research*, 36 (2002), p. 280.

First thoughts

Neuroscience and the developing power of the 50+ brain

Terrorism, wars and motorbikes have cracked many skulls, enabling brain science to make rapid progress! The effects of these head injuries have been studied by biologists, mathematicians, physicists, chemists, psychologists, pharmacologists, sociologists and philosophers. Their collective studies have given birth to what we now call cognitive science.

As cognitive science grew, so did ideas about the way the brain could enable you to think reflectively and creatively as well as critically. Your brain will give you the ability to respond differently at different ages and stages for the rest of your life. Your brain is the basis of your freedom to choose.

'I think, therefore I am.'

becomes…

'I can think differently, therefore I can change.'

You are not entirely a prisoner of your genes or your age. From the 1960s onwards, cognitive scientists were able to provide scientific support for important human values, like personal freedom, personal choice, personal responsibility and personal development, at a time when such ideas were under attack from postmodernist thinkers. Cognitive science helps you to challenge the idea that your life is determined by your economic or social circumstances, or your date of birth!

The electrical brain

One idea, popular in the 1970s and 1980s, was that it was useful to view the brain as computer hardware, and the mind as the computer software.

The idea is beguiling. There are many useful parallels. For example, when you turn off a computer, the software cannot work. Your brain needs a reliable supply of energy or it will suffer rather like your computer suffers. Also, a computer needs background software, for example, the software that periodically clears 'garbage' and consolidates memory files. Your brain is the same – it has autonomic activities that operate when you are asleep. Likewise, just because a computer is turned on, doesn't mean that all the software programs are running. Some programs need to be requested explicitly. In the brain, this 'requesting' is called metacognitive thinking. It involves the part of the brain called the frontal cerebral cortex. Many of the exercises in this book will help you to exploit the frontal cortex of your brain, so that you can learn to direct your own thinking. This part of the brain is very underdeveloped in young adults but matures with age.

So beguiling is the computer metaphor that it still holds sway, despite being seriously challenged by Professor Susan Greenfield in her book on the human brain, which was published in 1997. She described how traditionally viewed products of the mind, like ideas or images, could cause chemical changes in the brain. Importantly for this book, cognitive science has demonstrated that mental and physical exercises can develop the chemical structures that underpin your memory and your intelligence.

Brain research and brain scanning: the lessons and limitations

Recently, ideas on brain training have benefited greatly from our ability to watch images of brains while their owners are thinking about different types of decisions, problems and plans. CAT scanners use computers to combine X-ray slices of the brain and can be used to establish the structures of the brain, whereas PET scanners, which follow traces of radioactive isotopes introduced into the brain fluid, are better for monitoring brain activity. The uses of these two types of scanners are limited, because overdoses of X-rays or radioactivity would be harmful. Much safer is the use of MRI scanners which can be used to monitor blood flows in the brain, in real time.

Health warning!

The new technologies and tools of the cognitive scientist are impressive, but you should not suspend the healthy scepticism which brain training in critical thinking will encourage. Brain scans, for example, show what is happening when people think. This is a correlation. But a correlation is not necessarily a cause, or a consequence. Remember also that the person under the scanner is not you. Throughout this book, we offer you suggested plans of action that are clearly implied by the reasonable conclusions we have inferred from normally reliable sources. However, these tests were not carried out on you. As an individual you are unique. The action plans we offer may have been tried by our students, but it is for you to decide for yourself how well they work for you.

The chemical brain

From the 1970s onwards, we have been trying to imagine what happens inside your brain when you try to think. We and others have been trying to help students, teachers, managers, therapists, social workers and public sector workers to learn to think more effectively about the kinds of decisions they need to take, the kinds of problems they need to solve, and the kinds of plans they need to make.

At first, we were helped by the then prevailing model of 'brain-as-computer'. But we kept finding aspects of the ways our students were thinking that the computer model failed to explain. In 1997, Susan Greenfield's model of the brain as a chemical factory liberated us from the straitjacket of our computer model. Suddenly we could better understand the successes and the difficulties we were having with our students. Her neurochemical approach gave us ways to understand what we already knew.

At last, we could understand why, for many students, learning almost anything seemed to increase their capacity to learn, irrespective of the subject matter. For other students, lots of repetitions of relatively simple thinking tasks seemed to produce marked improvements in their capacity to think. This supported our emerging view that thinking was a combination of ten or so contributory skills (Figure 0.4).

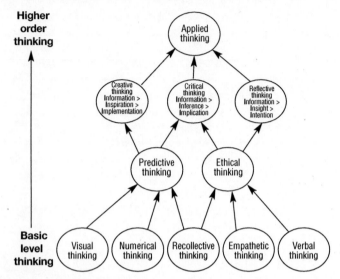

Figure 0.4 The hierarchy of thinking skills (Horne and Wootton, 2010).

Although logic (deductive and inductive) remains the backbone of clear thinking, it is a necessary, but not sufficient, condition for thinking at its best. Parts of the brain other than the frontal cerebral cortex have a role to play if thinking is to be first class.

The parts of your brain that control visual images, and the parts of your brain that empathize with the likely thoughts and feelings of other people, can work in concert with the parts of your brain that hold different facets of your memory. All these different parts of your brain can help the frontal lobe of your cortex to take a more logical decision or to make a more rational plan. Susan Greenfield's work gave us confidence to extend our ideas on combination thinking and to devise brain training exercises that involve the simultaneous use of different parts of the brain.

The structure and composition of the brain

If you want to train your brain, it can be helpful to find out something about the structure and composition of the brain you are seeking to train.

Inside your skull, your brain has the consistency of a sloppy undercooked egg. It has no moving parts. It is surrounded by a colourless fluid (CSF), which is circulating constantly. CSF contains mainly salt and sugar.

The brain itself is wrinkled and creamy in colour. Although it would fit into the palm of your hand, it is as heavy as three bags of sugar. The brain has two halves and looks rather like a small cauliflower whose stalk tapers to become the top of your spinal cord. The back of the cauliflower overhangs the stalk slightly. The overhang is called the cerebellum. The main part is called the cerebrum.

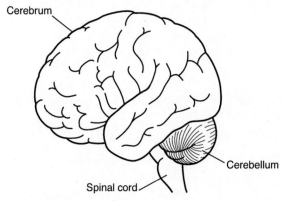

Figure 0.5 The human brain (taken from Horne and Wootton, 2010).

If you turn the brain over, you will see distinct regions that occur in pairs, so that the underside of the brain appears to be symmetrical about a central line running from the front to the back of the brain.

DIFFERENT JOBS FOR DIFFERENT BITS OF THE BRAIN

Your cerebral cortex is divided into about 50 different bits, many of which have a definite specialized function. In some parts of the cortex, towards the back for instance (the posterior parietal cortex), the distinction between the areas is more blurred. The posterior parietal cortex handles many sensations – sound, sight, touch and movement.

The frontal lobes of a mature brain become active when they are asked to empathize, make predictions, or tackle problems that involve planning, complex decisions or creative thinking.

Teenagers, or young adults under 25, often struggle with these kinds of thinking tasks. Often, the development of this frontal area of their cerebral cortex lags behind the bushing of the dendrites in the back of their brain, which is preoccupied with sensation and stimulation. Until the development of their frontal lobes catches up, young people are usually reluctant to volunteer verbal information, and they can appear to be anti-social and to have 'heads like sieves' when it comes to remembering things.

NEURONS – THE BUILDING BLOCKS OF THE BRAIN

Neurons have a squat, blob-like body called a soma, about 0.04 mm across. The soma sprouts tiny branches called dendrites. Commonly, neurons appear elongated, with dendrites at either end, sometimes on the end of a long, thin fibre called an axon. The axon is commonly two to three times longer than the body of the neuron, though spinal neurons can trail axons a metre long. So, squat somas, with stubby dendrite branches and long thin tails – these are your neurons. Neurons are the building blocks of your constantly developing intelligence.

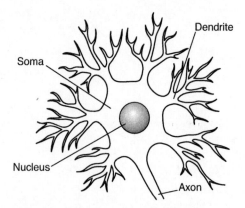

Figure 0.6 The nerve cell and branches (taken from Horne and Wootton, 2010).

DENDRITES AND AXONS – WHAT DO THEY DO?

The dendrites are receiving stations for chemical messages sent out by neighbouring neurons. The chemical messages converge down the dendrites into the neuron body. If the signals are strong enough, the neuron will generate an electrical charge, which will be conducted along the axon towards the dendrites of neighbouring neurons.

Figure 0.7 The dendrite.

The charges are carried either by positively charged sodium, potassium or calcium cations, or by negatively charged chloride anions. The charged anions and cations cannot normally pass through the fatty inter-layers of the neuron wall. However, an accumulation of negatively charged ions on the inside of the neuron wall will attract, rather like a magnet, ions and proteins of opposite charge to the outside of the neuron wall, thereby generating a difference in potential across the cell wall. This potential difference can be measured in millivolts. When the potential difference reaches about 80 millivolts, channels open through the neuron walls, to allow positively charged ions (usually sodium) to enter the neuron to neutralize the negative charges on the inside of the neuron. When the charge inside the neuron becomes about 20 millivolts positive, then potassium ions, positively charged, are allowed out through the wall of the neuron, until a negatively charged state is restored inside the neuron. All this happens in a thousandth of a second.

The direction of transmission of the electrical charges, and the speeds of the transmission, are determined by the directions and condition of the axons. If the axon is already connected to a dendrite of another neuron, then that predetermines the direction taken by the charge. If the axon is surrounded by a thick sheath of healthy myelin insulation, the transmission will be fast and accurate. Because you often wish to minimize the delay between one thought and the next, or between thought and action, chemical charges will hustle down your axons at about 400 km/hour, as long as the myelin insulation on your axons are in good enough condition. What happens when the electrically charged chemicals hit the synaptic gap between the end of the axon and the dendrite of a neighbouring neuron?

BRIDGING THAT GAP

With the advent of electron microscopes, which have magnification factors of over 10,000, chemicals can be detected in the synaptic gap. Among the chemicals detected in the synaptic gap are many differently shaped acetylcholine derivatives. These acetylcholine molecules belong to a general class of brain chemicals known as neurotransmitters.

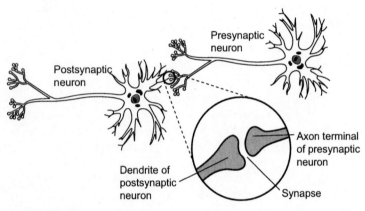

Figure 0.8 The synapse.

The more frequently electrically charged chemicals arrive at the end of the axon, the more often acetylcholine neurotransmitters can be seen launching themselves into the water in the synaptic gap. The small size of the neurotransmitters enables them to diffuse very quickly across the salty water that surrounds the axons and dendrites. They cross the gap in less than a millisecond, but how do they know which dendrite to choose?

Each neurotransmitter swimming across the gap is like a jigsaw piece, looking for a dendrite with a receptor molecule of exactly the right shape to make a perfect fit. Once the neurotransmitter finds and locks onto a right-fitting receptor, this signals to the channel in the wall of the second neuron to admit a charged chemical. An accumulation of charged chemicals moves down the dendrites of the second neuron into the cell body and out along the axon of the second neuron to the edge of the next synaptic gap, where it stares across the water at a third neuron. This is going on inside your amazing chemical brain a million times a second!

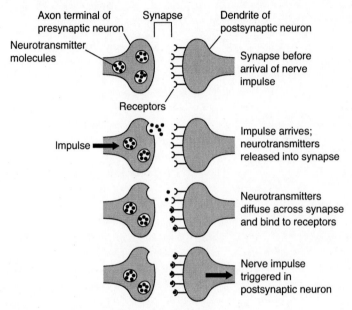

Figure 0.9 Synaptic transmissions (taken from Horne and Wootton, 2010).

While neurotransmitters like serotonin, dopamine and even acetylcholine frequently get a mention in popular accounts of brain chemistry, there is another neurotransmitter that rarely gets a mention but which is important to understanding why the 50+ brain is so powerful. It is called glutamate. It is important for memory. It can also cause neuron death. Too much glutamate appears to overexcite receiving neurons (by causing too much calcium to flood in), causing death by excitotoxicity. Excitotoxicity is one of the main causes of death in strokes, head injuries and Alzheimer's disease.

Your amazing brain

It is the quantity (and quality) of your neuron connections, not the number or weight of your neurons, that appears to determine your cognitive capacity and your mental performance. This has changed our view on the way the adult brain continues to develop. Work by

Siegler, at Carnegie University (USA) in the late 1990s, on embryos, babies, pre-school infants, teenagers, adults and seniors, indicates that brain development is ongoing throughout your life and that there is no cut-off in the development of your intelligence or in the development of your thinking skills (look back at Figure 0.4).

Every year, the young adult brain shrinks and loses weight. This loss is now thought to be due more to a loss of weight by individual neurons, rather than to the loss of individual neurons themselves. Losses can be compensated for by learning things, almost anything, because learning almost anything increases the density of your synaptic connections. Also, by applying, reciting or repeating what you have learned, or thought about, you increase the thickness of the myelin insulation around the axons of your neurons. This thicker myelin insulation results in quicker and clearer electrical transmission through your brain and more secure storage of information. Thicker myelination improves the recall of your memories and the speed and accuracy of your thinking. The brain training activities in this book have been designed to increase the number of synaptic connections in your brain and to thicken the myelin insulation of your axons. This process, whereby the act of thinking chemically modifies the route along which the thought has been chemically transmitted, is called neuromodulation.

THE YOUNG ADULT BRAIN

The brain growth spurt that began when you were a teenager started at the back of your brain, heightening your awareness and sensitivity to sounds, lights, tastes and touch. Because development in the middle of the brain comes later, young adults often do not feel in control of their emotional reactions and impulses. Young adults often feel awkward or clumsy. But the lag in the development of their frontal cortex is the biggest disability for young adults. This frontal cortex is involved in reasoning, planning, predicting and decision making. Small wonder the behaviour of many young adults often seems to you to be unreasonable and lacking in direction and to have little regard for risk and consequence. According to Giedd, reporting in 2004, this is because many young adults lack the ability of the 50+ brain to reason, to decide, and to assess risk and consequence.

THE MATURE BRAIN

Your brain can start to show a net loss of neurons if you drink alcohol or use certain other drugs (Chapter 1). Don't panic! You can still preserve and improve your IQ and the intelligence of your behaviour. This is because many of the thinking skills that contribute to intelligent behaviour (Figure 0.4 again) improve as you get older, as long as you learn to apply them explicitly when you need them. This kind of thinking – called 'applied thinking' – produces more intelligent behaviour (Chapter 5). It is a mistaken belief that memory necessarily deteriorates with age. In fact, your ability to recall early knowledge and experiences gets better. This is because recall benefits from repetition and you are more likely to have repeated a particular recall the older you get. On the other hand, what is likely to deteriorate from the age of 50 is the speed at which you can form new memories. New information processing often does slow down. There are brain training exercises in Part two that mitigate this. In Chapter 4 there are also exercises and activities that can help you to reverse any decline in processing speed and new memory formation that may have taken place already. You can also learn to use predictive thinking skills so that you can make an earlier start on thinking tasks that might otherwise be impaired by slower processing (see Chapter 8 in *Train Your Brain*, Horne and Wootton, 2010).

Risks of damage to the 50+ brain

It is fortunate that brain training can repair brain damage, because all of our brains are at risk from, for example:

- ▶ extended grief, depression, low mood or pessimism (Chapter 1)
- ▶ alcohol (Chapter 4)
- ▶ oxygen depletion and toxins, due to lack of exercise (Chapter 4)
- ▶ poor diet and the additives in processed food (Chapter 4)
- ▶ all manner of environmental threats (Chapter 4)
- ▶ raised blood pressure, often alcohol or stress related (Chapter 4)
- ▶ lack of stimulation or lack of conversational relationships (Chapter 6).

Mental performance does not inevitably decline with age, if you stay healthy. While it is true that certain diseases can lower mental performance, if you build up sufficient reserves of spare cognitive capacity such diseases will have less or no effect. This book is full of exercises, problems and games that can help you to create reserves of spare cognitive capacity. It also contains scientific advice on minimizing the chances that you will develop those diseases in the first place.

People who do not use their brains productively tend to drag down the average scores for older adults, and so obscure the high and increasing scores of those older people who use their brains productively.

Edward Coffey, of the Henry Ford Foundation, reported that adults aged 65 to 90 who used their brains actively, continued to perform well with no signs of loss of memory or reason, despite their MRI scans showing shrinkage in the size of their brains. In 2002, Quartz reported on a famous study of 4,000 nuns. This study was commenced by David Snowdon in Kentucky in 1986. The study is particularly interesting because all the nuns have very similar lifestyles, but some continue to teach and to be mentally active, and some don't. The nuns who continue to be mentally active are currently living, on average, four years longer, and their brain autopsies show, on average, 40 per cent more synapses and thicker myelin insulation on their axons. So, thinking helps you to live longer and thinking helps your brain to keep getting better and better. Thinking adds years to your life as well as life to your years.

The advantages of a chemical brain

Because chemicals react to different extents, and at different speeds, depending on the chemical environment in which the chemical reaction takes place, and because you have the ability to change the chemical environment in which your brain is trying to do its chemical work, you can affect the extent and speed of the chemical reactions in your brain and so improve its performance. You can change the chemical environment in your brain through diet, sleep, ergonomics, stress reduction, and by doing mental and physical exercises.

A chemical model of the brain can help you to understand how the frequent practice of the skills shown in the thinking skills model (Figure 0.4), even at a relatively undemanding level, can progressively improve the speed and accuracy of your thinking. As a result of the process known as neuromodulation, each repetitive pass through a neuron increases the thickness of its myelin insulation (for a systematic workout of all ten contributory skills, consult *Train Your Brain*, Horne and Wootton, 2010).

Excitingly, a chemical model of the thinking process leaves open the creative possibility that you won't come up with exactly the same response, or solution, even if a problem replicates itself. Because the first occurrence exercised neurons which were changed by that process, the chances are increased of a novel response, should the same problem or input be presented a second time. Not only do we think and learn, but the way we think and learn improves in the process. In a chemical brain, there is no need to threaten:

'Use it or lose it.'

The chemical model of the 50+ brain says:

'Use it as much as you can, it can get even better.'

However, it does seem to matter how you use it and for what purpose. More chemical connections are generated by activities such as drama, coaching, dancing or rock climbing, which involve memory, calculation, problem solving, decision making, prediction and oral presentation, than by physical activities alone.

A chemical brain predicts an improvement in mental functioning, rather than decline, as you get older.

Neurodegenerative diseases

Alzheimer's and Parkinson's are diseases. Diseases may cause premature ageing, but diseases are not a necessary consequence of getting older. The likelihood of disease can be lowered dramatically (Chapters 3 and 4). That is not to say that your neurons will not change as you get older. They will. Consequently, you may perform less well on time-constrained problem solving and on tasks that require rapid memorization of new information. However, these disadvantages can be more than compensated for by exploiting the many aspects of mental functioning that improve with age, like verbal reasoning, reflective learning, predictive thinking and creativity (see also Chapters 8, 9 and 10 in *Train Your Brain*, Horne and Wootton, 2010). In the end, what matters most is the extent and quality of your brain's interconnectedness and this is helped by working for yourself or for others (Chapter 5) or through social learning, thoughtful conversation and meaningful relationships (Chapter 6).

This book will encourage you to exploit the advantage which your 50+ brain already has over brains of younger colleagues.

You can build on these advantages. All other things being equal, your younger colleagues will find it hard to close the gap before you reach the age of about 100. By age 120, you will hit genetically imposed limitations. Beyond 120 is off our radar, and may depend on genetic re-engineering, which is beyond the scope of this book. We do not need to promise miracles – your 50+ brain is already miraculous enough.

The vista from the viewing point of neuroscience is awesome. We are so excited by what we have discovered about the 50+ brain that we need constantly to remind ourselves to balance our excitement with prudence, especially in relation to the most recent discoveries. Much as we try, throughout this book, to distinguish between well-replicated scientific findings, educated guesswork and hopeful speculation, you should not suspend the sceptical disbelief which we urge upon you in Chapter 5. As you have seen already, the state of your brain between now and your one hundredth birthday will largely be down to your own choice of lifestyle. It is wise to discuss major changes of lifestyle with people close to you or with a doctor, and then make up a mind of your own.

The 50+ brain – making up your mind

Your 50+ brain, as we have seen from Susan Greenfield's work, is a 1.5 kg chemical factory whose neurons fire a million times a second inside your skull. Your mind, on the other hand, is harder to define. According to Dr Jeff Victoroff, the very different words for the mind – the Greek ('nous'), as compared with the Roman ('mens'), or the more modern French ('esprit') – epitomize its 'Scarlet Pimpernel' nature ('they seek him here, they seek him there'). Your mind does seem to be located in your brain. When you think, your brain changes. When your brain changes, you change. So when you think, you change. That's how you make up your mind. You can use your 50+ brain to change your mind. As you continue to mature beyond 50+, your mindset of different ways of thinking will continue to get better and better. While learning languages is easiest done by your brain at age three, and learning mathematics is easiest done by your brain at around 17, your brain's powers of prediction, critical evaluation, reflective wisdom and creativity are just getting into their stride as you reach 50, and some areas of social science, art,

philosophy and law are dominated by the minds of the 70+.
But while a child can quickly memorize new information (and should
be encouraged to develop its brain capacity by doing so as often as
possible), the 70+ judges will likely need to take copious notes.

Living to a ripe old age

Your mind can continue to ripen till the day you die. Maybe that is
what is meant by living to a ripe old age. The ripening of the mind
does not, however, take place automatically with age. The ripening
of the mind takes place through experience. That is why you can
sometimes find 'old heads on young shoulders'. Clearly, the longer
you live, the more opportunities there are for formative experiences.
But you have to take the opportunities. To extract maximum value
from your experiences, practise reflective thinking (see Chapter 8 in
Train Your Brain, Horne and Wootton, 2010). By continuing to pack
in new experiences you can either play 'catch up' or you can ensure
that you 'stay ahead'. A ripe old age is everyone's potential. How ripe is
within your gift. How ripe depends, among other things, on the extent
to which you choose to implement the ideas in this book.

The reason we say 'among other things', is because it is self-evident
that this book alone cannot support an advance in the mental power
of millions of people – for you are each individuals. Each individual
brain will blossom, in part, according to its own biological plan – but
you can help shape the extent and direction of this blossoming. Your
neurons will continue to respond to whatever life experiences you
continue to put in their way, and the new neural pathways forged
by those experiences will increase your spare cognitive capacity, so
that you will have sufficient reserves to support increasing mental
performance. As your body becomes frailer, it does not follow that
your eyes will grow dim. Humans are not as other mammals are.
Humans have brains that are self-repairing and resilient, and which
can constantly adapt, improve and learn new things. At 50+, you
can deploy thinking skills that younger minds cannot yet muster,
let alone master.

ALL IS NOT ROSES

But it's not all roses. While younger bodies struggle with the threat
of facial acne, at 50+, you may need to fend off threats that bring

fatigue (Chapter 4) or reduced optimism (Chapter 1). You may come into a room and forget why you came in. You may become more hesitant to speak your thoughts, because your brain has more words to search through before it finds the exact one you want – the one that is on the tip of your tongue (Chapter 3). You may waste some time – not much in the scheme of things, but very irritating none the less – looking for keys or glasses.

Such things are worth learning to live with, in return for your increased ability to predict, to evaluate, to judge, to discern, to learn, to invent and to plan strategically. None of our 50+ students, feeling the power of their 50+ brains, have ever said that they would choose to be young again, despite having hairs in their ears, a near miss in the car, and the daily shock of seeing their parents in the bathroom mirror!

LIVING LONGER – LIVING WELL

In the Western world, neurological diseases are rapidly overtaking heart disease, cancer and strokes as the most frequent reasons why we fail to live to our full, genetically determined 120 years. According to the World Health Organization, mental illnesses have recently overtaken traditional killers, like bacterial, or insect- or water-borne diseases, as the world's most common cause of premature death and disability (Chapter 1). In the West we have learned to live longer, and now we must learn to live well.

Your 50+ increase in cognitive capacity is like boring out the cylinders in an engine under the bonnet of a car, or even adding an extra cylinder or two. To get the best from your bigger 50+ engine, you might now need to develop some more advanced driving skills. You might need a more advanced engine management system. The part of your brain that manages your thinking is called the metacognitive system and it appears to be controlled mainly by the frontal lobe of your cerebral cortex. You can strengthen and train this part of your brain by doing the exercises and solving the kinds of problems that you will find in Part two of this book.

HEDONISTIC BABY BOOMERS

If you are a hedonistic baby boomer, you may be looking forward to retiring between five and 20 years from now. You may think that brain training sounds too much like hard work. Perhaps you just want to relax and enjoy the prosperity that you have earned through years of sacrifice, saving and working long hours for some less-than-grateful organization.

All the more tragic, then, if the enjoyment of your well-earned prosperity is snatched away at the last moment by premature loss of your ability to enjoy stimulation, plan trips, choose a new car, feel pleasure or find love in an intimate, thoughtful relationship. The 50+ brain is ready to shift up a gear, not retire. There are alternative strategies (Chapter 5) that will help you to preserve and expand your 50+ brain, so that you can enjoy the things you have earned.

Do not retire to find yourself reading books on 'the problems of ageing'! As far as the brain is concerned, there are no problems – except those of physical health, or those of your own choosing. Baby boomers can continue to develop their brains and live the life they have worked so hard to fulfil.

THE ECONOMIC CONSEQUENCES OF CRUMBLING MINDS

The economic and social consequences of an epidemic of crumbling minds are so dire that governments might usefully promote brain fitness with the same urgency and resource allocation that they are now belatedly bringing to physical fitness, through the encouragement of sport, physical activity and accident prevention. Brain training at 50+ will bring benefits quite commensurate with costly campaigns for healthy hearts and cancer cures. Brains can be defended from disease-borne decline. Disease-borne decline could rapidly consume more economic resources than the present younger generation generate. It is time to rank brain fitness alongside body fitness.

We can turn this potential problem into an opportunity: advances in neuroscience and in brain scanning have shown that we can exploit the advantages and powers of the 50+ brain to generate great economic gain. The thinking skill set of the 50+ brain is well suited to entrepreneurialism. Last year, 50+ entrepreneurs added new business worth more than £24 billion a year to the UK economy (research undertaken for Yellow Pages). Companies set up within the past five years by people over 50 now account for 16 per cent of all new businesses in the UK. Professor Mark Hart, at Kingston University, says that because older entrepreneurs can draw upon years of personal experience, this helps to account for their high success rate and their growing importance to the UK economy.

FEET ON THE GROUND

To make a large leap forward, you need to start with your feet on solid ground. That is why we have started with Information about the brain – its construction and the science of how it works as a marvellous, 24-hour chemical factory. In this book, we will look at what we may reasonably Infer from this Information, in which we have justifiable belief. For each Inference we will examine the Implications for affordable, feasible and practical steps which you can take, the games you can play, and the types of problems on which to best train your brain. We have designed about 300 such problems and collected them together in Part two. This pattern of moving from justifiably believable Information, via reasonably believable Inferences, to practical and feasible Implications for action, characterizes the rest of the book. It is the basis of effective applied thinking, which is taken up again in Chapter 5.

10 THINGS TO REMEMBER

1 The brain used to be viewed as computer hardware, and your mind as computer software, and this view is too limited.

2 Brain scanners enable scientists to watch images of your brain while you think about decisions, problems and plans.

3 Your brain is more like a chemical factory than a computer.

4 Powerful thinking can combine ten or more separate thinking skills.

5 Each thinking skill can be developed by brain training.

6 The brain is wrinkled, creamy in colour and surrounded by fluid.

7 Different parts of your brain have different roles.

8 Neurons are the building blocks of your brain.

9 Dendrites and axons transmit and receive messages in your brain.

10 Dendrites and axons are linked by synapses.

Glossary

Axons – long, slender projections from a neuron. They conduct electrical impulses away from the neuron's soma, the bulbous end of a neuron.

Cerebral cortex – so-called 'grey matter' of the brain. The 'thinking cap', responsible for functions such as language, logic and information processing.

CT or CAT scanner – a machine that uses X-rays to take pictures of slices of the body and the brain.

Dendrites – the antennae of the neurons.

MEG scanner – a scanner that allows brain activity to be viewed while a particular task is performed. It measures the tiny magnetic fields generated by brain activity.

MRI scanner – a machine that uses a magnetic field and radio waves to show what is happening inside the body and the brain.

Neurons – electrically excitable cells in the nervous system that process and transmit information. Neurons are the core components of the brain.

PET scanner – a machine that detects radioactive material, which is injected or inhaled, to produce an image of the brain.

Serotonin – a neurotransmitter.

Synapse – a small gap separating neurons. The gap is between the axon of one neuron and the dendrite of the next. The gap contains neurotransmitters such as acetylcholine derivatives.

Suggested further reading

Quartz, S. R. and Sejnowski, T. J., *Liars, Lovers and Heroes* (New York: Harper Collins, 2002).

Greenfield, S. A., *The Human Brain: A Guided Tour* (London: Weidenfeld & Nicolson, 1997).

Gupta, S., 'Brawn and Brain' in *Time* magazine (May 2004).

Horne, T. and Wootton, S., *Train Your Brain* (Hodder Education, 2010).

Howard, P. J., *The Owner's Manual for the Brain: Everyday Applications from Mind and Brain Research* (3rd edn, Austin, Texas: Bard Press, 2006).

Kandel, E., et al (eds), *Principles of Neural Science* (4th edn, McGraw Hill, 2000).

Mesulam, M. -Marsel, *Principles of Behavioural and Cognitive Neurology* (2nd edn, New York: OUP, 2000).

Robertson, I., *Stay Sharp With the Mind Doctor* (London: Vermilion, 2005).

Schaie, K., *Intellectual Development in Adulthood: The Seattle Longitudinal Study* (Cambridge: Cambridge University Press, 1996).

Victoroff, J., *Saving Your Brain: The Revolutionary Plan to Boost Brain Power, Improve Memory, and Protect Yourself Against Aging and Alzheimer's* (New York: Bantam Books, 2002).

Wooton, S. and Horne, T., *Strategic Thinking* (London: Kogan Page, 2005).

1

The pursuit of happiness

In this chapter you will learn:

- *that chemical reactions in your brain determine whether you feel high or low, optimistic or pessimistic, and that they affect how well you think*
- *that you can control chemical reactions in your brain by what you do and what you think, and by what you eat and what you drink*
- *that the pursuit of happiness is largely fruitless and that you can more easily achieve a state of BLISS, through Body-based pleasures, Laughter, Involvement, Satisfaction and Sex.*

There is nothing either good or bad, 'tis thinking makes it so.

After William Shakespeare

Introduction

In this chapter, you will discover that chemical conditions in your brain change when you experience emotion, and when you think about the emotions which others may be feeling. Thinking thoughts and feeling feelings are chemical processes. Each affects the other.

The need for you to consider what you are feeling, as well as what you are thinking, arises in a number of thinking tasks, for example:

▶ An important part of *thinking critically* is the evaluation of an action's potential consequences for others. At 50+ you are much better at predicting likely consequences than a younger person. We call this empathetic thinking.

- ▶ When you need to ***think creatively***, your emotions are an important source of the mental energy needed to generate a long list of novel possibilities. At 50+ you have many more possibilities at your disposal than a younger person. Your emotional response to emerging ideas feeds both your intuition and your capacity and courage to make novel associations and creative connections between the many memories and images in your 50+ head.
- ▶ When recalling what was felt, as well as what was seen and said and done, you need to ***think reflectively***. At 50+, you have so much more experience from which to learn.
- ▶ In general, optimistic expectations correlate with the strength of your immune system – the probability that you will recover from serious diseases, like cancer, correlates to the likelihood that you will achieve successful outcomes on thinking tasks, like problem solving and strategy formulation.

Emotional intelligence

The capacity to link emotions to thinking was described by Goleman as 'emotional intelligence' in 1996, and as 'social intelligence' in 2006. Research by both Goleman and Damasio shows that you need to involve your emotions, particularly when thinking about problems and plans.

Emotional information is processed in a part of the brain called the amygdala. The amygdala is constantly sending messages to the prefrontal lobes of the brain. This means that there is a constant flow of emotional information to the parts of the brain involved in calculation and argument. McGaugh points out that the effect is not always helpful. For example, when fear or anxiety rises beyond a certain level, your ability to think and remember is impaired. On the other hand, when you feel positive or amused, the messages sent by the amygdala appear to improve your ability to think. Feeling positive or amused seems to increase the likelihood that you will come up with original solutions.

Insight
Emotions and the brain
Brain scans show that when people form intentions, on which they eventually act, certain parts of their brains need to be involved, while the problem, choice,

discussion or plan is being thought about. One essential area of the brain that needs to be included is the part which processes emotions. What you feel about the situation is an important component of your thinking about the situation.

To discover for yourself how closely connected are your thoughts and feelings, try the following activity.

A thinking and feeling experiment

Try the following experiment, either with a partner, or a pen and paper. Look around and write 'I am noticing…' (write down what you are looking at or listening to) and 'I am thinking…' (write down what you are thinking at that moment) and 'I am feeling…' (write down a single word describing that emotion). Keep this up for about 15 minutes. Review the results. Notice how many times you can change what you are feeling, even in 15 minutes. Notice what kinds of observations and thoughts are followed by what kinds of feelings.

Repeat, trying to increase the number of positive feelings you can experience in 15 minutes. Note that you can choose what you notice – what you look at, what you listen to. This increases the chance that you can find something positive to think about and this in turn means that you can feel better.

Try to complete the following sentences in succession. When you have completed number three, go back to number one. Keep going round the loop for as much time as you can spare. When you can do it easily, do it as often as you can. Keep it up to maintain mental fitness:

1 Right now I am noticing… (a person, a colour, a sound, a smell, a taste, a texture).
2 And right now I am thinking… (e.g. an opinion or a judgement).
3 And right now I am feeling… (e.g. an emotion – a simple word).

For increased mental suppleness, just keep going round the loop. For increased concentration span, increase the number of repetitions you do at one time. For increased mental agility and thinking speed, try to go round as quickly as you can without hesitation. You may notice that how you feel is changed by what you think, and what you think is related to what you notice. Because you can control what you notice by where you choose to focus, you can exert increasing control over your thoughts and your emotions.

Emotional and verbal thinking

The use of verbal thinking (Chapter 6) to identify and label the feelings you are experiencing, is more productive than just expressing the feelings impulsively. This is because, when you shout or otherwise give vent to your anger, for example, you leave a neural pathway between the amygdala and the brain's frontal lobes. This increases the ease with which subsequent stray feelings can disable your ability to think, especially under pressure.

> *Make me thoughtful not moody,*
> *Let me see good things in unexpected places,*
> *Let me see unexpected talents in unexpected people,*
> *And, oh, let me have the grace to tell them so.*

From a seventeenth-century nun's prayer

Insight
Internal dialogue
Conversations with yourself in your head (internal dialogues) need to explore what you are feeling about whatever you are thinking about – this means that you have to have as precise vocabulary as possible for labelling your feelings.

THE LIMITATIONS OF THE YOUNG ADULT BRAIN

In young adults, a hormone-driven dendrite explosion reaches the back of the brain, which deals with stimulation and emotion, well before it reaches the front of the brain, which deals with verbal reasoning. This leaves young adults vulnerable to confusing feelings, which they are not able to label, let alone challenge. Because their amygdalae are connected to the prefrontal lobes of their brains, the emotions of young adults take up short-term memory space which they need to make judgements, comparisons, calculations, decisions and logical arguments. Gottman realized that the thinking space of many young people, young men in particular, is quickly overwhelmed and disabled by their emotions. This is especially true following criticism. For example, for a typical male–female relationship between two young adults to survive, she has to make at least five positive comments about him for every one negative comment she makes about him.

Are you feeling anxious or are you feeling just worried?

At 50+, people can experience increased anxiety – often unattached to anything in particular and for no obvious reason. Anxiety can obsess your mind to the point where you no longer have enough free working space in your brain.

When people at 50+ are worried, it is right to take note. The 50+ have experience of the kind of things that can go wrong. Often a 50+ worry is a sensible preparation and rehearsal for things that may indeed go wrong. Worrying enables the 50+ to prepare contingency plans and these are often reassuring to others, as well as themselves. Contingency plans can be a good defence against chronic anxiety, which lowers performance on thinking tasks. One hundred and twenty-six studies of more than 36,000 students have shown that anxiety, and difficulty in managing emotions, is highly correlated with under-performance.

The biochemistry of emotion

According to US pharmacologist Dr Candace Pert, the brain signals the release of different chemicals, each of a different molecular structure, each time your feelings change. These molecules enter your blood and flow around your body until they find a receptor site which exactly fits their shape. These receptor sites thus pick up the messages from your body's hormones, like oestrogen and testosterone, and from your neurotransmitters, like serotonin and dopamine, and from other biochemicals called peptides. Your body's receptor sites also pick up messages from endorphins. Endorphins make you feel good. You can cause your 50+ brain to release endorphins into your bloodstream through exercise, or through sex, or by eating dark chocolate.

EMOTIONAL THINKING AND LEARNING

When you feel anxious, resentful, angry or bitter, or when you feel helpless, or very sad, this has an adverse effect on your ability to learn. Unmanaged emotion disables learning because it disables some of the thinking skills involved in learning. When you are emotionally distracted, it is hard to take interest in new information, or to persist with trying to make sense of information that is confusing or incomplete, or to recall accurately what you read earlier. You may find it hard to take decisions or think critically.

When young people are finding it difficult to take decisions there is brain-scan evidence of traffic between the amygdala, processing emotion, and the frontal lobes of the brain. Unmanaged emotions, like fear and anxiety, can lead to mental paralysis. This can happen during examinations, or when trying to work to someone else's deadlines or schedules.

Positive mental energy and motivation

As long ago as the 1980s, Horne found that adults needed to apply themselves over a long period in order to develop certain intellectual skills, like numeracy. The self-motivation to do exercises, to tackle questions and to practise presentations, comes from your emotions – like your fear of failure, or your desire to perform well in front of an audience. Emotions give you the mental motivation to deploy your full repertoire of thinking skills. The repetition involved in learning or rehearsing something new not only contributes to your present success, it also thickens the myelin insulation around your neural axons, enabling your 50+ brain to think more quickly and more accurately about future tasks. Repetition is often tedious or boring, so the motivation to study and practise needs to be based on strong overriding emotions.

Emotions can sometimes cause younger people to act impulsively. Often younger people close down thinking prematurely. In order to achieve a more thoughtful response, emotions like anger and anxiety need to be managed. By 50+, you will have had experience and practice at doing this. By 50+, you are more likely to have learned when to bite your tongue! Feelings, as well as facts, need to be thought about.

Getting to a 'yes'

If you are trying to get someone to make a decision, act on the assumption that they will need an emotional gain from the decision. Ask them to imagine a good feeling they will feel when they have decided in your favour. Then ask them what convincing reasons they could give to other people for having made the decision in your favour. People often feel the need to rehearse good reasons to give to others, even when their decisions are intuitive, emotional or irrational. The world often expects decisions to appear rational, even when we know they're not.

Those old familiar feelings

To understand some habitual but undesirable behaviour on the part of your 50+ friend or colleague, you could test the hypothesis that people will keep repeating behaviours that result in them feeling 'old familiar feelings'. 'Old familiar feelings' are feelings which they have become very used to feeling, possibly since they were children. One person's 'old familiar feelings' will probably differ from another person's 'old familiar feelings'. They may not be feelings that you would consider to be pleasant.

This can help you to understand why some undesirable behaviour gets worse when a young offender is punished. The culprit's familiar feelings may be ones that result from punishment. In which case, repeated punishment may lead to repeated offending. Study the pattern of the undesirable behaviour. Ask yourself, 'How does this person end up feeling?' Can you change how the person reacts to these behaviours, thereby thwarting the emotional pay-off which you suspect the person is getting?

IS OPTIMISM THAT IMPORTANT?

When the messages we receive, via television soaps and radio news or via the daily press and the internet, are so predominantly pessimistic, it can be difficult to feel optimistic. Does this really matter? How important is it to think positively?

True, the world is full of unhappiness and disease. But there is also love, compassion and joy. Research on selective perception has shown that you can observe things with a preconceived notion of how you think they should appear and that your perception can be so selective that you may find it difficult to change your mind, even when you see, or hear, contradictory evidence. Instead of reality, you selectively perceive what you expect to see. The older you are, the more likely you are to have had opportunities to reconfirm your preconceived views. To guard against this, you will need to be more deliberately 'open-minded', lest you draw false Inferences from mistaken Information, or draw false Implications from a false Inference.

Sports psychologists Bull and Rushall have tried to reverse 'negative' thinking in football teams and tennis players. They have discovered that optimistic self-confident moods increase a player's chance of winning. They have shown that optimism improves speed of thought and performance in sports like snooker, tennis and Grand Prix motor racing, and when taking penalties in soccer.

Memory, too, has been found to be very sensitive to optimistic suggestion. If you tell yourself, 'I'll never remember that', then the chances are you won't. Feeling pessimistic, for example about your prospects in a job interview, impairs your thinking skills during the interview, especially your memory. The main benefit of planning, or revising, or preparing, or rehearsing, is that not only are you likely to feel less anxious, but the condition of your brain will be enhanced by the repetition (as long as you don't cancel this out by staying up all night to do it! See Chapter 4). Consequently, you remember better and think better, even when answering questions on things which you haven't prepared. Written tests best suit people who are optimistic. People who are less confident do better when they are assessed through assessment centres, or through continuous assessment.

POSITIVE THINKING – THE EFFECT ON MIND AND BODY

The effect of mood on your chances of recovery from serious illness, or from major surgery and cancers, has been the object of much study. According to Fosbury, the management of diabetes has been shown to benefit more from mood management by cognitive therapists, than from information provided by nurse educators. According to Cohen, negative emotions, such as anxiety, increase the frequency with which people suffer from common colds. Colds impair breathing, lower energy, cause headaches and impair clear thinking. Cohen had found that swimmers could improve their performance by concentrating on optimistic thoughts.

Insight
Positive feelings
Expressing strong positive feelings, like hope, joy, excitement, optimism, gratitude, attraction, amusement, commitment, satisfaction and pleasure, raises mental energy and motivation and leaves chemical residues that favour thinking and creativity.

Seven types of negative thinking

Seven 'sick-making' types of thinking develop the kind of pessimism that has been found to impair health and mental performance:

1 **Black and white** – things are good or bad; pendulous, either/or thinking.
2 **Perfectionist** – less than perfect equals failure; nit-picking, blemishing.
3 **Comparative** – performance is judged only by comparison with other people.
4 **Generalized** – this sees a single event as part of a never-ending and inevitable pattern; characterized by use of 'always' and 'never'.
5 **Telepathic** – believing you can tell when others think negatively about you.
6 **Basket** – you give yourself one bad label and then assume any similar, or related, labels also apply to you.
7 **Guilty** – characterized by frequent use of the words 'should' and 'ought'.

Insight
Negative feelings

Identifying and labelling strong negative feelings is more productive than expressing them or enacting them. When you express or enact negative feelings (e.g. shouting at your children when you are angry), you leave in place neurochemical traces that will increase the risk that you will do it again. Readily accessible neuron tracks between your amygdala and the frontal lobes of your cerebral cortex will increase the frequency with which your thinking is disabled or impaired by strong negative emotions, like anger and jealousy.

Down on the farm

Many people regularly watch popular dramas or 'soaps', like *Emmerdale, Coronation Street* and *EastEnders*. These are frequently tragic. Hyams found that negative preoccupations undermine your thinking performance.

SEVEN STEPS TO OVERCOMING YOUR NEGATIVE EMOTIONS

1 Do an audit of your strengths (not your weaknesses). At 50+ you have skills and resources. At 50+, you have knowledge. At 50+, you have experience.

2 Forgive someone, if only in your head. Rehearse an imaginary conversation in which you forgive them. Let go of the negative memories that steal your headspace. You need your headspace for more positive thoughts. At 50+, you have nothing to lose by forgiving.

3 Visualize how things will look when you are succeeding. Hear the applause it is bringing and notice from whom (this is important). Feel how you feel when you are receiving applause and recognition for your success.

4 Applaud yourself. Discover that you do not need the constant approval of others, even though you are enjoying this as it is becoming more frequent.

5 Try things that are difficult and give them your best shot. When you are doing your best at difficult tasks, your best is good enough. Be the best that you can be.

6 At 50+, you can admit that you are not superwoman or superman (i.e. you can't be the cause of all that is bad, or the cause of the bad feelings of others). Others are responsible for how they feel.

7 Stop nagging and nit-picking and complaining. It lowers the mood of people around you. This in turn might lower your mood, because moods are contagious. Your good mood will lift the mood of others. Their good mood will then lift yours. When you see something you like, comment on it.

THE BLACK DOG OF DEPRESSION

Depression is the black dog that barks in the night and in the daytime. In 1999, mental disorders, like depression and manic depression, became the world's commonest cause of premature death and disability (World Health Organization). Seek professional or medical help if you think you might be suffering from depression. You would not try to cure yourself of pneumonia. Tell a counsellor or doctor if you have five or more of the following symptoms:

- ▶ fatigue
- ▶ loss of mental energy
- ▶ insomnia
- ▶ early waking
- ▶ overeating
- ▶ recklessness
- ▶ accident prone
- ▶ loss of confidence
- ▶ loss of enjoyment
- ▶ feeling hopeless

- no appetite
- loss of sex drive
- increased drinking
- increased smoking
- aches and pains
- piercing own body
- hurting yourself
- feeling helpless
- feeling guilty
- feeling worthless
- feeling agitated
- unable to work
- unable to concentrate
- thoughts of death.

Studies show that levels of work-related stress are a significant precursor to depression (for further details see Chapter 5 in *Train Your Brain*, Horne and Wootton, 2010). Building closer relationships with other people at work, and learning to participate in problem solving and decision making, can reduce stress and can improve your mental health.

THE BRAIN CHEMISTRY OF DEPRESSION

Adverse social and economic events are associated with biochemical changes in your 50+ brain. There is a strong correlation between the amount of serotonin and norepinephrine in your brain, and your mood. If your levels of serotonin (and norepinephrine) get too low, you will experience lowered mental energy, diminished pleasure from normally pleasurable activities and reduced sex drive.

The practical pursuit of BLISS

There are many books that offer you happiness in a few steps. Howard asserts that unless you are one of the 10 per cent who seem genetically programmed to be happy, searching for happiness will be futile. The difficulties experienced by seekers of happiness are compounded by living in a world that advertises and exploits this futile expectation of happiness. In the USA, happiness is a constitutional right. Americans have the right to life, liberty and the pursuit of happiness. Such expectations lead to much expenditure for some, and inevitable disappointment for others. In the end, everyone's mood is lowered by our failure to be happy. You are less likely to be disappointed if, instead of pursuing happiness, you pursue BLISS:

Body-based pleasure
Laughter
Involvement
Satisfaction
Sex

(Horne and Wootton, 2010)

The components of BLISS are not expected to persist. If they persist too long, or are repeated too frequently, your chemical receptors become desensitized. Imagine receiving non-stop applause and cheers, a standing ovation… for three hours. You would be desperate to get off the stage and sit down!

BODY-BASED PLEASURE

This first component of BLISS can be considered in relation to the five senses: taste, smell, sight, hearing and touch.

50 sensations to try before you die…

Eat: herbs and wild honey, cream and curries… and dark chocolate.

Taste: lips, skin, liquorice, aniseed… and dark chocolate.

Smell: cut grass, wood shavings, honeysuckle, pine resin… and dark chocolate.

Savour: a barbecue, a baby's neck, seaweed smells… and dark chocolate.

Gaze: at sunsets, distant hills, modern paintings and the faces of models.

Admire: cathedrals, temples, modern architecture, pottery and gardens.

Hear: babies babbling, Mozart's *Clarinet Concerto in A major* (2nd movement).

Listen: to running water, wind in trees, choir boys and bird song.

Enjoy: Mendelssohn's *Violin Concerto in E minor*, Status Quo, Berlioz's *Harold in Italy*, Pavarotti.

Stroke: clean hair, petals, warm sand, smooth skin, soft skin.

Feel: velvet, silk, fine cotton, linen, and dark chocolate melting in your mouth.

THE LAUGHTER (AND THE TEARS)

There is now much neuroimmunological evidence of the benefits of laughter. But the benefits of a 'good cry' have been less well publicized. There are many sorts of tears – tears of joy, anger, frustration, relief, hysteria or just of awe at the sight of a DB5 Aston Martin Volante! Witchalls found that emotional tears contain emotional brain chemicals, like leucine (associated with pain) and prolactin (associated with stress).

So cry me a river...

▶ Animal tears do not contain emotional chemicals. Is crying a hallmark of humanity?
▶ People suffering from depression, ulcers and colitis cry less than healthy people.

Is laughter the best medicine?

Laughter may not be the best medicine, but immunology studies confirm that it does augment other medicines that you take. The levels of immunoglobin in people's saliva are predictably:

▶ lower than average in people under stress
▶ higher than average in people who feel loved by others
▶ higher in people whose prevailing mood is optimistic or elevated
▶ higher in people who laugh, and in people who make other people laugh.

We counsel against abandoning conventional treatments to rely solely on positive emotions to cure disease (although there are 15 years of studies confirming the beneficial effects of laughter, positive mood and optimism in enhancing your immune system!). In research on heart surgery, men basing no optimism on religious beliefs were three times more likely to die, and men basing no optimism on the supportive optimism of friends and/or family were four times more likely to die. Clearly the impact of optimism is great and the supportive optimism of friends or family is particularly beneficial (Chapter 6). The impact of laughter is immediate. Cousins found that levels of life-threatening toxins were reduced after only a few moments of laughter. Laughter also appears to intercept emotional messages from the hypothalamus to the frontal cortex, thereby leaving the frontal cortex freer to be logical in its planning and decision making.

Ten things to do to raise your optimism

1 Collect qualifications and certificates.
2 Read anything from the 'Further suggested reading' sections of this book that catch your eye.
3 Commit a random act of gratuitous kindness every day.
4 Reduce the number of stressors in your life.
5 Spend time with people who share your sense of humour.
6 Dispose of some assets to release cash for shopping sprees.
7 Make a contact list of close family and old friends and keep in touch.
8 Improve your appearance, through exercise and self-tanning moisturizers.
9 Collect funny cards to send when people are ill, to say thank you, or for no reason.
10 Keep a file of funny stories or jokes, preferably at your own expense. Share one a day.

GET INVOLVED

The next thing you need to do is get Involved.

Involved in what? And exactly what does it mean to be Involved?

The object of Involvement is not sensory pleasure or emotional lift. The object is to become totally engrossed and totally absorbed in an activity, such as a game, a sport, a hobby or a conversation. You need to become so Involved that you lose track of time and, maybe, even lose track of where you are or cease to notice any physical discomfort that you may be suffering. When you really get Involved, little else will intrude into your awareness.

The seven elements of Involvement

1 Your goal is clear – you know what you are trying to achieve.
2 You feel you have a very good chance of achieving your goal.
3 You are able to concentrate and to push aside conflicting cares.
4 You feel up to it – you have sufficient energy, resources and skills.

5 You feel in control of the outcome.
6 Your sense of achievement is immediate.
7 Your sense of time is altered – how time flies when you are enjoying yourself!

(Wootton and Horne, 2004)

Your chances of getting Involved are greatest when the difficulty of the task and the level of skill needed are evenly matched. Too much skill required and you will be frustrated, too little and you will be bored. The beneficial effects of Involvement are more enduring than Body-based pleasure, or even Laughter, because they involve you in activity. Activity helps to fix things in your memory (Chapter 3). This is because it is you who is playing the game – you are not just a spectator. You are acting on the stage – you are not just sitting in the audience.

'I JUST WANT SOME SATISFACTION...'

You 'just want some satisfaction' of your needs. Horne and Doherty (2003) found it useful to classify human needs as:

▶ the need for **Warmth**
▶ the need for **Applause**
▶ the need for **Possession**.

The relative importance, to you, of each of these areas of need is unique to you, and their relative importance will have changed now that you are 50+ compared with when you were younger.

Your 'warmth' need is your need for persistent affection, acceptance, belonging, friendship, support and unconditional positive regard. This tends to grow, relative to your need for possession as you pass 50+. 'Warmth' needs have traditionally been easier to meet outside of work, but there is no real reason for this to continue to be the case (Chapter 6).

Improving the quality of working life is a preferable route to arguing for a better work–life balance. The nature of your work should not leave you needing to balance or compensate for it. Get the work sorted (Chapter 5).

Your 'applause' need is your need for some ephemeral things that will need constant reaffirmation, such as approval, admiration, congratulation, gratitude, recognition and success. The scale of your need for 'applause' should determine your choice of partner. Your need for applause will probably increase past 50+, so be prepared to discuss this with your partner (Chapter 6).

'Possession' need is your need to be able to say 'this is mine' (as in... this is my space, this is my child, this is my home, my garden, my hobby, my invention, my poem, my painting, my kind of music, my opinion, my idea). Normally, this need for possession is stronger when you are 30–5. Often, as you get well past 50+, you can take it or leave it. You can meet your needs for warmth, applause and possession at home, or at work, or in the community.

The 50+ can often meet their 'possession' needs just by thinking. For example, this is my idea, my poem, my thought, my memory, my experience, my opinion. The 50+ need not be dependent on money or on other people to meet their needs for 'possession'.

AND SO TO BED... (OR WHEREVER)

The final S in our state of BLISS is for Sex. It is easy to see why Sex is such an important source of wellbeing. Sex combines... Body-based pleasure (ideally from all five senses), enhanced mood (elevated by endorphin release), very focused Involvement (for both the male and the female brain – see Chapter 6), with the Satisfaction of all three needs, i.e. for 'warmth', 'applause' and 'possession'.

The effect of sex on your thinking depends on whether or not your pre-sex stress levels are excessive, whether or not you have an orgasm, and what type of thinking you are concerned about.

> Look at 'The seven steps in the sex life of your brain' on page 128 in Chapter 4.

Combating the obstacles to BLISS

While being 50+ can't guarantee happiness, you can minimize unhappiness. Five major obstacles to feeling good are anger, disappointment, fear, sadness and boredom. The table below suggests what you can do to minimize each.

The obstacle	What to do
Anger	▶ Have a pillow fight. ▶ Run, or walk briskly. ▶ Do something physical. ▶ Join a martial arts club. ▶ Dance, sway or shout to loud music. ▶ Talk to yourself, a pet, a tree or a hillside.
Disappointment	▶ Watch a heart-warming movie. ▶ Read *Chicken Soup for the Soul*. ▶ Perform an act of unsolicited kindness. ▶ Write a list of your lifetime achievements.
Fear	▶ Keep a diary. ▶ Write to someone. ▶ Call an old friend or cousin. ▶ Weed someone's garden (can be yours!). ▶ Rent an action movie (not a suspense thriller and not a mystery movie).
Sadness	▶ Exercise (Chapter 4). ▶ Watch *When Harry Met Sally*. ▶ Listen to *La Traviata* or *Madame Butterfly*. ▶ Arrange flowers or photographs or plant a shrub. ▶ Visit, mourn, discuss or commemorate the cause.
Boredom	▶ Join a club. ▶ Work with young people. ▶ Enrol for a class or a course. ▶ Volunteer to visit a hospital, a hospice, a prison or a school. ▶ Become a representative, e.g. councillor or school governor.

So, manage the five negative obstacles, i.e. anger, disappointment, fear, sadness and boredom, and pursue the five positive components, i.e. **B**ody-based pleasure, **L**aughter, **I**nvolvement, **S**atisfaction and **S**ex and you may not achieve happiness, but you can reasonably aspire to a state of BLISS and your 50+ thinking will benefit. Here are some further tips.

Tip 1 – Read a poem

'No longer gazing'

As I gaze upon the sky
Vague
Unattributable
Unattached
There descends
A drowsy unimpassioned sadness,
Having no relief in word, or thought, or tear.
In this mood, heartless,
Without thought, thoughtless,
I must gaze no longer on the sky.
For hoping from outward forms to win
The passion and the life whose fountains are within,
I might gaze forever.
We win but what we give
And through our lives
Alone
We live
And learn
And might hope to gaze forever.

Terry Horne, 1982

Tip 2 – Walk tall

Step 1 Slump in your chair and hang your head and your chin on your chest.

Step 2 Now try to remember a time when you had a good time and felt good. Hard, eh!

Step 3 Now try again, but this time, stand with your feet as wide apart as your shoulders, feet gripping the ground. Relax your knees. Breathe deeply, suck your belly button back towards your lower spine. Raise your head, pulling your chin back as far as comfortable. Look straight ahead into the distance and open your arms and chest as though to embrace someone. Notice how much easier it is now to remember a 'good time', and notice how the memory is raising your spirits now.

Step 4 Repeat and keep looking ahead. This time, without moving your eyes, see how far to the side and behind you can see with your peripheral vision. Use your imagination to complete the 360° around you. Relax your eyes and notice how much calmer you feel, less angry, less anxious.

Tip 3 – Maintaining morale

Keep tanned – even if it's only fake.

Live somewhere grand – even if only in one room.

Eat in a good restaurant – even if only one dish (e.g. a starter).

(based on a conversation with Aristotle Onassis)

Tip 4 – Keep up the talk

Some indication that bad feelings reside in the right (visual) rather than the left (verbal) side of the brain came in 1999 when psychologist Fred Schiffer used an EEG to find out why blanking the left eye on a pair of safety goggles lifted his patients' depression more dramatically than antidepressant drugs. The exposed right eye had to work harder, thereby stimulating the opposite left side of the brain – the side usually used for talking. Maybe that's why talking about things helps to lift mood (Chapter 6).

The effect of jealousy at 50+

Jealous feelings can completely overwhelm the short-term memory and working space in your brain, leaving the prefrontal lobes of your cerebral cortex – normally your logical mediators – very vulnerable to distracting emotional chemicals which will come from your amygdala. Clear thinking (and sometimes any thinking) will be nearly impossible. How prone are you to jealous feelings? How upset would you be in the following hypothetical situations?

Score: 1 = indifferent, 2 = quite upset, 3 = very upset, 4 = extremely upset	Score
1 Your best friend preferred to do things with others, not including you	
2 You kept finding yourself 'out of the loop' at work, or in a club, church or family	
3 You discovered a partner was having an affair	

(Contd)

Score: 1 = indifferent, 2 = quite upset, 3 = very upset, 4 = extremely upset	Score
4 A brother or sister seemed to be or had been favoured by your parents	
5 A partner flirted	
6 A partner who generally did not talk a lot to you or to your family was very animated and chatty with other people	
7 Your partner commented on a how attractive other people were	
8 Your partner had sexual relationships with other people	
9 At a party your partner repeatedly kissed someone else	
10 Someone flirted with your partner	
11 Your boss gave full credit for your hard work to a co-worker	
12 Your partner danced with someone else	
13 Your partner went out several nights a month without you	
14 Your long-standing boss supports the promotion of a new worker ahead of you	
15 Your partner is slowly developing more and more interests that exclude you	
16 Your partner constantly talks about someone else	
17 Your partner readily hugs others but no longer hugs you	
18 Your partner wants to meet up with an ex-partner	
19 Your partner shared a long and involved project with an attractive co-worker	
20 Your partner suggested that you were both free to develop other relationships	

HOW DID YOU DO?

20–45   85% of adults scored more than this.
46–53   70% of adults scored more than this.
54–57   Half of all adults scored more than this.
58–62   30% of all adults scored more than this.
63–67   Only 15% of adults scored more than this.

(Cautionary note: although the normed respondents were cross-cultural, they were not representatively so, and although many respondents were 50+, they were not controlled for age.)

The percentiles above are largely based on data collected in the 1980s. Are 50+ baby boomers less prone to jealousy? Are you more mellow and relaxed?

Only you know how jealousy affects you as an individual. Few emotions are more frightening, or more dangerous, or less amenable to clear thinking. Each day, husbands murder wives; wives murder husbands, mistresses or both. If your jealousy score is high, go back to your high-scoring situations and think about them now, rather than act impulsively in the middle of one of these situations. If any of these situations do occur, a well-rehearsed thought may be able to intercept messages from your amygdala before you say or do something you may regret. Your behaviour under provocation will depend on what you believe at the time – but belief is a combination of an emotion plus a thought. When you are jealous, your emotions are likely to be so strong that unless you have a very strong counteractive thought well rehearsed, and readily available, you are likely to be overwhelmed by your emotions and may act precipitately.

Jealousy is more than just insecurity. Insecurity provokes natural anxiety or fear of loss. Jealousy, on the other hand, provokes anger and aggression, betrayal, revenge and retribution. Jealousy feeds generalized pessimism, despair and low self-esteem – all of which lower performance on thinking tasks. Once feeling jealous, people can become obsessively hyper-vigilant, compulsively suspicious and even paranoid. All this takes up working space which the brain needs to think clearly about taking decisions, solving problems, making plans, learning from experience, or creating new ideas or developing greater intimacy in close relationships. The corrosive effect of jealousy extends beyond the person who is its object, and adversely affects wider family, social and working life.

Even if your jealousy score is in the highest band – over 70 – all is not lost. At 50+, you will find it easier to change than a younger person. You will need verbal thinking (Chapter 6) either as an internal dialogue or, preferably, with a thinking companion. If the jealous object is a partner, you will need to hug and welcome back your partner, even when your partner returns late. Even if your suspicions are well founded, anger will not make your relationship closer, which is what is needed (Chapter 6). Tell your partner how much you care. At another time soon, open a more general review of your relationship, of other problems that either of you may be experiencing.

Likewise, even if your score is very low – below 40, say – this is no reason to let someone take advantage of your unusually placid nature. You are entitled to respect and consideration. Say clearly that 'it makes me uncomfortable… embarrassed… anxious… etc. when you do X or Y'. Be clear, not judgemental. Stick to explaining, as clearly as you can, how you feel. If the transgression is serious, lay out your partner's options as clearly as you can. Share your feelings about the past and your thoughts on possible options for the future. By sharing your feelings, as well as your thoughts, you have a chance of getting things the way they need to be for you. If you are impulsively hostile and abusive, you may lose your relationship in the long run.

On being irritated – grumpiness at 50+

It is best not to blow grumpiness out of proportion or, in fact, to take any offence at it at all. Grumpy 50+ people generally know that they are grumpy and, whether or not they like the fact that they are grumpy, they are generally unable to stop themselves. In either case, they will not find it helpful to be reminded of the fact that they are grumpy. Being reminded of it is likely to make them grumpy! The scale of your irritation and the size of its cause will often be inversely related. It is the withdrawal of love that can make them irritating.

Irritation and grumpiness are useful (see Chapter 6) – if not endearing – in the 50+. They are emotions that do not lead to hatred. For example, say to yourself, 'I really like Neil, he is so irritating!'

And you can, of course, and frequently do, feel grumpy with yourself, for example when you catch yourself repeating what you have said many times before.

Insight

Grumpy old men and grumpy old women

You will get grumpier and less patient in some situations as you get older. This can be hard to control or avoid; you will need to work at 'tolerating fools gladly'. It is best to own up to this with any new group you meet or with people with whom you need to work. Once they realise that your irritation is neurochemical and not being directed at them, they will be better able to see the overwhelming compensatory benefits of your experience and superior thinking skills.

MOODS TOO GOOD TO BE TRUE

Low moods can lower your performance on thinking by reducing the energy you have available for thinking and also by reducing your optimistic expectation that you will succeed in thinking well. But very high moods also impair performance in thinking tasks by making it difficult for you to concentrate, or to pay adequate attention to relevant detailed information. Have a go at filling in tables 1, 2 and 3 below.

1 Mood level	Yes	No
Was there ever a time when…?		
You were so hyped that other people thought you were not normal?		
You were so irritable that you shouted at people or started a fight?		
You felt supremely confident in yourself or your ability?		
You slept much less than usual but didn't feel tired as a result?		
Your thoughts raced and you couldn't slow them down?		
You were so easily distracted you had trouble thinking straight?		
You had enormously more energy than usual?		
You attempted many more jobs than usual?		

(Contd)

1 Mood level	Yes	No
You rang people late at night or were very much more sociable or chatty?		
You did things that others might have thought were risky?		
You were much more interested in sex than you normally are?		
Your spending/shopping got you (or your family) into trouble?		
People complained that you were talking too fast?		
Total 'Yes' ticks		

2 Mood frequency	Yes	No
Were there more than three of the things to which your answer was 'yes' in 1 happening at the same time?		

3 Mood consequence	Yes	No
Thinking about such things as work, family, money, the law, and arguments, were the consequences of your actions in 1 ever moderately serious?		

HOW DID YOU GET ON?

If your number of 'yes' scores for section 1 was greater than seven, plus your answers in sections 2 and 3 were 'yes', you should seek professional help.

The 50+ feel insecure about...

Nuclear war no more – and terrorism neither. The 50+ feel insecure about identity theft, uncontrolled immigration and benefit fraud, insecure supplies of water and electricity, and unpredictable storms and weather. They are more anxious about corrupt public servants and organized crime, violence on the streets and rudeness in shops, and avian flu and superbugs in hospitals, than about Muslim fundamentalists. The insecurities of the 50+ electorate have not been reflected in the responses of their government. Since 1997, the UK government has spent £1,000 billion on 'national security'. Should more of it have been spent on things the 50+ actually feel insecure about?

Insight

Lacking confidence – what it does to brain performance

Lack of confidence, doubt, anxiety and insecurity all lower performance on mental tasks. As you get older some insecurities are inevitable; these are best identified so that they can be accepted, allowed for or, in many cases, addressed and removed.

AFFLUENZA – A VIRUS TO WHICH THE 50+ ARE ESPECIALLY VULNERABLE?

Still haunted by postwar hardship? The 50+ generation often resort to buying what they want, not what they need, according to marketing educator, Jeanne Hill, at the University of Central Lancashire (UK). Her favourite examples are big-screen televisions, luxury cars, facelifts, breast implants and new partners. Jeanne is concerned that we medicate our consequent unhappiness by using alcohol or antidepressants. Do you have the 50+ affluenza virus?

Do the following statements apply to you? Please answer 'Yes' or 'No'.

Do these apply to you?	Yes	No
I like to have luxuries in my life.		
I admire nice homes, cars and clothes.		
I spend a lot of time and research on purchases.		
I like to know what is fashionable.		
The things I own show how well I have succeeded.		
What I am paid matters as much as what I do.		
I compare myself with others.		
I like other people to say I am attractive.		

How did you get on? The more 'Yes' answers, the greater your infection!

Feeding your feelings – diet, dieting and depression

During 2008, chef Anthony Worrall Thompson provided recipes to the Mental Health Foundation, which helps to combat depression, anxiety and poor concentration.

His recipes contain fish, pulses and nuts to provide protein to keep your brain cells healthy, and fruit, salads and vegetables to provide vitamins and minerals needed by your brain's chemical factory. Rising levels of depression and anxiety are thought to be linked to the 50+ being the first generation for whom consumption of fresh food has fallen (down to 13 per cent in men and 15 per cent in women) at a time when the use of chemicals and additives in processed food has risen.

To perform well and stay sharp, your brain needs a balanced supply of water, complex carbohydrates, vitamins and the omega-3, -6 and -9 fats, found in fish, pulses, nuts and seeds and in unsaturated oils like olive oil, soya oil and oils from pressed nuts or seeds. Deficiencies in your diet can limit the capacity of your brain's chemical factory to produce amino acids, the neurotransmitters that transmit your thinking messages from one brain cell to the next. Serotonin, a key neurotransmitter, helps to regulate your feelings of contentment, anxiety and depression. Your level of serotonin is in turn regulated by tryptophan, which is why you should snack on nuts and seeds, not sweets and biscuits. Yo-yo dieting is bad for prevailing mood, as well as producing chemicals in your brain that impair thinking (Chapter 4).

Insight
Eating sensibly is important
As you get older, lowered physical activity will need to be compensated for by increased mental activity or you will gain weight, which can have some unforeseen and considerable consequences. The answer is not to diet. Yo-yo dieting has been strongly linked with depression and reduced performance in mental tasks, and there is little evidence that it works in the long term. There are many healthier alternatives and these are set out in the book. What and when you eat turns out to be more important for your mental health (and weight) than how much you eat.

A chip off the old block (of dark chocolate)

Since the 1960s, Helsinki and Oula universities have been studying the progress of 1,367 businessmen born between 1919 and 1934. They are now well 50+!

In 2007, in the *European Journal of Clinical Nutrition*, they reported that people who ate dark chocolate were healthier, slimmer and happier, better qualified and felt less lonely and more optimistic. Their predictive thinking was better and they were more likely still to be making complex plans for themselves and others. Eating the dark chocolate released endorphins into their brains, creating feelings of pleasure, while reducing sensitivity to the aches and pains of old age. So why not take a chip off the old block... of dark chocolate?

50+ hearts rule 50+ heads

In 2007, the journal *Nature* reported on the work of Professors Antonio Damasio of University College London, and Marc Hausser of Harvard University, who showed that emotion and intuition worked in tandem with logic (Chapter 5) to take decisions, especially when there was an element of moral reasoning or ethical thinking required. Damasio and Hausser's piece of brainwork looked at what happened in the ventromedial prefrontal cortex (VMPC) when 30 volunteers were separately asked to take decisions which could involve killing another person. For the first time, this work gave us some brain-based insight into how and why humans are humane, and not just robotically rational, in the way we decide things.

The group included six patients with brain damage in the VMPC. Unlike the rest of us, these six patients were capable of taking utilitarian decisions to kill individuals – 'for the greater good' – without compassion or compunction. For the rest of us, our emotions come into play *during* our decision making, not just *afterwards* as a reaction to the consequences of our decisions. Our humane human 'hearts' send lots of traffic to our frontal cortex, to contribute to the actual taking of the decision. Our 'hearts' really do try to rule our 'heads', thankfully!

Happiness at 50+

Research reported in the *British Medical Journal*, by Professor Gow at Edinburgh University, looked at people who took IQ tests at ages 11 and 79. Professor Gow found that self-assessed 'happiness' depended not on how bright you were as a child aged 11, or even on your lifetime gain in IQ, which was often substantial (Chapter 2), but on your ability to defend yourself against the loss of cognitive function. It was loss, or fear of loss, of cognitive functioning that caused unhappiness. The best defence against unhappiness caused by the loss of cognitive function is to make lifestyle choices to protect against disease (see Chapters 4, 5 and 6) and to train your brain to create spare cognitive capacity.

10 THINGS TO REMEMBER

1 The chemicals in your brain affect how well you think.

2 The chemicals in your brain change when you feel high or low, optimistic or pessimistic.

3 You can control the chemicals in your brain by what you do and what you think, and by what you eat and what you drink.

4 The pursuit of happiness is fruitless but you can easily achieve a state of BLISS, through Body-based pleasure, Laughter, Involvement, Satisfaction and Sex.

5 You need to explore what you are feeling, before you can think rationally.

6 Emotions can motivate, demotivate or disable thinking tasks.

7 High hopes enhance mental performance. Anxiety and fear diminish it.

8 Persistent low mood impairs thinking and health, and can have other serious consequences.

9 The pursuit of Body-based pleasure, Laughter, Involvement, Satisfaction, and Sex will benefit the speed and accuracy of your thinking.

10 The pursuit of happiness may be fruitless, but unhappiness caused by fear of loss of cognitive function can be reduced through lifestyle choice and by training your brain.

Suggested further reading

Berns, G., *Satisfaction: The Science of Finding True Fulfillment* (New York: Henry Holt, 2005).

Browning, G., *Never Push When It Says Pull: Small Rules for Little Problems* (London: Atlantic Books on behalf of Guardian Newspapers, 2005).

Fredrickson, B., 'The Value of Positive Emotions', *American Scientist*, 91 (2003), pp. 329–36.

Howard, P. J., *The Owner's Manual for the Brain: Everyday Applications from Mind and Brain Research* (3rd edn, Austin, Texas: Bard Press, 2006).

James, O., *Affluenza* (London: Vermilion, 2007).

Layard, R., *Happiness: Lessons from a New Science*, (New York: Penguin, 2005).

Psychology Dept., Edinburgh University: www.psy.ed.ac.uk

Schwartz, B., *The Paradox of Choice: Why More is Less* (New York: ECCO, 2004).

Seligman, M., *Authentic Happiness* (New York: Free Press, 2002).

Witchalls, C., 'Join the blub', *The Independent* (10 April 2007, p. 8).

Wootton, S. and Horne, T., *Strategic Thinking* (London: Kogan Page, 2000).

2

Exploiting the superior thinking skills of the 50+ brain

In this chapter you will learn:
- *how to exploit superior intelligence at 50+*
- *how to improve scores in employment IQ tests*
- *how to preserve your superior ability to think at 50+ by creating spare cognitive capacity as a buffer against disease.*

The young sow wild oats, the old grow sage.

Winston Churchill

Introduction

A study made in 1947 of the IQs of 70,000 11-year-old children in Scotland, has recently been rediscovered 60 years later by Professor Ian Deary of Edinburgh University. Professor Deary's study shows that smoking, bad food, lack of exercise and disease correlate with declining IQ scores, but age, in itself, does not. Quite the reverse!

So far, 1,500 of the people who took the IQ tests in 1947 have been traced and persuaded to retake their original IQ tests, to complete lifestyle questionnaires and to undergo MRI brain scans. In the absence of disease, or adverse lifestyle choices, average IQ improved by 10 per cent – a huge upward shift according to John Starr, consultant at the Royal Victoria Hospital, Edinburgh, when compared with a current assumption that IQs decline steadily from age 17 onwards. Staying physically fit, and eating foods rich in omega-3 fatty acids, were among the positive contributors to the gain in IQ with age. When adversely affected subjects were removed, the average gains in IQ with age were even more dramatic and were still increasing at age 70+.

The largest gains in IQ with age were associated with freedom from major illness and with persistent physical and mental activity. Chapter 4 shows how you can protect your brain from disease through simple physical exercises and by ditching diets and favouring the low-oxytoxic foods that are listed in the appendices.

Brain training is proven to maintain and thicken the myelin insulation on the neural connections between the different parts of your brain. As you age, your improving IQ seems to be a measure of the extent to which the different parts of your brain continue to connect to each other. Continuing to learn and create close relationships (Chapter 6), adds new connections. As neuroscientist Dr Barry Gibb says, 'If you think of the brain as a machine, you would not expect it to function for 120 years without good maintenance… "Neurobic" activities help to keep your head fit in the same way that aerobic exercises help to keep your muscles fit.'

Beyond a certain point, increased connectedness does not seem to go on adding to your tested IQ indefinitely, but what it does seem to do is to create spare cognitive capacity which you can hold in reserve, just in case you contract a disease that damages some of your existing connections. The important realization is that such damage is disease related – not age related. And the risk of damaging disease is lifestyle related. According to Professor Carol Brayne, at Cambridge University, you can control your own exposure to damage and reverse earlier damage.

Ironically, one of the pupils tested in the original 1947 study was Richard Wilson, who played Victor Meldrew, the elderly character in the BBC drama *One Foot in the Grave*. In some ways, the 50+ generation is guilty of helping to perpetuate ageism by colluding with prejudicial stereotypes of older people like Victor Meldrew (see the 'Final thoughts' section). Richard Wilson has agreed to help Professor Deary publicize his project and its important finding that IQ does not necessarily decline with age, and that it can, and does, improve with age. And if you train your brain, your IQ at 50+ can continue to get better and better.

The use of IQ tests for job selection

When you go for a job with an employer who uses psychometric selection tests, the battery of tests will almost certainly include some traditional IQ tests. These may be pen and paper tests or, more likely, they will be screen-based. You must attempt as many questions as you can within a time limit, which will be strictly enforced. There are always more questions than you can complete within the time. The questions will usually get harder as you work through the test, so relax, it is not you that lacks mental stamina – all the evidence points to the 50+ generation having more, not less, mental stamina than younger applicants. Since incorrect guesses do not count against you, you should make a quick, once over attempt at all the questions, before going back to the start to work systematically through all the questions you skipped over.

If you were allowed even a little more time, at 50+ you would likely have such an advantage over younger applicants that you could easily come out ten points ahead. This is a very significant difference – equating, for example, to senior executive and top civil service administration jobs, as opposed to senior clerical or executive grades. This argues for plenty of advanced practice, preparation and time efficiency on the day of the test. An employer using psychometric tests will almost certainly also have open-ended, less time-constrained, tasks in their test battery. These tasks will require creative thinking, reflective learning, general knowledge and judgement based on experience. This will give you, as a 50+ candidate, a tremendous advantage over younger applicants – just as long as you relax and enjoy it.

Insight
50+ and employment selection tests
The more thorough and up to date the selection assessment, the bigger the advantage you will have over the younger applicants. You will out-perform them on in-tray exercises, group work and presentations. Your social experience and your superior vocabulary will give you a big advantage – more modern tests increasingly focus on assessing 'streetwise' intelligence, which 50+ candidates have in abundance.

Modern tests of multiple intelligences

There is a trend, especially in US organizations, towards tests that assess multiple intelligences (see Table 2.1 on page 35). This trend gives 50+ candidates a clear advantage over younger applicants, because many of the additional intelligences measured in modern tests of multiple intelligences benefit from general knowledge and experience. Obviously, the older you are, the more general knowledge and experience you are bound to have. At 50+, you also have greater skills in prediction and in the 'streetwise' evaluation of what is likely to work in practice, as opposed to in theory.

Modern tests of multiple intelligences require applicants to use a lifetime of acquired information to infer the most likely answers (Chapter 5). Older people tend to score more highly than younger people on numerical, predictive and reflective thinking. The capacity for predictive thinking and reflective thinking, and the ability to estimate and quantify consequences, are key components of 'streetwise' intelligence. This confers further advantages on the 50+ candidate.

A MORE MODERN IQ TEST

Answer as many questions as you can.

1	Woman is to X, as Criterion is to Criteria.	Is X: Child, Father, Gender or Women?
2	Past is to X, as Spun is to Spinning.	Is X: Present, Participle, Predictive or Rotation?
3	Planes is to X, as Lines is to Cross.	Is X: Arc, Eclipse, Intersect or Chord?
4	Breakfast is to X, as Meal is to Hearty.	Is X: Continental, Full English, Light or Eat?
5	Plane is to X, as Polish is to Stone.	Is X: Flight, Hydrofoil, Timber or Wheat?
6	Buddhism is to X, as Median to Average.	Is X: Séance, Monk, Meditation or Religion?
7	Submarine is to X, as Helicopter is to Air.	Is X: Yacht, Fish, Lake or Water?
8	Meaning is to X, as Category is to Homogenous.	Is X: Acronym, Anonymous, Synchronous or Synonymous?

How did you get on?

The answers are at the base of this page. Our students range from 2–3 correct answers; 4+ is a good score.

Answers:

1 Women 2 Present 3 Intersect 4 Full English 5 Timber 6 Religion 7 Water 8 Synonymous

34

The disadvantages of youth and the 'streetwise' 50+

Older people have the advantage of having been young, whereas younger people have the disadvantage of never having been old.

Simon Wootton, 2007

Young people who have high verbal IQ scores can sometimes think and talk so quickly that they can defend the intellectually indefensible. They can argue for an unreasonable inference, or gloss over an impractical implication, especially when they are more quickly rewarded for doing a clever demolition job on a 50+ idea than they would if they took time to examine their own.

Intelligent young people are used to getting things right, from school onwards. Getting something wrong is unfamiliar. Intelligent people generally do not like the unfamiliar feeling of getting things wrong. Delusions of infallibility are often intact in younger people and the preservation of these delusions is sometimes more important to them than entertaining the possibility that they may be wrong.

Awareness of other possibilities and other possible consequences increases as you get older. According to Sternberg, this leads the 50+ to have 'streetwise' intelligence, which shows its wisdom through having 'good' or 'bad' feelings about people and situations. The 'streetwise' intelligence of the 50+ depends on broad general knowledge linked to experience. Both increase as you grow older.

Eminence

To be eminent, the 50+ need to exhibit only one type of intelligence. Eight possible types of intelligence have been identified.

Table 2.1: Eight types of intelligence (after Gardner 2004).

Intelligence type	The capacity...
Environmental	to observe and see patterns
Interpersonal	to empathize and respond
Intrapersonal	to know one's motives, goals and feelings
Kinaesthetic	to manipulate concepts, to use the body

(Contd)

Intelligence type	The capacity...
Linguistic	to use language (oral or written)
Musical	to use tone, accent, rhythm, pitch
Logical	to think logically, to calculate scientifically
Visual	to use graphics, to think spatially

Wordsworth, Beethoven, Einstein, Turner, Picasso, Freud, Winston Churchill, Gandhi and Darwin had some intelligences which lay dormant until they displayed them well after they turned 50 years of age.

Insight
Intelligence and how it changes with age (or does it?)
It is a myth that intelligence necessarily declines with age. Your intelligence reflects the extent to which different areas of your brain have readily accessible connections to each other. There are lifestyle choices and brain training exercises that can increase the interconnected feeders of your brain, as well as improving the quality of the myelin insulation along the neural pathways that help to form the connections.

Which intelligences could you display later in your life? Study Table 2.2 and then check out the 'Steps to eminence'.

Table 2.2: Types of genius often displayed in later life (after Gardner 1995).

Masters	Know all there is to know in a particular field. Masters are people with whom others feel privileged to work, or to whom others seek to be apprenticed, or under whom others seek to serve. One thinks of master painters, like Turner.
Makers	Know enough about the rules of a particular discipline to be able to break them. Like writing sentences without verbs! Makers bring new ways of thinking. People like Darwin and Freud.
Influencers	Work through others, often behind the scenes. They are the power behind thrones, like the 'silent accountant' behind Richard Branson. Philosophers like John Locke influenced Thomas Jefferson, who wrote the American Constitution. Karl Marx, Martin Luther King and

	Mahatma Gandhi illustrate how powerful an idea can be. Sometimes written. Sometimes quietly spoken in small circles.
Introspectors	Keep detailed diaries, write long letters or make extensive notes and leave them for posterity. Novelists, poets and politicians sometimes do this. People like Virginia Woolf, Wordsworth and Tony Benn.

Steps to eminence

Step 1 – First, decide which of the following interest you most. Ring the letter below your choice.

If...	Groups Management	Individuals Psychology	Nature Biology	Engineering Maths
Ring	A	B	C	D
If...	Bodies Sport	Words Teaching	Sounds Music	Appearance Art
Ring	E	F	G	H

Step 2 – Next, decide which of the following you think describes you best. Put a ring around the number below it.

If...	Planning Organizing Controlling	Articulate Numerate Logical	Good at learning Reflective	Curious Experimental Risk taking	Adaptable Easy-going Streetwise
Ring	1	2	3	4	5

Step 3 – You now have a number/letter combination, e.g. A2. If you find the position of your number/letter combination on the matrix below, it will be at the epicentre of words that enable you to explore the opportunities open to you in later life.

	1	2	3	4	5
A	Production control	Manufacturing Management	Quality control	Research Development	Sales Services
B	Planning administrator	Counselling Therapy	Academic research	Writing Editing	Social work Youth work

(Contd)

	1	2	3	4	5
C	Middle management	Editor Publisher	Academic research	Inventor Designer	Environment Ecology
D	Project management	Systems analysis	Purchasing Logistics	Design Engineer	Team leader
E	Own business	Commentator Sports writer	Dance Performance	Outdoor Active	Trainer Journalist
F	Literary PR/ agent	Actor/Editor Teacher	Critic Professor	Poet Writer	Journalist PR/ Media
G	Agent, Arts management	Lyrics Advertising	Music critic	Composer Musician	Teacher Accompanist
H	Arts admin., Museum	Designer Trainer	Exhibitor Development	Artist Creative	Director Innovation

Can you increase your intelligence and your IQ score?

Yes, you can. Reviews of more than 200 studies, including studies of adopted siblings and twins, have shown that less than 50 per cent of your IQ is determined by your genes – though good genes clearly get you off to a good start! In the longer term, you can improve your IQ score by 4 points just by what you choose to eat and drink (Chapter 4). You can add another 6–7 points by regular thoughtful conversations (Chapter 6). You can avoid short-term deficits of up to 15 points by following regular patterns of sleep (Chapter 4). According to Ostranger, you can add up to 14 points to your test score by preparation and stress reduction. That's a very significant increase when related to a 'normal' IQ score of 100.

Preparing for IQ tests – a six-point plan

1. If your diet has been haywire recently, then take the stipulated daily doses of vitamins B1, B5 and Vitamin C, plus mineral supplements of boron, zinc and selenium. Take with plenty of water (Chapter 4).
2. Practise mixing yourself booster drinks to find the mix and concentration that suits you. You may need a boost on the day,

especially if the tests are held in the afternoon. Booster drinks can be made from hot water and a spoon of honey mixed together in a mug. Add the juice of a lemon. Drink it with a capsule of vitamin E. Experiment the week before with one to four capsules but do not exceed the daily dose. Take the drink and the vitamin E capsules about one hour before the test. Sip sage tea during it (Chapter 4).

3 Make sure your prior sleep pattern is stable and sufficient (Chapter 4).

4 Raise or reduce your stress level so that you enjoy a sense of wellbeing. Use lavender oil if you need to calm yourself. On the day, put peppermint, basil, sage or rosemary oil on a tissue, so that you can control your level of mental alertness.

5 If you think you may be overtired and low in energy on the day, practise making 3G cocktails. A 3G cocktail comprises the herbs ginger, ginkgo and ginseng. It is important not to exceed the stated dose.

6 Career advice services, or job centres, will often let you practise taking tests under 'test' conditions. This is a good way to desensitize yourself to test trauma.

Does lifelong learning help?

In the first part of this chapter, we introduced Professor Ian Deary's discovery of 70,000 test papers which were taken when the candidates were 11 years old. The results of his subsequent study did not surprise those of us with experience of working with mature learners. Mature learners commonly improve their IQ scores by about 10 per cent during two years of part-time study. A 10 per cent shift, e.g. from 100 to 110, or 110 to 121, or 120 to 132, is a very significant gain. Professor Deary discovered that other IQ gains, especially among the physically fit candidates who had remained mentally active, were very high indeed. This 'elite' group are still being studied. It is already clear that on-going learning and on-going mental activity correlate strongly with these larger gains in IQ. The only vitamin supplements that appeared to have any long-term correlation with IQ gain were B12 and folic acid. The implication for those of you who wish to improve your IQ as you get older is to carry on learning, formally or informally, no matter what your age, and to train your brain much as you would train your body.

First of all, what you learn will likely add to the breadth of your general knowledge and this will support many of the thinking skills which contribute to your intelligent behaviour – like your capacity for critical, creative and reflective thinking. Secondly, how you learn can promote the formation of new neural pathways, newly connecting different parts of your brain. For this reason, you should consider the following advice on learning methods:

▶ Check out *how* you will be learning as well as *what* you will be learning.
▶ Avoid programmes that rely heavily on a traditional lecture/ seminar format, especially if seminar numbers are too high to support the kind of 1:1 conversations that foster cognitive development (Chapter 6).
▶ Be wary of academic courses that rely heavily on information transfer via IT, or distance learning packs, or handouts.
▶ Ask how much 1:1 face-to-face contact you will have.
▶ Ask whether paired learning will be used (Chapter 6).

Insight
Talk and learn
Learning activities that involve talking to others seem to increase your residual cognitive capacity. If you are thinking of formal study, find out whether the learning process involves any of the following: working in pairs with other learners; individual tuition or learning in small groups (2–4) with a tutor; oral assessment; presentations; coaching; monitoring; and peer- and self-assessment. These will contribute to your intelligence, while the syllabus will add to your knowledge.

The neurochemical basis of intelligence

So far, we have only considered ways to improve traditional IQ scores, but a multi-faceted model of intelligence leaves open the possibility of activities that can further enhance your intelligent behaviour. The work of Haier and Miller suggests that the better connected the different areas of your brain, the more intelligent you are.

Exercises such as cryptic crosswords may work, in part, by stimulating the growth, thickening and replacement rate of myelin, the insulation that surrounds the nerves in the brain. This is like replacing the poor-quality leads that come with a boxed set hi-fi or home cinema system with a more expensive set of leads. The more expensive leads enhance the definition of your television picture and the quality of the sound from your speakers.

The density of the neuron connections in your brain can be increased by learning new things and by tackling tasks and exercises that require you to use different parts of your brain in combination. As you will see in Chapter 3, activities that involve your memory will activate an extensive neural network, radiating out from your hippocampus.

Here are two sample combination thinking tasks for you to try.

Combining visual and emotional thinking

▶ A young child has returned home from school to find seven pebbles, a carrot, and a wet scarf on the grass outside the house. Why is the child crying?

Combining visual, numerical and creative thinking

▶ Because this is a dark chocolate cake, made to Sally's recipe, all eight people at the party want an equal slice of the cake. You are allowed up to three cuts.

Answer 1 = the snowman melted

Answer 2 = use two vertical cuts to cut into four and then one horizontal cut parallel to the base gives eight pieces in three cuts

Students doing combination exercises as part of their brain training circuits, often complain that such exercises make their 'heads hurt', a bit like muscle fatigue after working out in a gym. By undertaking exercises that combine a range of different thinking skills (e.g. visual, numerical, emotional, creative, reflective, predictive), you are really challenging your brain in your own mental gymnasium.

AFTER THE INITIAL BURN...

Haier's work, using brain scanners, has shown that when the more intelligent 50+ people first start thinking about a problem, many different areas of their 50+ brains light up and link up. Initially, your 50+ brain burns a lot of energy, while feeling its way around the problem area. Quickly, the frontal lobes of your cerebral cortex appear to delegate the brainwork to an appropriate selection of areas in the brain, which support the kinds of thinking needed to address the problem. This local area neural network then takes over, allowing the rest of your 50+ brain to relax.

50+ geniuses are created not born

Ellen Winner of Harvard has been studying prodigiously high IQ children. These high IQ children often do not even shine as adults (and certainly don't necessarily become geniuses). Twin research by Professor Michael Howe has shown that the role of inherited IQ in genius is overplayed and that motivation and intention, planning and persistence, and capacity for hard work are all big factors in genius. These are all factors that are in short supply in younger adults and in better supply as you reach 50+. Although this research is recent, the knowledge is not:

In life, it is the training, not the brain, that counts.

Ihara Siakaku (1642–93)

Insight
Becoming a genius

Research seems to point to genius being more often made than born – more a lifestyle choice than a genetic determinant. Eminence seems to be a more useful concept than genius, for there are many different ways in which it is achievable. It is important to choose the way that best suits your background, interests and personality.

THE VOLVO EFFECT

In discovering what he termed the Volvo effect, Professor Yaakov Stern studied the blood flow in the brain, using a zenon scanner. He discovered that people who did more learning in their lives had more reserve capacity and more resistance to Alzheimer-related intrusions, causing impairment of mental functioning. ('A tough car can keep rolling despite a bump or two.') The idea of cognitive reserve capacity had been earlier advanced by neurologist Robert Katzman and neuropathologist Robert Kerry. They had found extensive Alzheimer's plaques and tangles in the brains of their control groups – the ones with normal thinking abilities! The results have been replicated by Professor Caffey, using a PET scanner on the brains of 320 people with normal mental functioning.

Growing old gracefully and intelligently

As you grow older...

▶ You have the advantage of information and experience that can only be acquired through living long enough.
▶ You can use this information to feed your predictive thinking.
▶ You can use predictive thinking to remind you to make an earlier start on things that take longer.
▶ You can keep learning and trying new things.
▶ You can use the thinking skills in Appendix A to exploit your 50+ IQ.
▶ You can do brain training like that supplied in the brain circuits in Part two, in order to open up new neural pathways and add to the processing power of your brain. As you progressively complete more and more chapters, you will be able to combine the processing power of different parts of your brain. You will become more intelligent.

Insight
Keep on learning
When people who were 70+ were invited to resit IQ tests they had taken at school when they were 11, on average their scores were 10 per cent higher.

(Contd)

Many recorded even more dramatic improvements, and further research has shown that these high scorers had been involved in learning as adults. What seems to matter crucially is not so much what you learn as how you learn it: certain ways of learning leave neurochemical traces in your brain that can be used in subsequent learning.

'For I am 50+!'

Those people want it all.
But what these people do not know,
Is that the world is very complex, imperfect and oppressed.
What those people need is prophets, wise and not too stressed.
I am waiting for their call.
I'll have their problems soon finessed;
I'll rejuvenate the railways,
I will nationalize a mine,
I'll manipulate the mailways,
I'll use my intellect to shine.
I can illuminate their problems,
I can make them crystal clear,
But I saw your eyes go cloudy,
As you saw me lean to hear.
Yet, I had felt so confident
And I still feel very strong
Yes, I know that I am fallible,
Yes, I know I can be wrong,
Yes, I know my voice is nasal,
It has been boring all along.
You're right,
They did stop coming,
To stop and make a fuss,
I know that I am unstoppable,
Yes, that's me at 50+.

Terry Horne, 2008 – indebted to Pam Ayres, *Surgically Enhanced*

44

10 THINGS TO REMEMBER

1 You can exploit the superior intelligence that you have at 50+.

2 You can improve your scores in employment IQ tests.

3 At 50+ you can preserve your superior ability by creating spare cognitive capacity as a buffer against disease.

4 IQ tests measure some of the important thinking skills that contribute to intelligent behaviour.

5 In addition to the thinking skills measured in IQ tests, creative thinking, reflective thinking and predictive thinking are major contributors to intelligent behaviour and all these improve as you grow older.

6 Your scores on IQ tests can readily be improved by up to 14 points – a very significant improvement.

7 A high IQ test score is no guarantee of intelligent behaviour. For example, some fast-thinking people are more adept at defending poor thinking than they are at thinking well.

8 Genius requires intellectual virtues that can come with age.

9 Speed and accuracy of thinking are correlated with the quality of the myelin insulation surrounding the axons of the neurons in your brain, and this can be improved through brain training exercises.

10 Intelligence is linked to the number of neuron connections in your brain and this number can be increased by the way you use it.

Suggested further reading

Ayres, P., *Surgically Enhanced* (London: Hodder & Stoughton, 2006).

www.brainwaves.com. Conditioning exercises for six intelligences.

Cobb, J., 'Learning and dementia: the Framingham study,' *Neurology*, 45 (1995), pp. 1706–13.

Fixx, J., *Games for the Super Intelligent* (New York: Doubleday, 1972).

Gardner, H., *Changing Minds* (Boston: Harvard Business School Press, 2004).

Gould, E., 'Learning and neurogenesis in nature', *Neuroscience*, 2 (1998), pp. 259–66.

Howard, P. J., *The Owner's Manual for the Brain: Everyday Applications from Mind and Brain Research* (3rd edn, Austin, Texas: Bard Press, 2006).

Jarski, R., *Wrinklies' Wit and Wisdom* (London: Prion, 2005).

Miller, E. M., 'Intelligence and brain myelination', *Personality and Individual Differences*, 17 (1994), pp. 803–33.

O'Keefe, J., (1994) *Mind Openers for Managers*, Thorsons.

Rosenzweig, M., 'The effect of training and experience in the brain', *Behavioural Brain Research*, 78 (1996), pp. 56–66.

Snowdon, D., 'Linguistic ability and cognitive function: the nun's study', *Journal of the American Medical Association*, 275 (1996), pp. 527–33.

Stern, Y., 'Learning, occupation and Alzheimer's', *Journal of the American Medical Association*, 271 (1994), pp. 1003–11.

Stern, Y., 'Education, occupation and the rate of memory decline in AD: the cognitive reserve', *Neurology*, 53 (1999), pp. 1941–6.

Sternberg, R., *Successful Intelligence* (New York: Plume, 1997).

3

The superior memory of the 50+ brain

In this chapter you will learn:

- *that your long-term memory at 50+ is better than when you were younger and should continue to get better*
- *that the speed at which you can form new short-term memories will decline slowly from age 50+, but that this can be worked around*
- *that tips, tricks, tools and training can speed up new memory formation*
- *that as a bonus, memory training expands the already enhanced cognitive capacities of the 50+ brain*
- *how and why training your age-enhanced 50+ brain will help protect its increased intelligence and thinking skills against erosion by disease.*

> *I am growing older and will someday be old. I do not ask for improving memory but for lessening cocksureness,*
> *For greater humility when my memory clashes with that of others.*
> *Teach me the glorious lesson that occasionally I may be wrong.*
>
> Nun's prayer, circa 1600

Introduction

Millions of people around the world are worrying about their 50+ 'senior moments'. Names, keys, glasses, 'where's the car' or 'what was it I wanted in the first place!'. At 50+, it is normal to sense a dip in your ability to retain new information. None of this means that you are losing your mind or your marbles. Just the opposite – each of the ten thinking skills (see Appendix A) that contribute to your thinking power become more powerful as you get older. This chapter is about dealing with one, admittedly very irritating, aspect of only one of those skills: the speed at which you can form new short-term memory. If you don't learn to work around this (or just take more time over it), it can seem like you have lost the ability to do it altogether, and because it is the gatekeeper to many of your other thinking skills, it can undermine your confidence in your ability to think generally. This can be very disconcerting – alarming even – but your alarm is misplaced.

Recollection of long-term memory, on the other hand, actually improves with age – because, as you've grown older, you have had many more opportunities to recollect things, and each recollection thickens the myelin insulation around the neural pathways used to collect together the fragments of that particular memory. The earlier the original memory, the more likely you are to have had occasion to recall it. More recalls equals better retention.

It is perfectly possible to remain very sharp until you are very old – way beyond 50+. People like Winston Churchill and Golda Meir remained very sharp until they were much nearer 100 than 50.

For the sake of your body, over the last 15 years you may have become resigned to the need to adopt better eating and drinking habits, to perhaps stop smoking, and even to physically exert yourself more. You can now do exactly the same for your brain. You can, if you wish to, make lifestyle choices that will improve or maintain the fitness of your brain. You can affect the chemical conditions in your brain by the things you do and eat, and the way that you feel. Chapter 4 will detail some the choices you can make. This chapter will concentrate on your memory and how and why training your age-enhanced 50+ brain will help protect its increased intelligence and thinking skills against erosion by disease.

Is it wise to eat sage?

Apparently, if you rip sage leaves into small pieces and add a teaspoon of the ripped leaves to a cup of boiling water and sip your infusion during a test, or an interview or a presentation, you will improve your performance. Sage inhibits the breakdown of acetylcholine which the brain uses when it thinks.

Age is not a problem – but disease can be

Up until recently, we thought that certain diseases, like arthritis, erectile dysfunction, or Alzheimer's, came with age. We now know that this is not the case. These diseases often make people look older, but they are not themselves caused by age.

If you have already reached 50+, and you are still physically healthy, you should start planning what you are going to do for your one hundredth birthday! Sure, by then you will probably have become a lot slower at processing new information into short-term memory – but you can limit this, you can learn to work around it. Some other mental changes will be detectable, through specialist psychological testing, but they will not necessarily turn up as problems in your everyday living. You can add life to your living, not just years to your life. There are some tests in this chapter that will enable you to detect some changes, but there are also tips, steps, diet changes etc., that can help you to reverse, ward off or work around any changes you do detect.

From the age of 50+, you can sometimes start to lose up to 1 per cent of your brain cells each year, but that does not necessarily lead to loss of mental performance as long as your brain stays fit. You can tip the odds of enhancement and preservation decisively in your favour. You can add new brain cells. On tests, many 70+ brains outperform 20+ brains.

By 2003, Dr Jeff Victoroff had already pointed out that brain scientists were by now 'swimming in an ocean tide of promising discoveries'. By 2008, that tide had turned decisively. It is time to harness brain science into a movement for brain fitness that will rival the movement for body fitness.

Insight
Age and the brain
It is not true that age inevitably damages your brain, in fact age enhances the brain's performance. There are diseases which can lower the performance of your brain, but there is much you can do to prevent these diseases or at least to ameliorate their effects. Your risk of developing a neurodegenerative disease, like Alzheimer's, seems to be related to what you eat. You should favour foods with low oxytoxic and high ORAC scores (see Chapter 4).

Is there a 50+ memory pill just around the corner?

Not at the moment, but ask your doctor about:

▶ **Amparines** – it is a cognitive booster, even if you don't have Alzheimer's.
▶ **Donepezil** – it boosts concentration, even if you don't have dementia.
▶ **Modafinil** – it improves thinking, even if you don't have narcolepsy.
▶ **Ritalin** – it improves concentration and visual thinking, even if you don't have ADHD (look up vitamin R, on the internet).
▶ **Propranol** – it suppresses distracting or distressing memories, even if you don't have a heart problem.
▶ **MEM compounds** – currently under test in the USA.
▶ **Gene therapy** – neurological professor Matthew During reported on successful gene treatment of Parkinson's disease in the *Lancet* (June 2007) and one of the research team, Dr Kaplitt, believes it may be effective for other neurological conditions.

Memory and surgery at 60+

People aged over 60 are twice as likely to suffer a memory loss and mental sharpness after surgery, report doctors at Duke University in North Carolina, USA (*Anaesthesiology*, January 2008). Those who lose mental ability after surgery are also significantly more likely to die within a year of having the operation. Hence keeping both your mind and your body fit are equally important.

Memory test

TEST YOUR LONG-TERM MEMORY

1 What did you eat at your last meal?	
2 Where were you last Saturday?	

3 What did you do on the Thursday before that?	
4 Where were you at midnight on New Year's Eve?	
5 What was the title of the last film you watched?	
6 Where were you when you heard that President Kennedy had been shot?	
7 How did you last celebrate something?	
8 What was the last book you read?	
9 Where were you when you first remember being kissed?	
10 Who kissed you?	

To score: 0–6 is poor. 7–8 is average. 9–10 is good.

TEST YOUR SHORT-TERM MEMORY

Read one of the horizontal lines of numbers and look away.

How many numbers can you remember?

8						
13						
46	12					
7	10	35				
18	98	84	6			
4	69	25	38	13		
20	22	68	85	16	17	
78	56	88	91	24	46	80

If you can remember three or fewer, then your short-term memory is poor.

4–6, then your short-term memory is average.

7–8, then your short-term memory is good.

> **Insight**
> **Recall**
> The part of your brain called the hippocampus plays a central role in enabling you to recall things. Different fragments of the memory to be retained – images, numbers, sounds, and so on – are diverted to different parts of the brain. Connections to fragments already stored are sorted out and established. When recall is attempted, it is often only necessary to locate one fragment and the hippocampus plays a role in finding the other bits until the memory is recovered: sometimes not in its entirety, sometimes entirely accurate.

Sudoku is good, Scrabble is better, cryptic crosswords are brilliant!

Sudoku requires several parts of your brain to work together to support numerical, visual, emotional and critical thinking. As patterns emerge and fragments are remembered, many neural links are activated in over 30 different areas of your cerebral cortex. Many of these neural linkages involve your hippocampus, which plays a central role in your memory. When you play Sudoku or Scrabble or do cryptic crosswords, these neural links are run over and over again, thickening the myelin insulation around the axons of your brain cells and thereby improving the speed and the accuracy of your thinking. Emotional thinking is involved in managing your impatience, frustration, and the disappointment you feel as you compete with yourself or with others.

Your memory switchboard (the bit that looks like a seahorse)

Your hippocampus, the bit that looks like a seahorse, seems to act like a central switchboard. Your hippocampus links fragmentary components of your memory that may be stored in many different parts of your brain.

The hippocampus has been the focus of much of the research that has been done on memory and recollective thinking. Why? Is it just because it is distinctive in its appearance and therefore easy to see and isolate? In *Stem Cells: Controversy at the Frontiers of Science* (2006) and 'The Labyrinth of Memory' (2007), Elizabeth Finkel jokes about the preoccupation of brain researchers with the hippocampus:

> *A brain researcher is like a man who has lost his keys in the street. The brain researcher is found crawling about, on his hands and knees, near a street lamp.*

> *When asked if he has dropped his keys near to the street lamp, he replies, 'No, but it is too dark to search for them anywhere else.'*

A Sudoku puzzle is usually a 9 × 9 grid subdivided into 9 squares – like noughts and crosses.

6					1			
		9	7	5		2		8
	5	7		4		9	6	
5	6	2			3		8	
	4						1	
	8		6			5	7	3
	3	5		1		8	9	
1		4		6	8	3		
			2					7

The puzzle starts with some given numbers – called clue numbers – already inserted. The object of the game is to fill all the empty boxes so that each row, each column and each 3 × 3 large square, contains the numbers 1 to 9 – without repeating any number.

TIPS ON SOLVING SUDOKU PUZZLES

▶ Use an HB pencil with an eraser in the end, or a ballpoint that has more than one colour.

▶ Start by picking the 3 × 3 grid that has most number clues already given. Look at the rows and columns going through the square you have picked. Pick a row or column that has several clue numbers already in place. Pick a 'vacant' square in the grid you have chosen to work on.

▶ In pencil or in green ink, enter in a small font the 'missing' numbers, i.e. missing from the square, and from the row and the column in which the vacant square is sitting. If there is only one such number, you have found your first answer number. Enter the answer number in the vacant square by over-striking your missing numbers in black. Write the answer number as big as the clue numbers.

► Repeat for all the vacant squares in the row, the column and the 3 × 3 grid. By elimination, each time you enter a big black answer number, you can erase or strike out the small missing numbers that you have entered in other places in the row, column or 3 × 3 square. As soon as you have only one missing number left in a small square – that is, an answer number – overwrite it large and black.

► This will get you started and enable you to use basic Sudoku puzzles for brain training. Your brain will get most benefit from doing easier puzzles as quickly as you can. Note your times and note how much quicker you are getting.

The answer to the Sudoku above can be found at the end of this chapter.

Insight
The best game in town
The goal of a brain game is to connect together as many parts of your brain as possible. Sudoku, crosswords and chess are all good for this; backgammon and Scrabble are better, and a shared cryptic crossword is brilliant. According to the most recent French research, pencil and paper puzzles are more effective than their electronic counterparts. Each of the brain circuits in Part two will develop different combinations of thinking skills you need.

A myth about memory

'You are born with all the brain cells you will ever have.'

Not true. Memory researchers have discovered that your chemical brain is a complex organ which develops and changes with every thought that you have. This means that old, diseased or deteriorating brains can change and repair themselves with the right diet, exercise and brain training. This explains why it is that the brains of many older people show no deterioration in thinking performance (*Train Your Brain*, Horne and Wootton, 2010).

The myth of dementia

When pathologists dissect the brains of people who have remained mentally sharp and active up to the time they died, they sometimes find that these brains are riddled with Alzheimer's plaques! Yet those mentally active people had shown no signs of impaired memory when they were alive.

Michael Valenzuola's analysis (published 2006), covering 66,000 individuals, showed that people who kept their brains active, for example through work, leisure activities, or brain training, had half the risk of suffering dementia. The pathologists' reports in David Snowdon's nun study are particularly useful because the nuns with Alzheimer's who had impaired mental functioning had a virtually identical lifestyle/environment/diet etc., as the nuns with Alzheimer's who showed no sign of mental impairment. The only difference between the 'impaired' and 'non-impaired' groups was the level of on-going learning and mental exercise. In a convent, other lifestyle variables are largely controlled and comparable.

Memory, diet and dieting

Don't do it! Don't do it! Don't go on a fat-free diet.

Fats are the building blocks of your brain. If your fat-free diet is very successful, you may become slim and beautiful, but the only thing you will be fit for is reality TV.

Terry Horne, 2006, after George Burns

Your body fuels your brain by burning food. Brain activity can require your body to 'burn' more than 25 per cent of the food you eat – depending on how mentally active you are. Burning food (or calories) is more scientifically described as 'oxidizing' the glucose in your food, thereby releasing energy – physical and mental energies. Unfortunately, one by-product of the oxidation of glucose in our food is sometimes an 'oxygen free radical'. An oxygen free radical can attack a human cell and precipitate diseases like cancer or Alzheimer's. Alzheimer's disease may, in turn, impair your memory.

Normally, this chain of events would be interrupted because our bodies also produce antioxidants which can mop up oxygen free radicals before they can do any harm. If, however, you eat foods that are very rich in glucose, your body's normal production of antioxidants may not be sufficient to mop up all the free radicals that will be produced when your body oxidizes all the glucose in those

foods. In this book, we have called foods that are too rich in glucose
'oxytoxic' foods. There are low-oxytoxic versions of most of the
foods you eat. Appendix H lists the oxytoxic values of many common
foods, so that you can make an informed choice to eat foods which
are less likely to result in surplus free radicals and, thereby, lessen
your risk of precipitating neurodegenerative diseases. As an added
precaution, you can increase your consumption of foods that contain
antioxidants. Fresh fruit, vegetables and dark chocolate all contain
flavonols. Flavonols are the naturally occurring antioxidants found
in food. You can compare the flavonol levels of foods by consulting
the US ORAC index tables in Chapter 4, page 126 – dark chocolate
comes out very high!

OF MICE AND MEN

Eating less definitely increases the lifespan of mice and monkeys – by
up to 50 per cent. The lifespan of humans also increases if you eat
less. But it matters what it is that you eat less of. There is no point in
living much longer if you are brain dead for the last 10–20 years of
your life. So, do not completely cut out unsaturated fats, for example.
Your brain needs them or the walls of your brain cells may become
brittle and the brain cells may die. The amount of acetylcholine in
your brain is related to the quantity of omega-3, -6 and -9 fats that
you eat, and if you have insufficient acetylcholine in your brain, it
could mean that fewer messages will be passed between your neurons.

If you want to live longer by eating less, then eat less salty or sugary
or refined or processed foods. Eat less of foods that need little
chewing, or that are eaten quickly. Such foods have side effects like
diabetes and heart disease. Also such foods don't satisfy your hunger
for very long, whereas prolonged chewing sends messages to your
brain that you are becoming full and satisfied and that you will not
be requiring any more food at the moment. Refined sugary foods
provoke excessive insulin production, and this in turn produces
strong, hunger-like pangs in your stomach, which disturbs your
mental concentration and also causes you to eat more.

Incidentally, the mice not only lived longer, their brains were more
resistant to neurodegenerative diseases. In the case of people – as
opposed to mice – the incidence of memory problems caused by
Alzheimer's disease in China and Japan, where the average calorie
intake is lower but unsaturated fat intake is proportionally higher,

is about half of the incidence of Alzheimer's in the United States and Western Europe. A longitudinal study of 980 older volunteers in New York has reproduced the connection between Alzheimer's disease and higher daily food intake. The same study also found that the incidences of other brain diseases, such as Parkinson's disease and damage from strokes, also reduce when you eat less.

If you do decide to eat less, don't go on a weight-loss diet. Yo-yo dieting has deleterious effects on your mood and on thinking performance.

DOES STARVING YOUR BRAIN FEED YOUR MIND?

It's not as simple as that!

It's fitness that counts – not fatness. And it's what you eat less of that matters. For example, John might be a high-metabolic-rate consumer of junk food, might not be overweight and might have a body mass index (BMI) in the normal range – yet John may still be at risk of memory loss from Alzheimer's, because the total quantity of food eaten by him is not producing sufficient antioxidants to mop up all of the free radicals which are produced when his body oxidizes all the junk food he is eating. John will not have any antioxidants coming to his rescue from his junk food. The fat in John's junk food will have been converted to transfats – a form that his brain cannot utilize. All the salt in John's junk food will increase his blood pressure, risking further damage to his brain. Yet if John jumps on and off his bathroom scales every day and calculates his body mass index, he may think he's on a healthy diet.

The fact that John is not overweight will help, of course. Because he is not overweight, he will find it easier to exercise and that will help his brain. Exercise will increase the supply of blood to his brain and this will speed up his thinking. The exercise will also stimulate the production of new and replacement brain cells – particularly near his hippocampus, which is central to the working of his memory. Because John is not overweight, he is also less likely to develop diabetes or high blood pressure and so his brain is less at risk from stroke damage. While we do not advocate leaping from the frying pan of excessive eating into the fire of calorie counting diets, moving from a daily average of 2,700–3,000 calories per day of oxytoxic foods, to around 1,500–1,800 calories per day of less oxytoxic foods will at least halve your chances of getting Alzheimer's disease.

This does seem well worth considering. If you don't do physical work, and if you don't work in cold or wet conditions, an average of 1,500–1,800 calories per day is more than sufficient for your needs. If you live or work in a country with a knowledge-based economy, most physical work will be carried out by machines, and most of the machines will be minded by computers. However, an average is just that – an average. Each individual 50+ person has to work out whereabouts in relation to that average they need to be. Whether you need to be a bit higher or a bit lower will depend on your genes.

IS THERE SOMETHING FISHY GOING ON?

Your brain is at least 70 per cent fat. Fats and cholesterol are the building blocks of your brain. Brain fats are not the same kinds of fat that you store in your buttocks. Brain fats perform vital functions and your brain needs a constant supply of them to maintain and repair itself. Your brain also needs to be able to clear away any excess fat very quickly.

This tricky balancing act has been studied in around 700 people living in Rotterdam in the Netherlands. The study showed that your brain prefers the kinds of polyunsaturated fatty acids found in coldwater fish, such as tuna, trout, salmon and mackerel, but your brain is damaged by saturated or transfats, because any excess saturated or transfats are very hard to clear away. Saturated or transfats are found in meat, pastries and dairy products. You can easily recognize saturated fats as they are solid at room temperature. Transfats are produced when food is cooked at very high temperatures for long periods, for example by deep frying. In deep frying, the fat is often reheated repeatedly. The industrialized production of food often increases the content of saturated or transfats. Specifically, the Dutch researchers found that a diet high in saturated fats increased the risk to your memory from dementia, whereas only half an ounce of fish (20 g) a day was sufficient to lower the risk to your brain. This finding was replicated in 2003, when 800 people were studied in Chicago. Even eating fish only once a week was sufficient to reduce the risk of Alzheimer's by 60 per cent.

Neither of these studies proved that it was beneficial to take fish oil supplements instead of eating the fish. Dr Tan's Framingham study, in 2003, reported that blood cholesterol levels which are high enough to damage your heart do not necessarily increase the risk to your brain from Alzheimer's. The jury is still out on cholesterol. The cholesterol story is confused because someone with a low blood cholesterol level is more likely to be the kind of person who eats fewer calories, exercises more, enjoys learning, does Sudoku and cryptic crosswords and reads books on brain training – all of which are good for your brain. When it comes to a general link between fat consumption and the brain, the jury's verdict is definitely in on four counts:

1 The less you eat, the better for your brain (down to about 1,500 calories a day if you are a sedentary brainworker).
2 The 1,500 calories you eat must include some fats.
3 The fats you eat should be unsaturated. Saturated fats are definitely bad for your heart and may be bad for your brain too.
4 Eating coldwater fish, rather than taking fish oil capsules, may be the best way to get the unsaturated fats your brain needs. (The studies showed that you only need to eat a small quantity of fish: 20 g a day or 150 g a week.)

MEMORY, ALCOHOL AND OTHER MYTHS

It is widely believed that moderate alcohol consumption is good for your health. If we are talking about the health of your brain, this is not borne out by the brain science.

True, there is strong evidence that very light alcohol consumption, for example a 40 g measure of 11 per cent red wine per day, does benefit your heart. In so far as this reduces your risk of having a stroke, this also benefits your brain, because a stroke can cause extensive brain damage. Although brain training can greatly accelerate brain repair and recovery in stroke victims, it can be a lengthy process – taking up to 2–4 years – and it may be incomplete. It is better to reduce the risk of having the stroke in the first place.

However, drinking even only one small 40 g measure of alcohol is sufficient to delude drinkers into thinking that their mental judgement is improving, when it is, in fact, deteriorating. The immediate effect of alcohol is to depress many of your brain's functions. The longer-term effect is nutritional deficiency leading to permanent mental impairment and physical damage to your brain. Repeated exposure to alcohol damages tissue in many of your body's organs and your brain is not exempted. The more alcohol you drink, the more extensive will be the brain cell damage and the more memory problems you will have.

On the other hand, a study of 1,800 Swedish volunteers is reported to show a lowered risk of Alzheimer's in a group that drank alcohol compared with a control group that did not. The problem is that a control group of total abstainers in Sweden would likely have other stress-related lifestyle correlates that would increase their risk – so we might not be measuring the benefit of alcohol, just a risk associated with having an abstinent lifestyle. Also, the tradition in Sweden is to eat herring when drinking alcohol, so we may be measuring the benefit of eating the herring!

A study tracking 3,000 Japanese men, over a period of 18 years, showed that performance on memory tests worsened in line with increased alcohol intake. There could be a long-term beneficial effect on the brain of very light alcohol consumption, but that is not clear, whereas the short-term impairment in mental judgement, and in the speed and accuracy of calculation and thought, is very evident. Non-drinkers should not start drinking in the hope of protecting their memories in the long term. Existing drinkers might usefully cut their intake to seven units, or fewer, of alcohol per week, on the basis of first do no harm!

The role of physical exercise

Where possible, talking about life should supplement, not replace the muscular activity of living it.

Simon Wootton, 2004

It is about 2,000 years since the Roman poet Juvenal guessed that there was a connection between having a sound mind and having a sound body. By 2005, research by Dr Zaldy Tan was revealing why it is that having a fit body can help you have a fit brain.

Many benefits of having a fit body are already known – enhanced attractiveness, a more optimistic disposition and a heightened sense of wellbeing. Physical fitness is already known to help prevent heart disease, strokes, diabetes and osteoporosis. Connection between physical fitness and the prevention of Alzheimer's and the

60

preservation of memory, is relatively recent. In 2003, the *American Journal of Gerontology* reported on Dr Barnes's six-year study of 345 people, aged 50+, living in Sonoma, California. Dr Barnes's study showed that increasing your physical fitness did indeed increase your mental fitness and improve your thinking skills. This confirmed a five-year study of 9,000 people, aged 50+, in 36 urban and rural communities in different provinces of Canada. This Canadian study also showed that physical exercise reduced the risk of Alzheimer's. In Japan, a seven-year study of 800 people aged 50+ also showed that physical exercise not only deferred dementia but also could improve the mental performance of people who already had dementia.

In 2005, Kramer used an MRI scanner to show that the normal rate at which the brain loses weight with age can be reduced, or even reversed, as a result of physical exercise. William Greenough at Illinois, and researchers at Pisa, studied the effects of physical training and of brain training, and discovered that each encouraged the growth of new capillaries – the tiny blood vessels that deliver blood to the cells of your brain. The blood vessels of people aged 50+ who did physical and mental exercises worked as well as those of athletes who were half their age! The brain chemical nitrous oxide – yes, the one produced during sex (see Chapters 4, 5 and 6) – scours the blood vessels, and helps protect them against clogging and keeps them dilated. The nitrous oxide scouring system was found to work as well in 63-year-olds who did the exercises as in 27-year-olds. Of course, it might be that it is the continued sexual attractiveness, not the results from being physically fit and mentally alert, that result in more sex, that result in more nitrous oxide, that result in cleaner capillaries, that result in healthier brain cells, that result in fewer diseases, that result in better memory – but hey, take the sex – the memory of it will be a bonus!

Myers divided 65-year-olds into three otherwise matched groups that had either retired, or retired and exercised, or had continued to work. Within four years, Myers found that cerebral blood flows – a measure of the rate of supply of oxygen to the brain, and therefore of the rate at which the brain can work – had declined in the people who had retired, but had remained high in the groups that had either carried on working or started exercising on retirement. Why not do both? In other words, don't retire and start exercising!

WHICH KIND OF EXERCISE IS BEST?

Dustman divided 50+ men into three groups. For four months, one did aerobic exercise, the other did muscle body building, and a control group made no changes. Cognitive abilities were tested before and after. The scores of both the exercise groups improved over the control group – but the gain was greater for the aerobic exercisers.

Groups of 50+ women were studied for 12 months by a medical research institute in Australia. The 50+ exercisers did better on both memory tests and tests of rapid problem solving. According to Dr Victoroff, these findings have been replicated at least five times. Arthur Smith's case study of people who did a sport showed they were 3.5 times less likely to develop Alzheimer's, and that they had less beta amyloid in their brains. Beta amyloid is very debilitating to neuron activity. In 2001, Canadian researchers who had been tracking nearly 5,000 50+ people, found a 50 per cent reduction in the incidence of Alzheimer's among the 50+ people who took exercise three times a week (or more).

This does not mean that it is impossible for a 48-year-old marathon runner to get a degenerative brain disease – of course it is possible. You can only play the percentages and improve your chances of saving your brain for longer. The longer you live, the longer you need your brain to stay fit – or your longer life will only mean a slower death.

If possible, combine physical activity with social and mental activity. If you don't fancy a swingers' weekend with members of MENSA, try joining a Ramblers group or an amateur dramatic group, or a ballroom dancing class. It is never too late to learn rock climbing.

WHAT COUNTS AS 'VIGOROUS' EXERCISE?

Technically, subtract your 50+ age (whatever it is), from 220, and then take 85 per cent of your answer. Exercise till your heart rate/pulse rate, reaches that number. Ideally, do that five times a week, however briefly, but at least three times a week. This moderate regime – reaching 85 per cent, briefly, three to five times a week – seems to produce the same brain benefits as anything more 'vigorous'. Bodily fitness may be more demanding, of course. Anyone for a walk (briskly, of course)?

NEW TRICKS

When sluggish old rats are given exercise wheels, they develop more new mitochondria. Mitochondria provide power to brain cells.

So you can teach old rats new tricks! Importantly for the memory, exercise seems to regulate and reduce the production of inflammatory cytokines. Cytokines are believed to be involved in the production of Alzheimer's plaque deposits. So exercise seems both to offer increased protection of your memory and brain against degenerative disease, and, in the meantime, to increase the efficiency with which you can think and tackle mental tasks.

At the University of Irvine, scientists further divided the groups of rats into those who had an exercise wheel once a week, and other groups who had them two, three, four and seven times a week. The more the rats ran, the greater the level in their brains of BDNF, which is the protein involved in growing new neurons, especially around the hippocampus. The hippocampus plays a key role in memory creation and retrieval. Diets that are high in saturated fats lower BDNF levels, but older rats who had been fed a lifetime diet with excessive saturated fat, were able to reverse their decline in BDNF by doing exercise.

A tip from Dr Victoroff – get a TV treadmill!
If you are under the tyranny of a television, put a treadmill in front of it. Whoever is on the treadmill gets the best view of the screen!

Out-performing younger minds

Does all this reduction in brain disease, do all those billions more oxygen-rich blood cells, rushing through cleaner and more dilated blood vessels, reducing inflammation and increasing growth of new brain cells, does all this translate into brains that can actually perform any better on mental and thinking tasks? Yes, it does. Studies at universities in Ohio, Texas, Maastricht and Australia have shown that the 50+ brain becomes healthier and fitter following exercise and brain training. Average results on all cognitive tests improve. Because these are averages, there will always be exceptional sedentary cats who are still mentally brilliant, and fit butchers' dogs who are not so bright.

Exercise alone is not sufficient to determine your absolute level of cognitive capacity, because it does not improve scores on all of the necessary components of effective thinking. But one of the components that does benefit is memory. Memory does play an important role in many thinking tasks, especially those involving creative and reflective thinking, both of which get better and better as you get older, so long as you stay fit. Staying fit does not necessarily mean staying slim. Importantly and luckily, exercise and increasing physical fitness act to improve thinking components that might otherwise decline with age, i.e. the speed of new information processing, and hence of new memory formation. So there is only one age-related area of mental decline and you can reverse it if you want to – through physical and mental exercise. Alternatively, you can work around it, by using your improving predictive thinking to make an earlier start on thinking tasks. Why not do both?

> **Insight**
> **How to out-perform younger minds**
> Research has shown that results improve on all cognitive tests following brain training and exercise. A reduced risk of brain disease and an improved blood supply to the brain, combined with the reduced inflammation and increased growth of new brain cells, delivers better performance on mental tasks.

How to speed up your brain

The speed of new information processing is determined by the frontal lobes of your brain – the area that you use for planning and decision making – and this is one of the areas that responds most positively when you train your body and your brain. This explains why 50+ people who do not have a regime of physical exercise, or brain training, may struggle with navigation and driving a car in complex, fast-moving traffic, in a new town, in an unfamiliar hire car. But then, so do many younger drivers. The ability to perform such tasks is measured by using CRT tests – tests of complex reaction time. Following physical and mental training, 50+ people had much better CRT scores than 24-, 25-, 26- and 27-year-old comparators.

> **Insight**
> **Speeding up your brain**
> The frontal lobes of the brain, which determine the speed of new information processing, respond very positively to brain training. In complex reaction time tests, following physical and mental exercises, 50+ people out-performed 20+ comparators. Therefore, in your 50+ years, physical and mental exercises greatly improve the chance that you will retain your age-related mental advantage for longer.

Among nearly 7,000 UK men and women, aged 18–94, those who just occasionally walked, rather than drove/rode, had higher CRT scores than those who always preferred to ride. But a correlation is not necessarily a cause – perhaps an inclination to walk is a genetic, or socioeconomic, or lifestyle marker for other things that are the real determinants of high CRT scores. That is why a study of 222 Swedish twins, reported by Dr Victoroff, is important. Despite having identical genes, the twins that did mental or physical exercise scored higher in cognitive tests! In your 50+ years, fitness regimes greatly increase the probability that you will retain your age-related advantages for longer.

Flexible shoes – flexible brain

Check your footwear. Could you run to rescue a child from a road if you had to? Could you run for a train or a bus? Can you go quickly and safely up and down a flight of stairs? If not, next time you buy new shoes, buy something more flexible and make them your normal wear – just in case you ever fancy a walk at lunchtime, or a walk in the park with your thoughtful companion (Chapter 6).

IS 50+ IQ BEING ENHANCED, OR MERELY RESTORED TO FORMER LEVELS?

It is not certain that 50+ IQ is necessarily being boosted. It is possible that lifestyle choices may have degraded mental performance of the 50+, from the teenage years onwards, and that all we are doing here is reversing degradation in performance to a genetically determined capacity that was already there. Professor Ian Deary's comparison of IQ scores at 11 and 70+ (Chapter 2), suggests that there is definite enhancement in IQ just through getting older, and that exercise and brain training can add to that, or prevent that advantage from being eroded through lifestyle behaviour or other changes in your environment.

HOW TO MAKE CONNECTIONS

▶ Create as many links or associations as possible, so as to increase the number of future possible access cues, thereby increasing the chances of future retrieval. Since we can only hold up to 5 ± 2 new items of information in our short-term memory, making notes and associations, and linking and mapping things together, are essential steps in memorizing more than, say, three things.

- Associations can be simple – the 'g' in stalagmite reminds you that it grows up from the ground, while the 'c' in stalactite reminds you that it comes down from the ceiling.
- Sometimes whole sentences (acrostics) can be used to recall the initial letters of a list of words needing to be remembered. The acrostic 'every good boy deserves friends' gives you the musical notes, E, G, B, D, F, while the acronym FACE gives you the musical notes F, A, C, E for the spaces. The more bizarre the association, the more memorable it will be. Adding in emotion, texture, sex and smell is particularly evocative.
- 'I can't quite place it' is another way of saying, 'I can't remember it'. Over 2,500 years ago, the Greeks propounded the idea of finding a place for things in order to aid recollection. You can use a room in your own house in which you know from memory the relative positions of all the major items of furniture. You can then imagine a giant hammer on the chest, a teddy bear burning in the fireplace, the steam iron completely filling the sofa, a football bouncing along the piano keys, a hairdryer scattering the chess pieces. As you go round your room in your mind's eye, you can recreate your shopping list of hammer, teddy bear, steam iron, football and hairdryer!

HOW TO GROW NEW BRAIN CELLS

Physical exercise not only results in a stronger flow of blood, glucose and oxygen to the brain, it also stimulates the growth of new brain cells, especially in and around your hippocampus, which plays a key role in your memory.

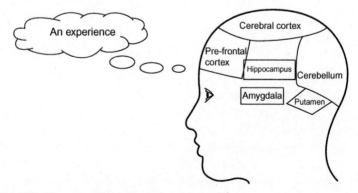

Figure 3.1 The different parts of the brain affected by brain training exercises.

Yes, you do have a photographic memory

It is so good that you can't turn it off – even after two and a half mind-numbing days of looking at over 10,000 boring photographs, many of them similar to each other.

In May 2007, Professor Richard Wiseman took over the ground floor of Waterstone's in London to expose people to up to 10,000 photographs and slides and then show them that they had remembered them (even though they denied it!). Recall rates ranged from 15 out of 16, after looking at 800 photographs for about 1 second each, to recognizing 86 out of 130 photographs after viewing over 9,200 photographs up to 3 days earlier. (The results replicated a similar study 30 years ago in Canada, when subjects also scored 98 per cent and 70 per cent, in equivalent tests of their photographic memories.)

MRI SCANS SHOWING BENEFITS OF DIFFERENT BRAIN TRAINING ACTIVITIES

Scratching the elephant in the room!

Images of the brain's response to scratching have revealed that the action suppresses activity in regions of the brain associated with unpleasant memories and emotions. In a study published in the *Journal of Investigative Dermatology* (2008), 13 volunteers were asked to scratch their legs. MRI was used to monitor the subject's brain while they were scratching. The results showed that the areas of the brain associated with unpleasant or aversive emotions and memories became significantly less active during the scratching.

The neurochemistry of memory

PASS THE PARCEL – A RELAY RACE DOWN MEMORY LANE

The memory messages from your hippocampus travel through your brain's neural network rather like a baton travels in a relay race.

In 2000, Eric Kandel was awarded a Nobel Prize for his work on the Californian sea slug. Kandel's work on the sea slug helped to

During meditation

While watching
videos

Thinking about
difficult problems

While writing
and redrafting

While discussing
or reading aloud

Chanting simple
sums fast

Figure 3.2 Based on research by Professor Kawashima (2007); his electronic exercises are available from Nintendo.

explain how the baton is passed down your neural memory lane. His work confirmed the central role played by sodium ions, which we encountered in Susan Greenfield's work (see 'First thoughts'). The sodium ions help to transfer the charge along the length of each of your neurons. At the end of the neuron's axon, the baton is picked up by neurotransmitter chemicals which then swim across a synaptic gap to the dendrites on your next neuron.

EMOTIONAL MOLECULES – THE 'CHEMICAL FIXATIVES' OF MEMORY

Your hippocampus receives messages from all areas of your brain, in particular from your amygdala. Your amygdala controls the production of what Candace Pert described as 'molecules of emotion' (Chapter 1). These emotional molecules seem to play an important role as 'chemical fixatives' of memory. These chemical fixatives help you to 'burn' learning into your memory. Hence the importance of emotional engagement when you are learning new things.

FLASHBACKS, EMOTIONAL TRAUMA AND 'CHEMICAL FIXATIVES'

When strong emotions, like joy, horror or disgust are associated with a memory, this causes a cocktail of chemicals, such as norepinephrine, adrenaline, enkephalin and vasopressin, to be released into your brain. Hooper and Teresi suggested that this cocktail of chemicals has the same effect as spraying varnish onto a chalk pastel painting. It stabilizes the picture, or the pattern, and reduces the risk of it getting smudged or distorted. The stronger the emotion, the easier it is for you to remember the incident later. Both Thayer and Maguire identified that each emotional state had its own library of memories. When experiencing pride in a success, for example, you may well recall a previous success. When expressing anger or resentment, you are more likely to dredge up earlier resentments which may not have been expressed at the time. It's a bit like collecting trading stamps of similar emotions you have saved up over your 50+ years and then cashing in 50+ years' worth of emotional trading stamps all at once.

DOES CELL LOSS NECESSARILY MEAN MEMORY LOSS?

No. This is because information is stored in the brain in many fragments, widely distributed around different areas of the brain. (This is why exercises involving your memory are so good for brain development). Even if there happens to be the odd cell missing on the neural route to a particular fragment, a diversionary route can usually be found. Even if one of the fragments cannot be located, the brain can generally join up the dots and recover the original memory.

Also, your brain does not shed cells dramatically as you age. The greatest loss of brain cells occurs in childhood. After that, even though your brain shrinks by up to 10 per cent by the time you die, this has recently been found to be largely because your individual cells shrink, not because your brain cells are lost. Cells can be lost through illness, or through drinking alcohol, which can kill up to 60,000 brain cells a day.

Even then it is not all bad news. Firstly, it is the number of connections in your brain, not the number of neurons in your brain, that determines your cognitive capacity. You can add daily to the number of connections you have in your brain through learning and brain training. Secondly, it has recently been discovered that your brain can continue to produce new neurons up until you die. Your hippocampus routinely produces new neurons. This has led to speculation that the new neurons might be needed for new memories. This adds to the importance of physical and mental exercise, because exercise has been shown to accelerate the production of new neurons near to the hippocampus. The carbon dating of brain cells in people who have died, shows that there are many cells that must have been added after their date of birth. As long as you avoid illness and keep your brain fit and well connected, senile decay is not inevitable.

LONG-TERM VS. SHORT-TERM MEMORY

In Australia, Clarke Raymond stuck electrodes into either end of slices of a hippocampus, and recorded the residual voltages in the receiving neurons. When he gave the hippocampus neurons a single charge, the residual voltages in receiving neurons rose slightly. But the effect did not last. The receiving neuron 'forgot' its recent experience. If Raymond repeated the stimulation – another ten times, say – a higher residual voltage was found in the receiving neurons. This time the effect lasted for weeks. In August 2005, the journal *Science* reported that Jonathan Whitlock had replicated Clarke Raymond's findings using the hippocampus of a living brain.

In the case of the short-term memory effect, the molecules of the receptor chemicals were modified by the stimulus. The memory faded because modified molecules were slowly replaced with unmodified molecules. In the case of the long-term memory effect, the repeated stimulus not only modified the molecules of the receptor chemicals, it also increased the number of receptor sites, and so made new synapses available to support further learning and extra cognitive capacity.

Alzheimer's disease

WHAT IS ALZHEIMER'S DISEASE?

Alzheimer's disease is the most common cause of memory loss and generalized dementia. Dementia is the term used to describe loss of cognitive capacity in the brain. Alzheimer's progressively impairs memory, and then the ability to concentrate, and then the ability to reason. Eventually, Alzheimer's affects verbal thinking and speech, and then emotional thinking and finally physical mobility. But fortunately, or unfortunately, you may not die quickly. Even with such severe Alzheimer's symptoms, it could take years of debility and disability before death does finally bring, perhaps, some kind of relief. It may be it is unwise of governments and individuals to prioritize body shape and body weight or even body fitness, over the fitness of your brain!

Insight
Alzheimer's disease

There are things you can do to prevent Alzheimer's disease, and to preserve your cognitive capacity if you do get it. The fitness of your brain is just as important as the shape and weight of your body. Studies have shown that if you keep your brain active you can halve your risk of suffering dementia.

WHO GETS ALZHEIMER'S?

Currently, in the UK, one in six people over 80 years of age have Alzheimer's disease, but if you are 50+ that does not mean that you have a one in six chance of getting it in the next 30 years. You can greatly reduce those odds by following the advice in Part one of this book. Also, by doing the kinds of sequences of brain training exercises that we have designed and collected together in the brain circuits in Part two of the book, you can greatly increase the spare cognitive capacity of your brain, so that, like David Snowdon's nuns, even if you do develop Alzheimer's disease, you may still have enough residual cognitive capacity to support your memory and your mind at the enhanced levels to which you will already have become accustomed at 50+.

THE CAUSES OF ALZHEIMER'S DISEASE

Some people's genetic make-up can give them a predisposition to develop Alzheimer's, but lifestyle choices play a big part in whether or not this predisposition is ever manifested. Smoking, high blood pressure, head injuries, for example, can each raise the risk of manifestation. So does dieting, so ditch the diet and favour foods with a low oxytoxic index (Chapter 4 and Appendix H).

Fitness matters more that fatness, as far as the brain is concerned. That is *not* to say that fatness is harmless. It isn't. Fatness competes for the oxygen supply that your brain needs. It's just that the effect of serial dieting in lowering thinking performance and increasing cortisol levels and the risk of neurodegenerative disease is far worse, especially as 90 per cent of people who diet regain the weight they lose within two years anyway. By contrast, 70 per cent of people who protect their brains by eating the low-oxytoxic foods which we have tabled in Appendix H, report losing weight and the weight stays off. People eating low-oxytoxic foods tend to have a BMI which is very stable and at the bottom end of the 'normal' BMI range in Western countries.

THE SYMPTOMS OF ALZHEIMER'S DISEASE

The symptoms of Alzheimer's include: putting things in strange places; failing to recognize people or places; cooking the same meal twice over; difficulty finding the right words; using a wrong or inappropriate word; dressing inappropriately for an occasion or time of year; feeling agitated or irritable; and also repeating the same conversation with the same person, just a few minutes later.

Alzheimer's disease – six ways to stave it off

1 **There's a word for it!** A 2007 US study showed that doing cryptic crosswords or playing games like Scrabble, adverbs, password or the association game (Chapter 6), slowed down production of the protein found in Alzheimer's plaques.
2 **Chill out:** Research done in California in 2006 showed that excessive stress increases Alzheimer's risk.

3   **De-saturate your fats:** According to Dutch research in 2007, saturated fats in biscuits, cakes, pastries, hard cheese and butter, increase the risk of Alzheimer's.

4   **Move it!** A Seattle study in 2008 reported that just three 15-minute exercise sessions a week reduce your Alzheimer's risk by 40 per cent.

5   **Lose the booze:** Limiting alcohol to seven glasses (40 g) of wine or seven measures of spirits per week, greatly reduces Alzheimer's risk.

6   **Stub it out:** The London Institute of Psychiatry says that smoking increases your risk of Alzheimer's by four times.

THE TREATMENT OF ALZHEIMER'S DISEASE

The rate of Alzheimer's advance, or of corresponding cognitive decline, can be slowed. Some of the effects can be treated. For example, the depression often associated with Alzheimer's can be treated with antidepressants, and irritable behaviour and violence can be sedated.

Alzheimer's disease – seven natural ways to sharpen up

1   **Omega-3:** In January 2008, the UK edition of *Health* pointed to the *Journal of Neuroscience* finding that omega-3 fats helped to break up plaques.

2   **Glutamine:** Patrick Holford has found that L-Glutamine boosts memory and learning.

3   **Sex and dark chocolate:** These raise dopamine and norepinephrine in the brain. This raises mood and performance.

4   **Vitamin B:** Vitamin B complex reduces the level of homocysteine in your blood. High homocysteine levels are associated with lower performance on thinking tasks.

5   **Acetylcarnitine:** This replaces missing acetylcholine. Your brain needs acetylcholine to transmit the neural messages that are used to collect up and piece together the fragments of your memories.

6   **Ginkgo biloba:** Ginkgo biloba boosts blood flow and this, according to the Brain Research Institute, slows the spread of Alzheimer's disease.

7   **Gotu kola:** This relieves memory problems and mental fatigue when these are caused by or exacerbated by stress.

1 The first Dansette multi-change record players
2 Half-timbered cars, like the Morris Minor Traveller
3 Bubble cars like the Reliant or the Fiat 500
4 Toys that you wound up with a key (no batteries)
5 Televisions... with wooden doors that hid the screens
6 Meccano sets and Box Brownie cameras
7 When a joint was something you ate for Sunday lunch

Memory – ten top tips

TIP 1: PICTURE IT

Take exactly two minutes to memorize as many as possible of the 30 words in the table. Then cover the words and write as many of them as you can remember in two minutes in the box labelled 'before visualization'. Note your score.

Story	Midday	Slice	Tube	Corner	Fruit
Tiger	Folder	Ceramic	Extract	Thought	Music
Dew	Office	Point	Shop	Watch	Life
Sister	Cardboard	Relax	Honey	Colour	Braces
Brain	Rain	Hole	Puzzle	Magic	Secure

Before visualization

Score

Re-read the original list and create an image in your head associated with each word – an image as large, as colourful, as weird as possible.

74

Connect that image with an equally colourful image of another word, until all the words are interlinked into a story, or a grand collage or picture. Imagine it hanging on a wall near where you are. Again cover the words, and this time, fill in the box below, again taking two minutes.

After visualization

Score

Note how much better your score is.

TIP 2: COUNT ON YOUR MEMORY

▶ Count aloud to 99 in threes as fast as you can. Note the time you take. Note how you get faster every successive day you do it. When your time stabilizes, start the exercise again, only this time count backwards from 99 to zero.

▶ Count in fives as quickly as you can while cleaning your teeth with your wrong hand. Notice how much further you can get in successive days.

▶ Repeat while moving your eyes back and forth from extreme left to extreme right.

▶ Once a week, count aloud from 1–130, as fast as you can. Notice how much faster you get each week. This uses both sides of your prefrontal cortex.

TIP 3: PUT A NAME TO IT

'I can remember your face, but I just can't place...'
People are irrationally offended, or delighted, by whether or not you forget or remember their names. The names – the words, especially if foreign – are hard to remember, because they are only letters, devoid of meaning, or of any associations that could be placed in your brain to be picked up later as cues. You must repeat the name out loud. Check the spelling. If it is a foreign name ask what it means, and

if appropriate, ask why their parents chose it, etc. The more you talk about it and repeat it, the more likely you are to find a way to associate it with a feature in their face.

If you have forgotten a name, you've forgotten a name. It's not surprising and you just need to admit it. You will probably find they have forgotten yours and you will both be grateful for a second chance to swap names. Because you will associate their name with the embarrassment of forgetting it and having to ask a second time, you will be less likely to forget it a second time.

TIP 4: PIN IT DOWN

'The number of times I have forgotten…'
Numbers are hard to PIN down because they are even more devoid of meaning than letters and words.

You have to create a meaning, a strong visual meaning.

For example, one (1) might be a mast or a tower near your home or work; two (2) a pair of white swans on black, still water; three (3), her moist pink lips; four (4), a white sailing yacht on blue water against the green edge of a seaweed-smelling coastline, and so on. Whatever works for you. You can then connect these images in a daft story to make a sequence, or place them with the objects on your memory walk (look at 'Take a walk' below).

If numbers have more than three digits, they may exceed your cognitive limits, i.e. 5 ± 2. The first task is to 'chunk' them – to break them up into groups. Get into the habit of reading numbers like 9922196833369 as, say, 99, 22, 1968, 333 and 69. Read them aloud to add sound and rhythm to what you are trying to remember. The next task is to make each chunk personally meaningful. For example, 99 might be a parent's age – picture the parent as you say 99 aloud; 22 might be the number of a house – visualize the door with the number on it as you say 22, etc. Now imagine your 99-year-old parent going into the doorway of the house numbered 22. Perhaps 1968 was the year of a famous sporting event – picture it taking place on the television inside the house numbered 22, and already you can remember 99221968. Continue the process, by associating 333 and then 69 with people, addresses, historic dates, birthdays etc. and then connect all these images together in a story or sequence, adding movement, colour, sound, smells and tastes wherever possible.

TIP 5: LEARN THE LINGO

Joining a language conversation class ticks many brain training boxes. Learning second languages involves social and emotional intelligence (Chapter 6), as well as recollective thinking, speaking aloud and much useful repetition. Learning a second language also involves a different part of your brain from the part that you use to speak your first language. It develops some of the parts you also need for mathematics and for music. This results in a lot of 'neural' traffic back and forth between the amygdala region and the prefrontal cortex. This is very good for synaptic growth generally and for myelination.

TIP 6: SPELL IT OUT

Obtain a list of the 100 most commonly misspelt words in your language. At 50+, you can probably spell a lot of them already. If so, generate your own list. Stick it up in the toilet and learn one a day. Cumulatively recite the spellings of the ones you have already learned. After 100 days, make a new list, for example 100 words that describe emotions. Important as it is to spell accurately, it is the practice of memorizing – even a word a day – that is as important as what you memorize.

Your verbal thinking (Chapter 6) is limited by your vocabulary, so it is a good idea to expand it. A word a day = 1,000 new words after 3 years. To put the value of that extra 1,000 words into perspective, some daily newspapers can be read with a vocabulary of 100 words (Chapter 6)!

TIP 7: GET A WHIFF OF THAT

Get a book and find a paragraph you would like to remember. Then:

1 Inhale a favourite scent (e.g. sage, lavender, basil).
2 Underline the key words.
3 Give the paragraph a subtitle, like you would see in a newspaper.
4 Read the paragraph aloud, as if you were a newsreader – stand up and give it the same drama and emphasis.
5 Write out all you can remember, sounding out the words as you go.
6 Next day, inhale the same smell and write out the paragraph again.

TIP 8: MAP IT OUT

When constructing a shopping list, group like things together, for example vegetables/fruit, tins, chilled, dairy, sweet, frozen, hardware. Put the groups in the order in which they appear in the store.

TIP 9: DON'T FORGET IT

Remember that to forget is normal and healthy. It is your healthy default to forget, unless you deliberately decide to remember. To give yourself a fighting chance to not forget, put your car keys, or door keys, on top of what you must remember to take with you. Put your watch on the other hand to remind you.

N.B. Make a note of it
> *'The horror of the moment,' the King went on, 'I shall never, never forget.'*
> *'You will though,' the Queen said, 'if you don't make a memorandum of it.'*
>
> Lewis Carroll, *Through the Looking-Glass and What Alice Found There*, 1872

Always make notes. Take a pad, or ask for a page from someone else when you need one. Map what is being said. Three chunks of three. Most people can remember three new things.

TIP 10: TAKE A WALK

Go for a walk that you can reliably reproduce in your head. As you go round your walk, identify, say, 27 distinctive objects on your way from A to B. Be sure that you can see, or imagine, each object clearly as you retrace the walk in your head. Then associate each object with something you want to remember, for example a point in a presentation, speech, exam question, sales pitch or job application. The crazier, more bizarre, more emotional, or sexier the association you make between the object on your walk and the point you are remembering from your walk, the better. You will then be able to recall your points in any order or even amaze your audience by telling them what points you are skipping over, so as to finish on time. You can, of course, remind them in reverse order of the 27 points (3 groups of 3 groups of 3 points = 27 points) you have just covered. (What a speaker, and without notes!)

WINSTON'S RULE OF THREE
> *If you have a point to make don't try to be subtle – use a pile driver:*
> *Hit the point once;*

Then come back and hit it again;
Then hit it a third time – this time with a tremendous whack.

Winston Churchill, aged 80

Eight steps to a better memory

1 *NOVELTY*

Every year, pick a novel topic, skill, craft or country, as foreign
to your previous life or experience as possible. Research the
possibilities. Select one and aim to get to the bottom of it, within
the year.

2 *IMAGINE*

Go for a mental walk every day – somewhere familiar. Report, in
detail on everything that you can see in your mind's eye. Count
things as you go, for example 'tree number'. Describe the details out
loud as you take your mental walk. Preferably, describe what you
see to a partner. Do mental arithmetic by visualizing yourself doing
it on paper or on a whiteboard. Learn lists of words by imagining
a vivid image that you can associate with each word. Imagine odd
connections between one image and the next.

3 *MAKE A SLIDE SHOW*

Practise trying to turn what you read in a book or magazine or
on the internet into a slide show – a sequence of images that
are interconnected in your mind. Hear yourself giving a talk to
accompany the slide show. Afterwards, recall what you have read as
best you can. Your visual memory will back up your verbal memory
and will eventually become a faster, more comprehensive way for you
to remember things.

4 *BE A POET AND KNOW IT!*

When words rhyme, they are easier to learn, for example: one is a
John, or a con, etc. (whatever is easiest for you), two is a shoe, three
is a tree, four is a door, five is a hive, six is sticks, seven is heaven,
eight is a gate, nine is a mine, ten is a hen.

Make sure you learn your rhyme off by heart. Then whenever you
want to remember ten names, ten items, ten points for a speech,

you can link an image for each of your points to the image of your number. The more absurd the images and their juxtaposition, the easier they will be to recall – especially if they evoke a strong emotion like disgust, or argument, or laughter, or sex. Neurons that fire together – wire together.

5 ADD SENSATION

In addition to visual images, smells, sounds, emotions, touches and tastes can also be used as effective associations with the thing you want to remember. Try adding a sound, or smell, or feeling to your visual images and so double your chances of locating a retrieval clue when you are next searching for the item you have remembered. Most 50+ people find visual or auditory clues the easiest to think of and use. It is more difficult to associate smells with items to be remembered, but if you can, smells can be deeply evocative.

Examples of sounds might be imagining the grunts of a sweaty weightlifter lifting a ton for item one; the sound of heels clicking, echoing down a hallway for a shoe (smelly?) for two; trees for threes, rustle or creak; four is a door – hear it once more; the buzz or a drone goes live with the hive for five; sticks for six can crackle and hiss and spit on a fire (can you smell the smoke?); seven is heaven (can you hear the choir singing?); eight is a gate so creaky it needs oil (the smell of WD40?); nine is a mine so hear the explosion, or the noise of drills; ten is a hen, a fat clucking hen, or a crowing cock. The more neurons that are firing, in more places in your brain, at the time you remember, the easier your subsequent recall will be. Remember, neurons that fire together – wire together.

6 QUESTION, LIST AND LINK

When trying to remember something you have read, for a subsequent meeting or presentation:

▶ Decide on the **questions** it is trying to answer. (A handy checklist of possible questions is 'who?' (has done, needs to do), 'what?', 'when?', 'how?' and 'why?'.)
▶ **List** the answers to the questions as bullet points. Group the bullet points, three to a group.
▶ Number the bullet points and **link** your image of the number to an image you can associate with the bullet point.

7 MIX IT TO MAX IT

What does not quite kill us makes us stronger – or so Nietzsche tried to reassure us. Multi-layered, multi-faceted, multi-topic, multi-recall memorization does not quite kill us, but it does take longer, and therefore it does stick stronger. The more arduous the process of memorization, the stronger the memory. A quick cram the night before an exam is gone the day after. What a waste. A waste not only of the value there might have been in the topics that you revised, but what a wasted opportunity to extend and strengthen the neural structure of your brain.

At 50+, if you can enrol for a few night classes, or weekend courses, do not choose closely complementary or mutually supportive modules. Instead, go for chalk and cheese contrast, for example chemistry, computing and conversational French. Have several books on the go at once. Progress will be slower and more tortuous, but much more beneficial in the long run. The more of your neurons that are active at the time you are trying to memorize something, the better. As Professor Ian Robertson says, 'neurons that fire together, wire together'. That is why you are more likely to remember something if there is a lot else going on – for example, if you are moving, smelling and listening or having strong feelings about what is happening. That is why some memories are so vivid that they can be a problem – vivid flashbacks of emotionally exhilarating or devastating events can play havoc with your attempts to concentrate on the thinking task in hand.

8 THE CHURNING IS THE LEARNING

The important thing about memory games is the taking part. Even if at first you don't succeed, eventually you will make 'head' way! It is the very act of trying that produces the development. All your attempts to run and re-run your neural pathways – trying to find your memory fragments – that's what thickens the myelin insulation around the axons of your neurons. That is what is going to make your subsequent storage and retrieval of memories quicker and less prone to interference and error. The more mistakes you make – the more false starts – the more restarts and re-runs, the stronger your memory will become.

N.B. Because each of the eight steps above are multi-faceted and intentionally complex, just pick one technique and practise it until

you have mastered it – or have become bored with it. Then pick
another, until you have mastered all eight.

The effect of stress chemicals on memory

In 1994, the *Journal of Neuroscience* reported that 19 adult volunteers
had been given a stress chemical, glucocorticoid, or a placebo, for
four consecutive days. The volunteers listened to a tape and were
asked to recollect what they had heard. The placebo group found
this easier and easier on successive days, consistent with the idea of
neuromodulation (see 'First thoughts'), whereas the recollections
of the group receiving the stress chemical deteriorated significantly.
Worryingly, none of the stressed group seemed aware of the
deterioration in their mental performance, even though observers
had very quickly noticed considerable and rapid deterioration in their
memories, even under low levels of stress! If you think your memory
may sometimes be made worse by excessive stress, read Chapter 5 in
Train Your Brain (Horne and Wootton, 2010).

Protecting your brain from disease

1 LEARNING

It is never too late to learn. It does not seem to matter so much what
as how. Learning in pairs is especially good for your brain.

2 BRAIN TRAINING

Brain training exercises have been shown to be effective, however
late they are started. There are specific memory workouts in the
recommended readings (Dr Tan and Professor Robertson). An
electronic brain training game like *Brain Training: How Old Is Your
Brain?*, by Dr Kawashima (Nintendo DS), works if you keep doing it.

3 PHYSICAL ACTIVITY

You literally need to win hearts to win minds! The health of your
memory will be limited by the health of your heart. If it doesn't
pump hard enough, your brain will be short of oxygen and mental
energy. If it pumps at too high a blood pressure, you risk damaging

your brain. By warding off depression and raising self-esteem, self-confidence and optimism, physical activity improves thinking and promotes growth of brain cells.

4 DITCH THE DIET – EAT LESS OXYTOXIC FOOD

Ditch diets that deprive your brain of the unsaturated fats it needs. Select foods with a low oxytoxic index (Appendix H) and choose foods that mop up random free radicals that you might still produce (Appendix I).

5 POP SOME PILLS?

Check with your doctor, pharmacist or health worker, the advisability of supplementary vitamin E, vitamin D, vitamins B6 and B12, folic acid and the minerals zinc and selenium. If you have significant memory loss symptoms already, or if you have a family history of severe forgetfulness in old age, ask about statins, ibuprofen and homocysteine now.

6 IMPROVE TO PROTECT

Many of the memory improvement techniques also have a role in protecting the brain. They encourage myelination and create reserves of cognitive capacity that act as a buffer.

7 KILL THE STRESS, BEFORE IT KILLS YOU

The impact of stress becomes more detrimental as you get older. Your brain reacts to perceived threats, or stress, by inducing your adrenal glands, next to your kidneys, to release cortisol, which in turn increases blood sugar, breaks down proteins and releases fat. This is great for an immediate fight or flight situation, but if it is persistent, it destroys your brain. Stress is manageable, but unmanaged can lead to depression. Depression greatly impairs thinking and is much harder to treat. Depression is not the same as psychological sadness, or grief, or feeling a bit down. It is a brain chemical imbalance and you may need to see your doctor for a treatment to restore that balance. Not only can depression make it hard for you to concentrate on thinking tasks, it can also shrink your hippocampus and affect your memory. At 50+, it can precipitate dementia. Selective Serotonin Reuptake Inhibitors (SSRI) treatments often stimulate the production of new brain cells, though their effectiveness in lifting depression may be a placebo effect. Talking helps.

If you, or more usually someone else, suspect that you are already showing symptoms of Alzheimer's, you can get the symptoms treated. There are treatments that slow, or temporarily arrest, the spread of the disease. At present, there is no certain cure – but many possible cures are on the horizon, so it is well worth trying to hold your situation in the meantime. You could consider volunteering to take part in a current medical trial.

Ask about Aricept, Exelon and Reminyl, which are acetylcholinesterase inhibitors. These can improve memory and performance on other thinking tasks, even if you don't already have Alzheimer's. In general, they can restore your level of performance to what it was about a year before you commenced treatment. That is why it is so important to act quickly, before your performance drops significantly. In 2004, the Food and Drug Administration in the USA approved Memantine for treatment of Alzheimer's that is already well advanced. Memantine has been in widespread use in Europe for at least 13 years. Memantine works by blocking the dendrite receptors that would otherwise overstimulate the movement of calcium ions in your neurons. Excess calcium kills neurons. Ask also about Cerebrolysin, which is widely used in China, and also about the trial result for ginkgo biloba, if you would prefer herbal treatment.

Insight
Protecting your brain from disease
It's never too late to learn, especially using paired learning. Focus your brain training on memory workouts and your physical workouts on your muscles and your breathing. Select foods with low oxytoxic scores and high ORAC scores and don't yo-yo diet to lose weight.

IN SHORT...

We have evidence from the research on nuns, from studies of occupation and mental activity, and from the neurochemistry of the brain, that brain training not only improves your memory, but also improves your brain's capacity to resist and reverse the effects of disease, and increases the power of your brain to support more effective applied thinking and more intelligent behaviour. Time to train your brain.

Here is the answer to the Sudoku puzzle from earlier in this chapter (page 53):

6	2	8	3	9	1	7	5	4
4	1	9	7	5	6	2	3	8
3	5	7	8	4	2	9	6	1
5	6	2	1	7	3	4	8	9
7	4	3	5	8	9	6	1	2
9	8	1	6	2	4	5	7	3
2	3	5	4	1	7	8	9	6
1	7	4	9	6	8	3	2	5
8	9	6	2	3	5	1	4	7

10 THINGS TO REMEMBER

1 Forgetting is normal and necessary.

2 When you need to remember, take deliberate steps to counter the normal mechanisms, which are designed to make you forget things.

3 Effective strategies for countering forgetfulness exist and can be learned.

4 Loss of long-term memory is not an inevitable consequence of age.

5 Long-term memory normally improves with age.

6 Memory loss can be caused by diseases like Alzheimer's.

7 Your risk of developing Alzheimer's disease can be drastically reduced.

8 Even if you do develop Alzheimer's, there are strategies and treatments for slowing down the effects, or for avoiding them altogether.

9 Memorizing new things stimulates new neuron growth and forges new synaptic connections. Memorizing things involves repetition, which strengthens myelination.

10 Memorizing things develops spare cognitive capacity. Having spare cognitive capacity helps you to protect your ability to think, as well as to remember, should you develop a disease like Alzheimer's.

Glossary

Alzheimer's disease – is commonly characterized by progressive loss of cognitive functions, often termed dementia.

Amygdala – comprises almond-shaped groups of neurons located deep within the medial temporal lobes of the brain. It performs a primary role in the processing and memory of emotional reactions.

Dementia – is a decline in cognitive function due to disease, not ageing.

Suggested further reading

Barnes, D., 'Fitness and cognitive function in older adults', *American Journal of Gerontology*, 51 (2003), pp. 458–66.

Cotman, W., 'Exercise, brain health and plasticity', *Trends in Neuroscience*, 25 (2002), pp. 294–302.

Dumas, S., 'Neuron plasticity during mood disorders', *Biological Psychiatry*, 48 (2000), pp. 731–40.

Evans, D. A., 'Fish consumption and Alzheimer's disease', *Archives of Neurology*, 60 (2003), pp. 939–47.

Finkel, E., *Stem Cells: Controversy at the Frontiers of Science* (Sydney: ABC Books, 2006).

Finkel, E., 'The Labyrinth of Memory' *Cosmos*, 13 (2007).

Fratoglioni, L., 'Alcohol and dementia', *Clinical Epidemiology*, 55 (2002), pp. 958–65.

Gedo, M., 'Depression not age shrinks the hippocampus', *Journal of Neuroscience*, 19 (1999), pp. 5033–44.

Hultsch, D. et al, *Memory Change in the Aged* (Cambridge: Cambridge University Press, 1998).

Joseph, C., 'Drinking and cognitive performance', *American Journal of Public Health*, 90 (2002), pp. 1253–60.

Kalmijn, S., 'Dietary fats and dementia', *Neurology*, 42 (1997), pp. 775–83.

Kawashima, R., *Train Your Brain* (Penguin, 2007).

Logan, A., *The Brain Diet: The Connection Between Nutrition, Mental Health and Intelligence* (Cumberland House Publishing, 2006).

Mattson, M., *Diet–Brain Connection: Impact on Memory, Mood, Aging and Disease* (Kluwer, 2002).

McKay, R. and Cameron, H. A., 'Restoring the production of hippocampal neurons in old age', *Nature Neuroscience*, 2 (1999), pp. 894–7.

Mori, A., 'Stress, aging and brain oxidative damage', *Neurochemical Research*, 14 (1999), pp. 1479–97.

Otten, L., 'Brain activity predicting recollection', *Nature Neuroscience*, 90 (2006), pp. 488–92.

Robertson, I., *Stay Sharp With the Mind Doctor* (London: Vermilion, 2005).

Rupp, R., *Committed to Memory*, (London: Aurum Press Limited, 1998).

Tan, Z. S., *Age-Proof Your Mind: Detect, Delay, and Prevent Memory Loss-Before It's Too Late* (New York: Warner Wellness, 2006).

Victoroff, J., *Saving Your Brain: The Revolutionary Plan to Boost Brain Power, Improve Memory, and Protect Yourself Against Aging and Alzheimer's* (New York: Bantam Books, 2002).

Wiseman, J., *Quirkology* (London: Macmillan, 2007).

Yosipovitch, G. and Carstens, E., 'Report from the 4th International Workshop for the Study of Itch', *Journal of Investigative Dermatology*, 128 (2008), pp. 256–7.

4

Oxytoxic food and mental fitness

In this chapter you will learn:
- *to eat food your brain needs, when it needs it*
- *to convert food into nutrients that your brain needs in order to think clearly, quickly and creatively*
- *to minimize damage caused by alcohol, tea, coffee, cannabis, cola, ticks and dieting and to avoid 'oxytoxic' foods that increase the risk of brain diseases like Alzheimer's*
- *to use sleep, exercise, smart drugs, dark chocolate and sex to rejuvenate your brain.*

> *The state of your brain is as much a lifestyle choice, as a genetic inheritance.*

Terry Horne, 2003

Introduction

Thinking is a chemical process. How well your 50+ brain thinks depends on how well those chemical processes work. The chemical processes in your 50+ brain are affected by the presence in your brain of water, acids and other trace chemicals. You can affect the chemical conditions in your brain by the things that you do, the things that you eat and the way that you feel. Chapter 1 looked at what you can do about the way that you feel. This chapter will look at the effect on the brain chemistry of the 50+ brain of the things you choose to do, and the things you choose to eat. The chemical conditions in your brain are largely down to lifestyle choices that you can make. You can choose to create conditions in your 50+ brain that favour high-performance thinking and intelligent action, or you can do and eat things that greatly increase the risk of brain diseases and dementia.

Your brain can change in response to the way you exercise and the way you breathe. It can also change in response to what you eat and drink and smoke. It is changed by what you do, and by what you don't do, in and out of the bedroom. Your brain can change in response to your lifestyle. Your brain is able to adapt because, according to Colin Blakemore (CEO, UK Medical Research Council), your brain is not only a chemical factory, it is an extremely busy chemical factory. Your brain needs energy for more than a million chemical reactions every second!

The chemistry of your brain can be changed by what you do with it – so let's look at how to optimize the chemical conditions in your brain to increase its performance.

Sharper synapses at 60 – a six-point summary

1 NUTRITION

Omega-3 fatty acids, found in oily fish such as smoked mackerel, sardines, salmon and tuna, will improve your cognitive ability, as long as you maintain a balance between omega-3, -6 and -9. B vitamins are important and they can be found in Marmite. Complex carbohydrates can be found in fruit, vegetables, salad and wholemeal grains. Complex carbohydrates not only fuel mental energy, they also release mood-enhancing chemicals, like serotonin, that raise mood, optimism and hence performance on mental tasks (Chapter 1). Fat-free diets destroy memory and kill your brain cells, and serial dieting does your head in. We suggest you 'ditch the diet', and eat as much as you need of low-oxytoxic food (see Appendix H). Saturated fats, such as those found in crisps and biscuits, will increase your risk of dementia. Blueberries, strawberries and spinach are rich in flavonoids which will help protect your brain from attack by free radicals – but dark chocolate (must be dark) has ten times more flavonoids than all of them put together (Appendix I)! Your brain is 80 per cent water – so things that dehydrate it, like alcohol, salt, strong tea, cola and coffee are bad news. Drink two to four pints a day of water, preferably plain, or weak tea – preferably fruit or herbal.

2 EXERCISE

Walking, jogging and cycling improve the supply to your brain of the oxygen that it needs to oxidize your food, thereby fuelling the chemical reactions that need to take place when you think. Exercise also stimulates the production of new or replacement brain cells, especially round the hippocampus – an area crucial to memory, especially in the brains of the 50+ (Chapter 3). Exercise also helps to protect the brain against the cortisol derivatives produced by excessive stress. Don't yo-yo exercise, i.e. don't join a gym unless you intend to use it for life. Paul Williams studied 23,000 exercisers. His report, in *Science of Exercise* (Feb. 2008), shows that if you stop working out, your metabolic rate will fall to lower than before you started. Your thinking will slow and your waist will grow bigger than before you started.

3 RELAXATION

Breathe in counting five; hold your breath counting five; breathe out counting five. You feel better already! That's because you have just relaxed your body and boosted your brain. Yoga, meditation and breathing exercises rejuvenate your brain by reversing the effects of stress-induced cortisol which can cause neuron damage, cell death, depression and memory loss, especially in the 50+ brain. Lowered mood and lowered optimism reduce performance in mental tasks (Chapter 1).

A study at Boston University has identified breathing exercises that can restore and even increase the levels of gamma-aminobutyric acid (GABA) in your 50+ brain, thereby restoring or elevating its performance. A 2005 study in Massachusetts found that meditation exercises will thicken the prefrontal lobes of your cerebral cortex. Cortical thinning, which has contributed historically to a slowing down in the speeds of new memory formation in the 50+ brain, can now be reversed (see later for details of the exercises).

4 SLEEP

People who claim to sleep like babies have never had one.

Les Burke

Find out how much you need. At 50+, you need less sleep than when you were younger – but maybe not as little as you think. Shortage of sleep, or disturbed patterns of sleep, produces a dramatic deterioration in performance on thinking tasks. The time it takes you to restore your performance to normal levels also increases from 50+ onwards. Power naps do help but you need deep sleep to rest your 50+ brain and to aid long-term memory (Chapter 3). You also need shallow dream time sleep (REM sleep) to help you make sense of new information.

5 SEX

During four of the seven stages of sex, from arousal to afterglow, the chemicals released in your brain favour better thinking. In women who have orgasms, sex may boost the number of neurons in their brains.

6 THINKING SKILLS

Appendices A–F at the back of this book show that the three pillars of effective applied thinking are critical thinking, creative thinking and reflective thinking, and that these are supported, in turn, by skills in predictive, ethical, verbal, emotional, recollective, visual and numerical thinking.

All these thinking skills, like any skill, profit from repetitive practice. One way to practise them is to keep learning new things – what you learn does not seem to matter as long as the learning involves using new combinations of thinking skills. If the learning involves lots of repetition, like juggling, ballroom dancing, skiing, mountaineering, playing a musical instrument or speaking a foreign language, so much the better. In 2004, older people in Toronto were found to have faster mental reflexes and longer concentration spans after they learned another language.

Another way to practise your thinking skills is to do (much as you would in a gymnasium) brain training exercises that work each area of your brain. Such brain 'circuits' need to be graded and systematic, and to be based on the most up-to-date models of what happens chemically in your brain when it thinks. For example, cryptic crosswords don't just test your brain power – more importantly, the attempts you make to solve the cryptic clues leave new neural traces and connections in your brain.

Insight
Sharper synapses at 60

To have sharper synapses at 60 add omega fats 3, 6 and 9 and ORAC foods to your diet, and reduce oxytoxic foods. Exercise your muscles and your breathing but don't join a gym. Relax and improve the quality of your sleep. Have sex if you can and train your brain to improve your critical, creative and reflective thinking through brain training exercises that combine their basic components: words, numbers, feelings, images and memories.

Food for thought

Under normal circumstances, the brain uses mainly glucose for energy. The glucose is oxidized to produce water, carbon dioxide and energy – enough to fuel a million chemical reactions a second! Neurons, and the sheaths surrounding their axons, need to be kept in good condition, and phosphatidyl choline is essential for that maintenance. However, in order to work, Maguire discovered that phosphatidyl choline needs certain B vitamins. Folic acid and selenium boost cognitive functioning. Folic acid is found in dark, leafy green vegetables. Selenium is found in seafood, wholegrain breads and nuts.

Folic acid sets back ageing

In 2007, the *Lancet* reported that 818 participants aged 50–70 had been given 800 micrograms of folic acid per day and had then out-performed younger subjects on tests of memory and thinking speed – the only area in which the 50+ brain normally lags behind the younger brain. Added to this, all 818 of these superior performers had been diagnosed with partial atrophy of the hippocampus, an area of the brain important for consolidation of memories.

Connors reported that boron, iron and zinc improved mental activity. Boron is found in broccoli, pears, peaches, grapes, nuts and dried beans. Zinc can be found in fish, beans and wholegrains. The vitamin C in citrus fruits and salads enhances the absorption of iron. Iron helps to form ferroxyhaemoglobin, which is used to carry oxygen through the blood to the brain.

In humans, neurotransmitters like dopamine and norepinephrine are essential for mental alertness and acuity, for high-speed calculation, and for evaluation and critical thinking. Eating protein increases the supply of neurotransmitters. Eat more protein if you wish to be more mentally alert and quick thinking. (Some of the lowest rates of dyslexia in the world are found in Japan, which has the highest per capita consumption of fish.)

Importantly for the 50+ brain, blueberries, strawberries and spinach contain chemicals that appear to reverse the deterioration in thinking ability caused by previous lifestyle choices. (Note that, ounce for ounce, dark chocolate has ten times as many flavonols as the berries and the spinach, but it must be dark chocolate (like Malagasy, for example) not the dairy stuff! (See Appendix I for more information.))

Insight
Food for thought

Your brain is more interested in the content of the food you eat and when you eat it, than how much of it you eat. It is especially looking for folic acid, selenium, zinc, iron and vitamins B and C. You will think more accurately if you eat protein and complex carbohydrates for breakfast and lunch, and leave sugary foods until around 6 or 7 p.m.

Vitamins – to pop the pills or not?

At least ten different B vitamins can affect the neurotransmitters in your brain. For example, Anderson found that people had difficulty in thinking when their B1 levels were low.

The beneficial effects from B1, B5 and vitamin C, and the minerals boron, zinc and selenium, are best obtained by adjusting your diet rather than taking vitamin pills. You can usefully increase the proportion in your diet of berries, such as blackcurrants, redcurrants, bilberries, strawberries and, especially, blueberries. Also, try increasing your intake of spinach, green cabbage, broccoli and watercress. If you are anaemic, do not take iron tablets unless your doctor has investigated possible causes of your anaemia other than iron deficiency.

Food for thinking – a day plan

On days when you are involved in mainly mental, not physical, activity, try to eat complex carbohydrates (like fruit, salad and vegetables) and proteins (like fish, poultry, lentils, pulses and nuts) during the daytime. Keep grain carbohydrates, like bread and cereal, and fats, like avocado and liver, until after work in the evening. Drink before bed – but no driving – a smoothie, made from low-fat yoghurt and 80 g of fruit (especially mango) which will make you sleepy. According to Dr Buxton, of the British Nutrition Foundation, writing in the Nutrition Bulletin in May 2008, it will also contribute two of the five portions a day of fibre that you need. If you like your smoothies thick, add fat-free powdered milk.

For enhanced thinking speed and accuracy...

MORNINGS

If you can face protein first thing, start with it. Try eggs – boiled, scrambled, poached, or a Spanish omelette. Any kind of coldwater fish, especially oily fish like kipper, mackerel or salmon, is excellent. Try stewed fruit, berries, blackcurrants, nuts or seeds. Try soaking dried fruit overnight in hot weak black tea with a dash of fresh orange juice. This reduces the concentration of the sugar in the dried fruit, as well as producing a delicious syrup to add to low-fat yoghurt. For preference, have fresh fruit if possible. Avoid bread and cereals in the morning if you can – keep them until evening, when you should favour wholegrains. Drink plenty of water on getting up, before and after cleaning your teeth, and just before leaving the house. Top up a sipping bottle of water to carry with you.

Eating a good breakfast and other myths

While it is true that children at school find it hard to concentrate and think if they feel hungry, at 50+ it matters crucially what you eat for breakfast. White toasted bread and jam rapidly metabolize into glucose and produce insulin-driven pangs of hunger well before lunchtime. Even milk and cereals (especially if sugary) will burn up in about two hours. To work best, breakfast should be based on protein and on complex carbohydrates, like those found in fruit.

DAYTIME

Again, any protein is good (especially oily fish like mackerel, herring, salmon and sardines) with dark green vegetables (like spinach and cabbage) or with salad. Try to eat vegetables raw, especially carrots, cabbage and celery. Eat the protein first. If you need afters, try fruit salad or just fruit. Avoid biscuits, bread, pasta, pizza or pastry. Drink as much cold water as you can. If you need a hot drink during the day, choose weak tea – preferably green or herbal – rather than coffee.

EVENING

Wholemeal bread and cereals eaten in the evening will help you to relax and to sleep. Rapeseed oil or linseed oil will give you omega-3 fatty acids. Corn or soya oils contain omega-6 and omega-9. Flax, hemp, sesame and pumpkin oils will help you to maintain the balance between omega-3 and omega-6. Because these oils are degraded by hard cooking, it is better to stir in a teaspoonful before serving, after the hot cooking is finished, or drizzle them onto your salads or raw vegetables. Good quality non-stick pans make this easier. The wholemeal bread will give you your selenium. Pasta will give you the energy you need for physical exercise the next day. This is the time of day when puddings will do least harm to your thinking and they may help you to sleep. Try fresh fruit crumbles made with bran and oat toppings, or homemade ice cream made from a blend of low-fat yoghurt, skimmed dried milk powder and fresh fruit.

The effects of dieting, snacking and grazing on thinking

Sow wild oats when you're young and grow sage when you're 50+.

After Winston Churchill

SNACKING AND GRAZING

Jenkins took people with normal eating habits and divided them into two groups: one group ate the traditional three meals a day; the other consumed identical food, but 'grazed' on it up to 17 times per day. The 'grazers' maintained a more stable insulin level and had lower cortisol levels (Chapter 5). Research undertaken on students either 'grazing' or not eating at all during a thinking test, showed that those permitted to snack on raw vegetables, achieved higher scores than the matched group who were not allowed to snack.

Thinking consumes energy and needs fuel. If it suits you, have more snacks and fewer large meals. Large meals are often preceded by reduced ability to concentrate and followed by periods of drowsiness. However, do not snack on sweets or biscuits or on refined, salty carbohydrates. Snack on protein, such as low-fat yoghurt, nuts or seeds. Salads are good but are often not convenient, unless pre-prepared from finely chopped leaves, rocket, cabbage, fresh spinach or watercress, and well mixed with, say, salmon, egg, tuna, smoked fish, nuts, broad beans, lentils, peas or poultry. Raw vegetables, like carrots, celery or cucumber, are easy to nibble. Fresh fruits like apples and pears are socially acceptable snacks at any time.

Insight

The effects of dieting, snacking and grazing on the brain

Snackers and grazers score highly on thinking tests, but if you snack on sweets, biscuits or salty carbohydrates, you will likely have problems concentrating after two hours, due to insulin rush or dehydration. Do not yo-yo diet to control your weight, if you want to avoid damage to your brain and your mental performance. If you must lose weight use the 3T method (described below).

DITCHING DIETS

I took off all my clothes and straightaway the doctor said,
'You'll have to diet.' I said, 'What colour?'

Ken Dodd, octogenarian

The British Association for the Advancement of Science reports that whether or not people who diet frequently lose weight, they certainly lose mental performance.

The dangers of fat-free diets!

By all means eliminate solid, saturated transfats from your diet. Transfats have few unsaturated bonds in them and so it is very hard for your body to break them down and get rid of them. They tend to be stored in your body, eventually clogging up your arteries and destroying your waistline. Stored fat cells compete with your muscles and your brain for the oxygen they need to work effectively. Transfats also interfere with two fats, omega-3 and omega-6, that your brain really does need.

Without unsaturated fats in your diet, your brain can't produce acetylcholine, and without this, the walls of your brain cells will become stiff and brittle, and the cells may die. You will suffer memory loss and your thinking speed and accuracy will deteriorate. Such a fat-free diet will not only kill your brain cells, it may also kill you! De Angelis found that low-fat diets increased death rates from depression, suicide and accidents. Of course, obesity and heart disease also threaten your life and your social life and so it is understandable that you might want to reduce your weight. But yo-yo dieting or a very low-fat diet are not safe ways to do it. If you use the tables in Appendix H to eat what you normally eat but choose the low-oxytoxic versions, then you may lose weight as a side-effect of protecting

(Contd)

your brain. It is known that in countries with a low risk of Alzheimer's, where people live on low-oxytoxic foods, people's body mass indices are also much lower than in countries where people eat high-oxytoxic foods.

If you want to reduce your weight or body size at the same time as protecting your brain then, according to research by Professor Fletcher in 2007, you should not buy fad diet books, especially those based on cooking and eating! Yo-yo dieting seems to be one cause of dead brain cells and depressed thinking ability. Try the 3T approach – TTT.

THE 3T APPROACH TO DIETING

T1 – Take Aim

Taking aim will help your body to settle slowly to an equilibrium weight, such that your body mass index (BMI) will be somewhere between 18 and 25. If it's already below 18, that's unhealthy – bad for your body as well as your brain. If it's more than 25, you are carrying more flesh than you need as a buffer against illness or hard times. Surplus body mass competes with your brain for the oxygen it needs in order to think quickly and well for sustained periods. If your BMI is already between the values of 18 and 25, ditch the diet!

To calculate your BMI, get some scales, preferably digital, that read in pounds or half kilos. Weigh yourself in your underwear (if you weigh yourself in outdoor clothes and shoes, for example in a pharmacy store, deduct 5 kg or 10 lbs). Put a hardback book or board horizontally on your head and mark off your height when standing, barefoot, with your back pressed up against a wall. Measure the height of the mark from the floor, preferably in metres. (If in inches, divide the measurement by 10, and then by 4.) Multiply your height in metres by itself. Divide this number into your weight in kilos. That is your BMI, i.e. BMI = kilos ÷ (metres × metres).

If your BMI is not between 18 and 25, then divide 20 by (your height in metres × your height in metres) and Take Aim at this target weight. The World Health Organization says that your weight can change by up to 4 kg per month without threatening your health – but slower is better. Now put away the scales for 12 months or so. Select low-oxytoxic foods from Appendix H and follow steps T2 and T3. Use the more comfortable fit of your clothes, or comments of friends, as your feedback mechanism.

T2 – Take Note

The point of taking note of your feedback is to teach your brain what moves your weight, and in particular what the things are that you do *often* that move your weight. Things you do occasionally throughout the year – parties, celebrations, holidays, trips – do not in the end determine your stable BMI. It is the things you do regularly – often by habit – that move your weight. The trick is to spot your habits, then Take Note and Take Action to break them. Habit breaking is good for your brain, whatever the habit, so food-eating habits are as good a place to start as any! The following are typical food habits to look out for and take note of. Check them out now:

▶ I can't have just one, I eat the whole box.
▶ I've always struggled with my weight.
▶ I diet every year, or before every holiday.
▶ I am always pecking.
▶ I just get cravings for…
▶ I tend to eat on the move.
▶ It's just that I'm not as active as I used to be.
▶ I eat properly in public, but when I get home…
▶ I eat properly in the daytime, but during the evening…
▶ I keep finishing the children's leftovers – waste not want not.

What habits can you add to your list?

How often do you…? *Score: always = 6, usually = 4, sometimes = 2, never = 0*	*Score (0, 2, 4, 6)*
Do the same thing on the same day of the week?	
Go back to the same place for a holiday?	
Repeat purchases and from the same retailer?	
Watch a regular scheduled television programme?	
Eat the same things for the same meal, e.g. breakfast?	
Say things that are boring?	
Dismiss the ideas of other people?	
Wear the same style or brand of clothes?	
Sit in the same place in a restaurant or in your lounge?	
Do things that are not good for you?	
Total score for negative habits =	

(Contd)

How often do you...? Score: always = 6, usually = 4, sometimes = 2, never = 0	Score (0, 2, 4, 6)
Seek out people who might be interesting?	
Forgive people?	
Surprise others?	
Vary your daily newspaper?	
Deliberately look for a challenge?	
Make changes to make things more interesting?	
Try a new place for a meal or a coffee?	
Learn something new?	
Do something you don't find easy?	
Listen quietly with full attention and empathy?	
Total score for positive habits =	

Add your positive and negative habit scores together. How did you get on?

0–25	You have good habit-breaking skills. Use them to ditch diets. Use them to bust food habits that push your BMI where you don't want it to be.
26–50	You need to strike a balance between your good and bad habits. Is there a positive that you could do more or a negative you could do less?
50+	You are habit prone. Perhaps you border on obsessive or compulsive. Do you need professional help or counselling? Discuss your score with another person (Chapter 6). A friend can often spot hidden habits. Once spotted, most habits are easy to break, given a little support.

T3 – Take Action

I'm on two diets at the moment. I simply don't get enough to eat on one.

Jo Brand

Now you have Taken Aim, and Taken Note of the habits that stand between you and your aim, you are ready to Take Action to change your unhelpful habits around eating and drinking, so that you can ditch that diet. Here are five useful questions for you to ask:

▶ Is this a habit that was useful in the past, but is now past its sell-by date?
▶ Are you good at this habit? (This might be why you are stuck – people tend to stick with what they're good at.)
▶ Is the habit copied from someone who used to be a useful role model who is no longer an appropriate model for you?
▶ How did you learn this habit? If you learned it, you can unlearn it!
▶ Do you see a habit as an expression of your personality? Well it's not. It might be an aspect of your 'style' of operation in some situations, but you can adapt your style to varying circumstances as you get older. The state of your brain is a lifestyle choice.

Get into the habit of breaking habits. Start by ditching habitual weight-loss dieting. Weight-loss diets can damage your brain (low-fat diets), or deprive you of mental energy, or of B vitamins or minerals that you need to think clearly and well over sustained periods. Your body will follow your mind. Try this…

Exercise 1: immediate proof that your body will follow your mind

Stand with your feet the same distance apart as your shoulders, toes turned slightly in. Extend your right arm out and in front of you, fingers at eye level. Focus on the finger tips of your right hand and rotate your trunk as far as you comfortably can and notice at what your finger is pointing. Centre your body again. Close your eyes and, in your mind's eye only, see yourself rotating further this time. Watch your hand swing well past its original stopping place.

Without opening your eyes, rotate your trunk again and, in your mind's eye, see your finger going past the original stopping point. Allow your body to follow your mind. Open your eyes. Amazing, eh! In the same way, your brain will adjust the weight of your body and your BMI as you Take Aim, Take Note and Take Action to break habits.

Exercise 2: fold your arms – developing your second nature

Fold your arms. Now fold them so the other arm is on top. Difficult, hey? Now relax. Fold your arms. Notice that the original arm is back on top again! You have to be quite deliberate and methodical to do things differently from the way you habitually do, especially if it's a habit of a lifetime. So never give yourself a hard time about relaxing back into an old habit. It's normal 'first' nature. Many repetitions of a 'new habit' are needed before it becomes your 'second' nature – that is where emotional intelligence comes in (Chapter 1). Repeatedly feel the good feelings you will feel when you see yourself breaking a habit.

Breaking eating habits works because your appetite is controlled by a part of your brain called the hypothalamus, which is about the size of a clementine and weighs about 14 grams. Your hypothalamus is involved in your emotional thinking (Chapter 1). That is why eating food is often such an emotionally charged matter. Harvest now the good feelings you will feel when you have ditched your diet. In the meantime, listen to your hypothalamus and eat when you are hungry. Your brain tells you that. (Do not wait until you are 'starving', because your brain will naturally go into some emergency mode and instruct your body to 'binge' – to stock up against the threat of imminent starvation.) Indications of hunger include your stomach rumbling, your head aching, being irritable, restless and unable to concentrate and having a dry or bad-tasting mouth. Many of these are also symptoms of dehydration, so always drink a glass of water first to be sure that what your brain is debating is the need for food, and not just a need for water. If you do need food – eat, and as soon as you can, whatever the timetable says! However, if your hypothalamus is signalling an emotional need – not a genuine need for food – this food will only make you fat. Check whether you are an emotional eater. Do you:

▶ eat more when you are alone?
▶ eat more when you are happy?
▶ eat more when you are sad?
▶ think about food a lot?
▶ feel guilty about food?

- ▶ eat when you're bored?
- ▶ eat when you're upset?
- ▶ cheat on diets?
- ▶ eat under stress?

Doing something different – thinking twice

If, for the wrong emotional reasons, you always do what you've always done, you will always have what you've always had. If you have always got an overweight body, you will always get an overweight body. To achieve something different, you have to do something different.

To do something different, you have to think differently:

- ▶ **Think twice before jumping on the scales.** Random variations – like fluids, sweating and constipation – play havoc with bathroom scales. Only use scales when you are certain – for example, from the fit of your clothes – that things are going the way you want them to.
- ▶ **Think twice** before eating. Have you had a drink first? Do you have time to eat slowly? Are you ready to take 20 minutes? Are you able to leave some food on your plate?
- ▶ **Think twice** about whether you feel stressed or low. Is it a break or some reassurance that you really need (rather than this sweet food)? A talk or a phone call to someone might take the pangs away.
- ▶ **Think twice** about eating when you're not at home. Some fast food or food that is convenient to eat on the move is very oxytoxic. But not all fast food is (see Appendix H). Fish and chips are not as bad as most fast food and some snacks have a very low oxytoxicity. Carry small apples in your pocket. Carry water in case it's water your brain needs. It may only be a taste in your mouth – carry minty sweets such as Tic Tacs or Fisherman's Friends. The mint smell will also help you to think more clearly.
- ▶ **Think twice** about using food or drink as a treat or reward or a pat on the back. Instead, buy a magazine or an expensive moisturizer (or a smaller size of jeans and smaller top!).
- ▶ **Think twice** about 'red light' food warnings about sugar, salt and chemicals. You are what you eat, and so is your brain.
- ▶ **Think twice** before shopping. Make a list. Don't buy offers if they are not on your list. Don't buy on impulse. If you really

need it, it will be on next week's list. Check whether any of the following are (or should not be) on your shopping list.

Thoughtless shopping list	Thoughtful shopping list
Crisps	Fresh fish
Biscuits	Pasta
Pies	Eggs
White bread	Bananas
Mayonnaise	Red fruit
Cook-in sauces	Chillies
Hard cheese	Ginger
Bacon	Olives
Liqueurs	Skimmed milk
Strong cider or ale	Low-fat yoghurt
Cappuccino/lattes	Yeast
Coconuts	Fast fish and/or chips
Peanut butter	Chicken
High oxytoxic ready meals	Chicken liver
(see Appendix H)	Kidneys
	Avocados
	Nuts
	Melons
	Seeds
	Molasses
	Maple syrup
	Onions
	Leeks
	Herbs
	Blueberries
	Apricots
	Tofu
	Beans
	Peas
	Olive oil, nut oil, hemp oil
	Dark chocolate

The oxytoxic index

Do not seek diets to die for. Ditch any chronic diets. These diets make you irritable, lower your ability to concentrate, reduce your mental stamina, lower your mood, cause depression, damage your self-confidence and lower your optimism. These side effects lower your performance on thinking tasks. Stressing about your weight and obsessing about food releases cortisol derivatives into your blood. If excess cortisol gets into your brain, it may damage your brain cells and wreak havoc with the chemical reactions that need to take place if you are to think clearly, quickly and accurately. Additionally, if your diet is too low in fats, the walls of your brain cells may become brittle and may die. It really will be a diet to die for – slowly, and in distress.

As far as your brain is concerned, what you eat matters more than how much you weigh. Although your brain will undoubtedly have less competition for oxygen in your blood if you weigh less, being fit is more important than whether or not you are fat. To perform well on a day-to-day basis, your brain needs enough fuel and chemicals and vitamins to catalyze the chemistry of its thinking.

Moving on from improving the day-to-day thinking power of your brain, by giving it 'food for thought' you will also be protecting it, as far as possible, from attack by diseases. We have explained how brain training can be used to create reserve cognitive capacity, in case you do get a neurodegenerative disease. What we are concerned to do next is to tip the balance strongly away from you getting a neurodegenerative disease at all. This will add life to your years, as well as years to your life.

Many degenerative diseases start when a cell or cells start to mutate, and when the mutation then reproduces. Cancers or tumours often start this way, and so might diseases like Alzheimer's. Cells can mutate if they are attacked by oxygen free radicals. Free radicals are sometimes produced when oxidation takes place. The more your food requires a lot of oxidizing, the greater the chance of you generating an oxygen free radical as a by-product. For each category of food, we have given a common member of that category an **oxytoxic index**. Its **oxytoxic index** is a comparative measure of how much oxidation takes place in your body when you eat it. The more oxidation, the greater the risk of free radicals. So, eat when you need to eat but, where possible, favour the foods with lower **oxytoxic indices**.

Many people want the convenience of branded processed foods as well as the benefits of fresh produce, so we have included the oxytoxic indices of many branded processed foods. There is a great variation from brand to brand. The choice is yours.

The state of your brain and your thinking power is a lifestyle choice for you to make. You may be able to make a better informed choice if you first cast your eye over the **oxytoxic index tables** in Appendix H.

A daily total oxytoxic score of 100 for women and 120 for men is found in Japan, China and Asian countries where the incidence of Alzheimer's (and some cancers) is very low compared with the USA and Europe. For example, the incidence of Alzheimer's in parts of the USA is seven times higher, and in Europe three to four times higher, than in Japan, China and Vietnam. We do not advocate keeping a daily score, but it might be prudent to favour lower, rather than higher, oxytoxic foods. And, just in case you still produce the odd oxygen free radical, include some of the foods from the ORAC (oxygen radical absorbance capacity) table below. Free radicals will likely attack any of these ORAC foods in preference to your brain cells. The relative power of these brain-friendly foods to absorb free radicals is shown in Appendix I. Note that dark chocolate is at least ten times more absorbent of free radicals than any other food in the table.

Table 4.1: ORAC (free radical absorbing, brain-friendly) foods.

Alfalfa	Apple sauce	Artichoke	Asparagus
Aubergine	Avocado	Basil	Beans
Bell peppers	Black-eyed peas	Black pepper	Blackberries
Blueberries	Broccoli	Cherries	Chillies
Cider vinegar	Cinnamon	Cloves	Cocoa
Dates	Elderberry	Figs	Ginger
Green tea	Kale	Nuts	Oats
Olive oil	Oranges	Oregano	Parsley
Peaches	Pears	Plums	Pomegranate
Prunes	Purple carrots	Purple potatoes	Raisins
Raspberries	Red cabbage	Red grapes	Spinach
Sprouts	Strawberries	Tangerines	Turmeric
Wholegrains	…and dark chocolate		

The **oxytoxic index** has been created on the grounds that there is little point in dieting, if dieting reduces your ability to think well when you are alive, and only extends your life by adding 10 or 20 years in which you are almost brain dead – i.e. unable to recognize, remember or reason. Maybe your starting point in deciding what to eat should be the health of your brain.

Insight
Do oxytoxic foods kill your brain?

The more oxygen your food needs to metabolize it, i.e. any foods with a high oxytoxic index, the greater the chance that you will produce oxygen free radicals which can damage the cells in your body and brain. However, oxygen free radicals would rather attack the cells in high ORAC foods, like dark chocolate, than brain cells, so eating high ORAC foods helps to absorb any oxygen free radicals you do produce.

Feeling full

How much you eat should also be determined by your brain. Your brain will tell your stomach to produce hunger pangs in response to the chemicals present in your brain. For example, if your blood contains a lot of insulin, perhaps because you have overloaded your digestive system too quickly with simple sugars, your brain will scream 'hunger' and nag you until you eat (probably more sugar). During this time, it will be very difficult for you to concentrate on thinking tasks. On the other hand, your brain will produce chemicals that send messages like 'full', 'satisfied', 'sated' or 'bloated' in response to the action of swallowing, tasting and, particularly, chewing. It takes about 20 minutes for your brain to produce the chemical message 'full'. You should start by drinking water, since it is easy for you to confuse a signal for dehydration with a signal for hunger. The dehydration signal is likely to persist even after you have mistakenly eaten food to no avail. You may then eat even more unnecessary food and still not extinguish the brain call for water. After swallowing half a pint of water slowly, you may well find that you are not hungry after all. If the signals persist, try changing the taste in your mouth – try mints, Cox's apples, or a square of good quality dark chocolate. Wait a while. You may notice that your brain is no longer signalling hunger. When you are sure your brain really needs to eat, eat a nutritious balance of foods and favour foods with lower oxytoxic indices. Maintain a nutritious balance over the day.

Ensure that you eat without distractions (television, radio, books) because if you are not fully aware of the texture and smells of what you are eating, your brain may under-produce chemicals that signal 'satisfied'.

Favour hard, chewy foods and chew them deliberately and slowly –
a mouthful at a time. This will maximize the production of 'full'
chemical messages in your brain. Foods that have been blended or
processed to make them mushy or easy to swallow trick your brain into
allowing you to eat much more than is needed by your brain or body.

> **Insight**
> **How to feel full**
> If you feel hungry you may actually be dehydrated. To get your brain to signal
> 'full' instead of 'hungry' drink some plain water. If your brain still signals
> 'hungry' try a square of dark chocolate, or an apple, or mints.

Brain-based cooking tips

*As I'm getting older, I decided to cook more healthy meals, so I bought
Gordon Ramsay's new book called 'Take Two Eggs and F*ck Off'.*

Jack Dee

Having created the right conditions, under which your brain will
tell you that you are not hungry when it has had enough to eat,
it still matters what you choose to eat. You need to pick from
each of proteins (meat, fish, pulses, eggs, lentils, nuts), complex
carbohydrates (fruit, vegetables, salad) and unsaturated oils or fats.
Your brain needs the complex carbohydrates to provide mental
energy for your thinking tasks. The proteins provide many of the
neurotransmitters and minerals and vitamins involved in your brain's
chemical reactions. Your brain needs fats to repair and maintain its
brain cells, and to create replacement cells.

To reduce the likelihood that your brain will be attacked by disease,
when you make your daily choice of proteins, carbohydrates and fats
you should favour those foods that have lower **oxytoxic indices** and
try to include at least one of the foods from Appendix I.

Make a start:

1 Use anti-inflammatory herbs and spices, such as turmeric and
   ginger.
2 Eat raw foods or choose ingredients or ready meals with a low
   oxytoxic index.
3 Avoid simple sugars and syrups. Favour complex carbohydrates
   as found in fruit, vegetables, salads and wholemeal grains.

4 Cook for the minimum time, at the lowest possible temperatures.
5 Use a non-stick pan. Wipe with a little oil on a tissue before cooking. Add a little olive, or sesame, or hemp oil *after* cooking.
6 Eat fresh fish three times a week. Cook in foil in the oven with lemon, or a quick hot sear in a pan (for example a sea bream fillet takes only 90 seconds per side!).
7 Eat five to ten helpings per week of deeply coloured fruits, vegetables or salads, including at least one per week from Appendix I.

There are also some easy, low-oxytoxic recipes for you to try in Appendix J.

Fitness, health and training your brain

Our low oxytoxic index enables protecting your brain and enhancing its performance to be given a higher priority than losing weight at 50+. What matters more than fatness is fitness. Fitness is of two sorts: healthy fitness – the sort that helps you to fend off illness, thereby allowing your brain to perform better and better as you get older; and sporty fitness – the sort that goes further than healthy fitness because your work requires it, or your sport demands it, or because you are mad or vain!

Healthy fitness requires only 15–20 minutes of modest exercise three to five times a week. At least three times a week, you should get a bit puffed or even slightly sweaty for a few minutes. Begin and end with simple stretches after you have warmed up your muscles by walking briskly for a few minutes first.

Sporty fitness, i.e. 4S fitness, involves S for strength, S for speed, S for suppleness, S for stamina. Get a book, a friend, a gym or a coach to give you a regime for each. Sporty fitness will help your healthy fitness too – and both will benefit your brain.

Swinging along at 50+

You are far more likely than a 16–25-year-old to be able to walk upstairs holding a normal conversation without becoming breathless. You are far more likely to catch that bus.

PILATES – THOUGHTFUL EXERCISE

The main brain benefit of aerobic exercise is the residual increased rate of supply of oxygen to your brain. The main drawback is that aerobic exercises like jogging, running, rowing and power walking can be so boring that they appear to actually numb your mind. Aerobic exercise can be leavened by trying aerobic dance classes or by playing basketball, or better still, korfball, which is a kind of cross between netball and basketball played in mixed teams. Aerobic workouts to music using a DVD or better still in a live class, bring variety to ease the tedium.

Fortunately, exercises you do for suppleness and posture are much more mentally demanding and so bring additional cognitive benefits to your brain. Yoga is a well-known example, but a system more recently developed by Joseph Pilates is also demanding because 'Pilates' exercises require constant awareness of the position of your limbs and the state of tension of many of your muscles. Pilates provides a mental workout that mirrors your physical workout. This is intensified when you are copying visual demonstrations or watching your movements in a mirror. In 2003, the Pilates Foundation published an excellent guide written by Trevor Blount and Eleanor McKenzie.

PREJUDICE AGAINST FAT PEOPLE

With extra body weight, brain oxygenation through exercise is less appealing, as more of your body will compete for the oxygen which your brain needs. This adds to the prejudicial image of overweight people as slothful mentally, as well as physically. In job interviews, overweight people are at a disadvantage even when competing for jobs where mental (as opposed to physical) agility is being sought. Unfortunately, too few interviewers know that it is physical and mental fitness that matters – not body bulk or fatness.

THE POSITIVE EFFECTS OF RELAXATION ON THINKING

Gelb found that the tested cognition and memory of people taught how to relax was 25 per cent higher than in a control group. He found similar gains when posture was improved prior to thinking tasks.

Movement and the mind – how to sit and stand

Avoid lifts and escalators. Seek out stairs. Do not lie if you can sit, or sit if you can stand, or stand if you can walk, or walk if you can run, or ride if you can cycle.

When sitting on a chair, push your buttocks into the back of the chair. Do not cross your legs. Place feet firmly apart on the floor, about the same distance apart as your shoulders. Imagine you were trying to crumple a rug under your feet. The same applies when standing, but relax your knees. Once an hour, rub the palms of your hands together as vigorously as circumstances allow. Keep rubbing while you count backwards from 100 to zero.

When standing, sitting or lying down, try to imagine that your navel is a large nut connected by a bolt through to your backbone. Imagine the bolt slowly tightening as you breathe in. Keep your navel bolted to your backbone.

According to McWilliams, massage and yoga not only relax you, but can also help you to control the frequency of the electrical brain waves in your head. This is because excessive stress impairs thinking and relaxation lowers the cortisol associated with the stress. But if you are not at all stressed or anxious, the effect on your mental performance may be adverse. A quarter of students, for example, require stimulation and mild anxiety (about deadlines, presentations or prospective questioning) to get them into the zone of proximal readiness to think!

Exercise 1: Memorable yoga

To improve your mental concentration and memory, try removing your shoes and standing tall with your feet together. Breathe in deeply and transfer your weight onto your right foot, placing the sole of your left foot as high up the inner thigh of your right leg as you comfortably can, with the toes of your left foot pointing down your right leg at the floor. Press your left foot against the right leg and with the right leg

(Contd)

push back against the left foot. If you can, raise your arms upwards on either side of your head and press the palms of your hands together. Focus the eyes on something just above head height and breathe deeply in and out, counting backwards from eight. Repeat with your weight on your left leg.

Exercise 2: Respire to inspire

For creative and imaginative thinking, force every last bit of breath out of your body, especially by squeezing the muscles of the stomach and buttocks. Hold this state for as long as you can and then allow the breath to rush in and appear to fill all the cavities of your body, from your abdomen up to the upper regions of your chest. Raise your shoulders to suck in the last breath. Hold for as long as you comfortably can. Repeat three times. Use a finger to gently close one nostril and breathe normally. Jot down every new idea that occurs to you – however crazy these ideas might seem.

Now change from the slow, deep breathing rhythm that is needed for creative thinking to the quicker, shallower, upper-chest breathing that favours critical thinking. To do this, stand with knees relaxed, your feet about as far apart as your shoulders, and imagine you are squeezing a rug on the floor between your feet. Hold your arms straight out in front of you and slide your palms back and forth over each other as fast as you can without a break, while counting backwards from 100. Do not ease off. Try to accelerate for the last 50 counts. When you reach zero, straighten your knees and drop your head as near to the floor as you can. Use one hand to tap up the opposite side of your body, from your ankles to your head, as you slowly straighten up. Bend down again and repeat with the other hand, tapping the other side of your body. Your electrical brainwave cycle will now be much quicker. You will now be better prepared for a quick 'thinking-on-your-feet' evaluation of the creative ideas you just produced when you were breathing deeply and slowly through one nostril.

You can do this exercise in a seated position. Just push your chair clear of the desk or table.

THE EFFECTS OF AEROBIC EXERCISE

My grandmother didn't take up serious walking until she was 57.
She is 97 today and we don't know where the hell she is.

Ellen DeGeneres

Dienstbier reports that aerobic exercise enhances thinking performance. Brain activity is fuelled by oxygen. Aerobic exercise increases the supply of oxygen to the brain. Herman divided people into three groups: group one was given vigorous aerobic exercise, group two was given moderate anaerobic exercise and group three was given a placebo activity not involving exercise at all. The two exercise groups consistently showed significantly higher scores on reasoning and thinking tests than the non-exercisers. The exercise regimes were rotated around the groups and the most enhanced reasoning and thinking scores continued to be achieved in the group that was exercising aerobically. According to Bagley, anaerobic exercise is better for enhancing creative thinking, although it will improve critical and reflective thinking as well, if your overall thinking is temporarily impaired by anxiety or stress (Chapter 1).

The 50+ come out to play

In Germany in May 2007, the daily paper, *Der Spiegel*, commented that 'pensioners are taking over power, while children become extinct'. In Berlin, and next in Nuremberg, the pensioners are certainly taking over the children's playgrounds! (This would not be news in China, where public places commonly have keep-fit equipment for adults, but it is still rare in Germany.) The pensioners' playground in Berlin – Prussia Park – was designed by Finnish researchers from the University of Lapland. The playground cost only £13,500 for eight exercisers – a fraction of the cost of a typical children's playground. More are planned, after Nuremberg, based on evidence that physical and mental exercise delay dementia – often indefinitely.

JUST STEP OUTSIDE – JUST WALK THIS WAY

Provided you are brisk enough about it, walking can provide all the low-impact aerobic exercise your brain needs without risk of injury, and without special shoes and socks and other gear you need for running. Pull your stomach in and push your hips forward. This engages your muscles – abdominals and lower back and bottom – the core muscles. No wonder you look and think better. Roll your feet outwards as you walk, so as to keep your knees and ankles in a straight line. It's not as difficult as it sounds, and all the repetition is brilliant for your brain.

Walking the talk
According to Joanna Hall, you reach your optimum speed just before you feel tempted to break out into a run. You should be able to talk to a fellow walker – but only just. Buy a pedometer and build towards 10,000 paces a day, five days a week. According to Shinsha University, interval walking is as effective as interval running – i.e. slow–quick–slow. The Ramblers Keep Walking project provides a free 12-week programme with guided walks and social events (www.ramblers.org.uk).

Go through the wall

Use endurance anaerobic exercise to manage anxiety or stress (Chapter 1), or to raise your metabolic rate to speed up the flow of oxygen to your brain, and maybe even to lose weight. You will get the calming effect of increased serotonin without eating, because tryptophan will be bumped off your body fat. In this way, you can manage your stress and lose weight at the same time, if that is what you want to do.

TACTILE STIMULATION
Give time to hobbies that involve physical contact, tactile stimulation or intricate handwork. Try massage, swimming, rock climbing, planting, sailing, DIY, or contact sports like rugby or judo. Try painting, weaving, printing, model making, working with clay, or ballroom dancing. Walk in the rain or a strong wind. Try a sauna, jacuzzi or steam room.

Exercise 3: Put your head in your hands

▶ Start the day with your head in your hands! Sit on the edge of your bed, or the seat of your lavatory, and support the weight of your forehead in the palms of your hands, with your fingers in your hair. Allow your chin to fall slowly onto your chest, your hands stretching the skin of your forehead, and your fingers running through your hair.

▶ Sit up again. This time start with your finger tips on either side of your nose. Allow the weight of your head to fall slowly through your hands, which should graze your ears until your fingers touch at the back of your head.

▶ Sit up again and restart with your finger tips under your ears. Again allow your head to fall slowly against the friction of your palms and fingers until your finger tips pass in front of your ears and touch at the top of your scalp.

▶ Repeat with your finger tips passing upwards behind your ears this time, before meeting at the top of your head. This can literally make your hair stand on end.

▶ During the day, brush or comb your hair as often as vanity or local custom allow.

The effects of sleep on thinking

To achieve optimum performance, people need good quality sleep. Horne found that impaired sleep reduced performance on many mental tasks. Mitler's studies of catastrophes, such as the Three Mile Island nuclear power accident and the Challenger space shuttle explosion, concluded that poor sleep quality had impaired decision making and contributed to each.

The amount of sleep people need varies greatly from one person to another. It ranges from four to ten hours. For adults, quality of sleep seems to be more important than quantity. Quality of sleep can be impaired by listening for a baby, the return of a missing teenager, or by fear of not hearing the alarm clock. Sleep quality can also be impaired by snoring.

Many people who work shifts never get the chance for a high quality sleeping pattern to develop. People who work continuous night shifts perform better at mental tasks than people whose shift patterns change. Travel across time zones and the accompanying jet lag impairs performance on mental tasks. Going to bed later than usual has a more deleterious effect than getting up earlier than usual. The time taken to re-stabilize mental activity after a disturbed sleep pattern increases with age. Even with young adults it can take up to four days. At 50+ it can take more than one week.

Getting to sleep

Remove televisions and radios from your bedroom. Try going to bed later each night until you find a time at which you ordinarily drop off to sleep without delay. Talking to a partner prior to sleep can be desirable but such conversations should not involve complicated feats of memory or planning. Use a bedside notepad to park things until the next day. The deep breathing exercises described above will help you to settle your mind and slow down your brainwaves.

If you are physically tense, squeeze and then relax all your muscles in turn, from your toes, through to your ankles, calves, thighs, buttocks, stomach, back, hands, arms, shoulders, chest, neck, face and right up to your scalp. If a massage is on offer, seize the moment! If early sleep is the goal, imagine a line down the centre of the body and another across the body, intersecting at the groin. Taking each quadrant in turn, direct the massage so that the flow of pressure is towards the head or feet, away from the groin. Start by lying face down. You may fall asleep without ever turning over! If you like to make love prior to falling asleep, then ask to be massaged so that the flow of pressure in each quadrant is towards the groin. Avoid direct contact with the groin.

According to Coren, scores on intelligence tests decline cumulatively on each successive day that you sleep less than you normally sleep. The daily decline is approximately one IQ point for the first hour of sleep loss, two for the next, and four for the next. After five successive days of sleeping two hours less than you need, your IQ can be lowered by up to 15 points. This means that a person of normal intelligence could have an effective IQ of only 85, the level at which you would need special education in order to learn. Even a very 'bright' person (IQ of 120 plus) can be reduced to robotic thinking, as though on automatic pilot.

According to Griffey (writing in *The Independent* in April 2004), in the UK in 1910, people averaged nine hours' sleep per night.

In 1990, they averaged eight hours' sleep per night. By 1995, according to a survey by First Direct, they were averaging seven hours and 35 minutes a night. By 2004, the average had fallen to seven hours per night. Are we sleeping less because we are more stressed, or are we more stressed because we are sleeping less? Certainly, levels of neurotoxic cortisol derivatives are raised in our brains.

THE DANGERS OF DISTURBED SLEEP AT 50+

Once you have found a convenient time at which you fall asleep easily, without reading, radio or television, try to stick to it. At weekends do not set an alarm. Notice the time when you wake naturally – however early. Record your natural length of sleep time. Notice how short your 'natural sleep time' can be, especially when you are 50+. Whenever you are forced to sleep less than your 'natural sleep time', your performance on IQ tests, and the kind of mental aptitude tests used by employers, is likely to drop. The consequences can be serious. You may be incapable of learning something you need to learn, or thinking about some emergency that is new or complex or fast moving. Your reaction to unusual events will be poor, as will the reactions of a younger person. You should minimize your driving after sleep loss or sleep disturbance. Do not negotiate, or give presentations at which questions will be asked, immediately after travelling across a time zone, particularly as you get older.

EARLY TO BED... EARLY TO RISE

A study at Southampton University, based on 1,200 men and women, showed no evidence that 'early to bed, early to rise' made anyone 'healthier, wealthier or wise'! What seemed to be important was to be a regular riser – whether early or late. It is disturbed sleep patterns that disturb health, wealth and wisdom. The 50+ tend to sleep less and to rise earlier, so 50+ brains have more hours of daily brain power available to them than younger brains. This more than compensates for the few mental tasks for which more time is required as you get older. For example, you need more time during recall, because at 50+ you have more possibilities to search and select from than when you were 25 (see Chapter 3).

15 TIPS FOR SLEEPING BETTER AT 50+

1 First, are you sure you really need to sleep any more or any better?

2 Don't eat or drink late into the evening.
3 Evening food should include carbohydrate and not be very spicy.
4 Evening drinks should not be caffeinated or alcoholic (warm milk is good because it contains tryptophan which will relax your brain).
5 Don't do aerobic exercise in the evening (unless it's sexual).
6 Warm baths and ritualistic cleansing help.
7 Remove computers, radios, televisions, rowing machines and bright lights from the bedroom.
8 Substitute the above with aromatic oil burners. Try lavender or chamomile.
9 Use fresh-air ventilation and keep the temperature at around 16–18°C.
10 Use blackout blinds on your windows.
11 Try relaxation breathing and exercises.
12 Park any intrusive thoughts on a notepad by your bed.
13 Don't resort to listening to the radio, or worse, the television. A relaxation tape of sea sounds or wind noise will work better.
14 If you wake early, get up and do something nice, for example have sex, eat dark chocolate, drink freshly squeezed juice or read a car magazine. You may not sleep, but you can dream!
15 If midnight insomnia is recurrent, seek medical advice.

DEAD DRUNK OR DEAD TIRED (OR JUST DEAD)?

Drink driving is dangerous. Tired driving is more so, causing more than one in ten accidents.

Coren tested a group of drivers after they had been awake for one hour after their 'normal' bedtime. Their thinking processes and reaction times were worse than a control group who had drunk more than the UK drink–drive limit for alcohol consumption! In countries like the United Kingdom, where the clocks are changed by one hour in the summer, car insurance accident claims rise by 25 per cent in the first four days following the one-hour sleep loss. Out of all UK motorway accidents, 25 per cent of drivers admit to feeling sleepy prior to their accident. Add in people not admitting this for fear of self-incrimination, plus the drivers who did not live to tell the tale, and the effect of sleep loss is likely to be a much more serious contributor to accidents even than alcohol. The effect is more marked in 50+, 60+ and 70+ drivers and increases with age.

The magazine *What Car* organized a test by Professor Parkes of the Transport Research Laboratory. The tired subjects fared much worse than subjects over the legal limit for alcohol.

Action:

1 Have an especially good night's sleep the night before a long drive. Don't stay up packing!
2 Do stop if you find yourself whistling, singing, opening windows, turning up the radio, hitting yourself. Drink one coffee and sleep for 20 minutes – but not longer – before trying again.
3 Try to avoid driving at night.

Power naps – do they work?

New York, the city that never sleeps, is sprouting Metro-Nap soporific salons – £10 for 20 minutes. London has snooze booths, 30 minutes' shut-eye for £27.50. Who said sleep was priceless! At 50+ you can learn to do it for free!

The effects of alcohol on thinking

Heavy drinkers risk a brain disorder called Wernicke-Korsakoff syndrome, a progressive memory deficit. Sufferers normally recover their ability to speak and walk, but do not recover their ability to think. The condition seems irreversible and untreatable. Alcohol depletes vitamin B1, which is essential for the thinking process. As we have seen already, there are other ways to feel more relaxed and less stressed that do not impair thinking or damage your brain. The effect of alcohol is likely to be more damaging as you get older than 50+.

THINKING AND HITTING THE BOTTLE?

▶ Minimize your consumption of alcohol, especially during the day. Between one o'clock and four o'clock in the afternoon it can have up to ten times its usual effect.
▶ Do not drink alcohol on an empty stomach.
▶ Drink plenty of water before and after drinking alcohol.
▶ Drink spirits only with a double mixer plus plenty of ice.

▶ Do not mix alcohol with analysis. Even small amounts of alcohol can lead to a dangerous combination of error proneness, over-confidence and increased risk taking.

The effects of tea, coffee, cola and caffeine on thinking

Caffeine is found in tea, coffee and cola drinks and in some food products. Caffeine can quicken your reaction time and prolong your vigilance during demanding tasks. However, there is a need to keep doubling your intake of caffeine to have the same effect. Eventually a plateau is reached. The caffeine also acts as a diuretic. You keep urinating, causing dehydration. This produces lethargy and reduces your cognitive performance. Nutritionists recommend that you drink eight to fifteen glasses of water a day, depending on your body size, the weather and your activity level. Water is preferable to strong tea, soft drinks or fruit juices. David Kerr found that the caffeine lift, or 'buzz', was an illusion. Within 30 minutes of taking caffeine, he observed that the flow of blood (and hence oxygen) to the brain had reduced by 10–20 per cent. There is, however, an antioxidant protective element to good quality black coffee.

COFFEE – GOOD FOR YOUR BRAIN (AND NOT THAT BAD FOR YOUR BODY)

For years we have recommended one cup of cafetière filter coffee each day, because the benefits to your brain, and your performance on thinking tasks, seem to outweigh the risks to your body. Our more recent interest in brain protection, especially from degenerative diseases like Alzheimer's, has unearthed further potential benefits from drinking real coffee.

Many coffees – like Arabica coffee from Madagascar – are so rich in beneficial phytochemicals that, as reported by Dr Yanagimata in the *Journal of Food Chemistry* (2004), a small daily consumption of good quality coffee (not instant coffee), may be sufficient to reduce oxidative attacks on the fat components of the cells in your brain (remember, we think that oxidative attacks are possible precipitants of neurodegenerative diseases like Alzheimer's and Parkinson's, Chapter 3). When you add this to our observation that stimulation, whether from coffee, aerobic exercise or dark chocolate, is associated with increased energy, enhanced sense of wellbeing, improved self-confidence and greater sociability, motivation and stamina, then, on balance, the additional protection that comes from drinking a cup a day of good quality coffee, seems worth some risks, but not if your anxiety levels, or blood pressure, are already high.

Over a period of eight years, 130,000 people who consumed at least one cup of real coffee a day were less likely to attempt suicide (and also showed a 30 per cent reduction in diabetes, liver disease, colon cancer and gallstones). In studies in Norway (Svilaas, 2004), the USA and Europe (Frost, 2006), coffee was found to be people's number one source of protective antioxidants. Further indications of coffee's protective value against degenerative brain disease came from a longitudinal study of 8,000 people (of whom half were not coffee drinkers). The non-coffee drinkers were five times more likely to get Parkinson's disease. It is not certain whether the protection came from the coffee or from low levels of dopamine in the brain, without which there is no 'buzz' from being a coffee drinker. Similar levels of protection can also be achieved by eating up to six squares a day of dark chocolate (70–75 per cent cocoa). In the same way that chocolate should be dark to confer protection, coffee should preferably be drunk without milk – skimmed milk if you must, and no sugar.

Watering the brain

▶ Dehydration has a major adverse effect on mental activity. Coffee, strong tea and cola, like alcohol, make things worse because they are diuretics.
▶ The adrenal boost from the caffeine in coffee, tea, and cola is short-lived. The first buzz from the first cup is eventually negated by fatigue.
▶ Tap water, hot water, fruit teas or herbal teas all produce greater benefits with less detriment.

The effects of sweets on thinking

People who become anxious frequently often crave the tranquillizing effect of the serotonin that is formed from the tryptophan released into their blood when they eat simple carbohydrates. Perhaps that is why people who are over-anxious often crave something sweet. Sweet things are usually sweet because they contain simple carbohydrates like refined sugar. For the anxious person, the advantage of refined sugar is that it is very rapidly absorbed by the body, so the calming effect is almost immediate. A serious downside, however, of eating food containing refined sugar, is that it can cause an overproduction of insulin. Excess insulin provokes hunger-like pains and makes mental concentration very difficult. It also produces craving for more sweet food and so the cycle gets worse. If your diet contains too much processed or refined carbohydrate, like sugar, then the insulin-producing systems in your body may become exhausted, or even diseased. This risks type 2 diabetes, heart disease, damaged eye sight and other neuropathic complications.

The effects of smoking on thinking

I smoked my first cigarette on the same day I kissed my first girl. I have never had time to smoke since.

Toscanini, aged 87

Smokers self-report increased mental alertness and improved performance on a host of cognitive tasks after one cigarette. However, this positive effect is soon countered by an adverse effect on the oxygen-carrying capacity of your blood. Smoking ties up the haemoglobin that carries the oxygen in your blood.

Damage to your lungs limits your body's ability to absorb the oxygen needed to support mental activity.

Stubbing out dementia at 50+

The December 2007 issue of *Health Magazine* reported research showing that if you give up smoking now, even at 50+, you will reduce your risk of dementia by 50 per cent (as well as immediately improving your thinking power in the short term!).

The effects of drugs on thinking

CANNABIS – THE URBAN MYTH OF HARMLESSNESS

This is a dilemma because the use of cannabis for pain control is rising in the 50+ age group and certainly chronic pain lowers mental performance. However, over a three-year period, Mathews studied people who were regularly using cannabis (or marijuana) at least ten times a week. He found that regular users progressively reduced their baseline of brain activity, compared with a matched control group. Regular users show lower energy levels, lower completion rates on personal goals and plans, lower reported pleasure in anything and reduced interest in using their bodies or their brains.

COCAINE – THERE HAS GOT TO BE A BETTER WAY... THERE IS

When an endorphin molecule in your body jumps a synaptic gap and finds a receptor site, you experience pleasure. Normally the endorphin will then detach. A cocaine molecule will lock the endorphin onto the receptor site so that you will continue to experience the pleasure. You will crave for a repeat of this pleasurable experience. You are hooked. The more cocaine you use the more the blood vessels in your brain will become constricted. This constriction will impair your ability to think and will eventually damage your brain. This constriction is more likely, and the likely damage more extensive, as you grow older than 50+.

'Just a tick' – avoiding the brain bug

Lyme's disease is a disease once found only in African countries. It is carried by ticks which bite their prey, suck their blood, and sometimes leave a red ring around the bite. Lyme's disease can cause a swelling of the brain (encephalitis), a complication from which about 1 in 50 victims die. Even if you do not die, you can be left with severe neurological damage and be unable to walk or move your joints.

Today there are carrier ticks in 27 countries in mainland Europe, including the UK (in the New Forest, Exmoor, South Downs, Yorkshire Moors, Scottish Highlands and the Lake District). If you are bitten and you get a red ring, or flu-like symptoms, you need a large and sustained dose of strong antibiotics immediately. If you wait for a blood test it can be too late for the antibiotics to be effective. Since the 50+ are more likely to be walkers, they should cover their arms, not wear shorts, and check their bodies for red rings after country walks.

Designer brains and cosmetic neurology – the effects of smart drugs

In May 2007, Peta Bee, writing in the *Times*, questioned the fairness of students who were buying drugs, like Modafinil, which enhanced intellectual performance. According to Dr Danielle Turner, from Cambridge University, Modafinil improves memory, planning, information processing, emotional and reflective thinking and decision making, and seems to have only benign side effects. Peta Bee reviewed a number of other 'smart drugs', including Ritalin, which was originally developed to treat attention deficit disorder in children. It is now claimed to improve alertness, memory, and visual and spatial thinking in 50+ adults.

Mice memorized five times faster when given these drugs. That kind of memory acceleration would come in handy if you needed to learn a second language, or wanted to play a musical instrument, or needed to revise for an exam – especially if your speed of new memory formation had declined (see Chapter 3).

However, you might remember everything, but understand nothing. What matters is not what you can remember, but what you can do with what you can remember. What matters most is your ability to think, and your ability to apply your thinking.

Insight
Designer brains
'Smart' drugs, which can improve memory, are now widely available on the internet. However, what matters more than simply remembering is the use you can make of your memories. That requires thinking skills which you can develop.

Dark chocolate boosts the brain

Dark chocolate boosts your brain while protecting your 50+ heart from disease and your 50+ body from cancer. Eating dark chocolate can improve your learning and your memory. Improved blood flow carries more oxygen to the brain, enabling you to think more quickly for longer. Your blood vessels relax, reducing blood pressure, brain damage and risk of heart disease. In February 2007, the American Academy of Science, from two separate studies, one in the USA and one in the UK, reported that dark chocolate was not an old vice, but a modern-day life saver. Welcoming the news, nutritionists pointed out that the finding applied only to dark chocolate and warned chocoholics to avoid the pale dairy stuff. In a way we have come full circle, because chocolate was originally brought from South America to the court of the Spanish Empire as a medication and brain stimulant. It was a state secret which they believed helped their intelligence and their military dominance.

Dark chocolate is high in antioxidants. Professor Ian MacDonald found the increased blood flows in the cerebral cortex persisted for three hours after eating dark chocolate. Dr Helen Berg of Harvard found that rates of heart disease were only a fraction of Western levels in parts of the world (such as Panama) where drinking dark chocolate was part of the everyday diet. Deaths from cancer were similarly very low. Rates for strokes and diabetes were also low. Dark chocolate contains epicatechin – a mineral so vital to health that Professor Hollenberg would like to see it classified as a vitamin. The efficacy of epicatechin is undermined by sugar and dairy products. Hence the need to eat your chocolate dark!

Insight
Dark chocolate

Dark chocolate can boost your brain while protecting your heart from disease, your mind from depression, and your body from cancer. Dark chocolate improves learning and memory. The theobromine in dark chocolate relaxes the muscles around your blood vessels; it reduces your blood pressure, while still increasing the flow of blood and oxygen to your brain.

THE NEUROSCIENCE OF DARK CHOCOLATE

A heart-felt plea

According to Dr B. Jensen, you need the magnesium in dark chocolate to decrease the coagulation of your blood. This will help your heart to deliver more oxygen to your brain. This will not only raise the thinking speed and thinking power of your brain, it will also protect your brain from the damage that is caused by high blood pressure.

Dark chocolate lifts depression

Dark chocolate contains monoamine oxidase inhibitors (MAOIs). These allow the levels of serotonin and dopamine in your brain to remain higher for longer, alleviating depression and producing feelings of well-being.

Dark chocolate – the new vitamin

Free radicals attack and oxidize the DNA in your brain, creating growth points for tumours and other degenerative brain diseases like Alzheimer's, Parkinson's and motor neurone disease. Cheng Lee at Cornell University, showed that dark chocolate is rich in antioxidants, called flavonols. Flavonols mop up the free radicals, before they can oxidize your brain. Dark chocolate is twice as rich in antioxidant flavonols as red wine is and three times richer than green tea. The flavonols in dark chocolate also make your blood platelets less likely to stick together and cause brain damage through a stroke. Cheng Lee found that a normal cup of drinking chocolate, based on dark chocolate, contained about 600 mg of epicatechin.

Dark chocolate – better than broccoli

The US Department of Agriculture compared the oxygen radical absorbance capacity (ORAC) scores of well-known brain foods like spinach, blueberries and broccoli with dark chocolate (ORAC scores measure the concentration of flavonoid antioxidants in foods):

Broccoli	890
Sprouted alfalfa	930
Plums	949
Sprouts	980
Raspberries	1,220
Spinach	1,260
Strawberries	1,540
Kale/cabbage	1,770
Blackberries	2,036
Blueberries	2,400
Dark chocolate	13,120

Dark chocolate a safer 'buzz' than caffeine

Eating dark chocolate substantially increases your mental speed and energy because it contains the brain stimulant theobromine.

(Dark chocolate is virtually free of caffeine when compared with the levels found in coffee, strong tea and Red Bull.) Caffeine also gives your brain a temporary boost, but it can raise your blood pressure, which can be serious if it is already too high. Dark chocolate contains about 21 per cent of theobromine. Theobromine works as a brain stimulant by relaxing muscles and so dilating veins, arteries and blood vessels thereby allowing more blood to flow to the brain. The effect of theobromine is gentler and more sustained than that of caffeine. It lasts four times longer and is kinder to your heart. Theobromine has actually been prescribed for heart patients to help lower blood pressure.

Get involved

Dark chocolate contains PEA (phenylethylamine). PEA activates the neurotransmitters in your brain, which control mental attention, concentration and alertness. Your levels of PEA go up naturally, without chocolate, when you are gripped by a great movie, or are enjoying a good book, or are wholly engrossed in a football match, a work project or a computer game. Elevated levels of PEA can cause us to lose track of time. This is why time seems to fly when you are enjoying yourself. PEA is present in higher levels in 'blissful' people (Chapter 1). It is also found in dark chocolate.

The brain's BLISS chemical

Dark chocolate contains an anandamide – a cannabinoid brain chemical which is known as the 'BLISS chemical' because it is produced in the brain when you feel good (Chapter 1). The anandamide released in your brain when you feel good acts on your brain in the same way as the THC in cannabis, but because anandamide does not act on the whole of your brain, like cannabis does, you can feel good without losing your mind. You do not feel 'out of it' like you would on cannabis (or marijuana). Anandamide is a natural brain chemical that is not known to have harmful side effects, unless you would regard BLISS as harmful. In fact, BLISS is strongly correlated with good health (Chapter 1) and the anandamide in dark chocolate is the brain's own bliss chemical.

The secret of eternal youth?

According to Dr G. Cousens, MAOIs (monoamine oxidase inhibitors) in dark chocolate work by allowing increased levels of anandamine and dopamine to circulate in the brain. It is the high level of anandamine and dopamine that distinguishes the brains of children from the brains of most adults because, in general, as you get older the levels of these neurotransmitters decrease. This decrease is associated with a decrease in physical and mental spontaneity and joy. You are as young as you think and feel and the MAOIs in dark chocolate can help to keep your anandamine and dopamine levels nearer to the levels of your youth.

And so to bed
Dark chocolate produces endorphins that induce the loving feelings which often lead to sex. The same endorphins also facilitate the euphoria of the 'afterglow'.

The effects of sex on your brain and your thinking

The effects of sex on your thinking depends on whether or not your pre-sex stress levels are excessive, whether or not you have an orgasm, and what type of thinking you are concerned about.

THE SEVEN STEPS IN THE SEX LIFE OF YOUR BRAIN

1 You and your partner each need to have sufficient testosterone in your brain. Low levels of testosterone are the most common cause of low levels of libido. Stress, fatigue, disturbed sleep, and hormone imbalance due to pregnancy, hysterectomy or menopause, are common causes of inadequate levels of testosterone.

2 Given you have sufficient testosterone, then a rising level of oestrogen can generate a feeling of desire, triggering the release of pheromones under your armpits. These may create a reciprocal sexual desire in your partner (the jury is still out on this one).

3 Sexual desires release dopamine. Dopamine helps you to think visually. Dopamine will help you to visualize, imagine and fantasize about the different possible places and ways in which you might have sex with your partner. This will further raise your level of desire and the level of nitric oxide in your bloodstream.

4 The nitric oxide increases your rate of blood flow. Besides helping you to dilate the labial lips of your vaginal area, or to engorge the tumescence of your penis, the increased rate

of supply of oxygen to your brain will enable you to process information faster and to assess problems more quickly. (The increased rate of oxidation will leave your head clearer afterwards for calculations, decisions and action.) Nitric oxide readies you for action.

5 If the action is sexual, your oxytocin levels will rise, causing pelvic contractions and raising the possibility of female orgasm. The oxytocin heightens a sense of being wanted, safe and secure. It is sometimes called the 'trust hormone'. It increases preparedness to think of novel or riskier solutions. It aids creative thinking.

6 The pleasure of sexual activity, especially following orgasm, raises the levels of serotonin in the brain. Serotonin calms agitation, stress and anxiety. Cortisol levels associated with stress are moderated, making calm, logical decision making and calculation easier. High levels of serotonin favour creative thinking.

7 With stress relieved, head cleared, and visual and creative thinking empowered, there is an 'afterglow' of satisfaction associated with a rise in the level of phenylethylamine (PEA). PEA produces feelings of wellbeing and a tendency to smile involuntarily! PEA is the brain chemical associated with romance and falling in love. It is also produced by eating dark chocolate. (Sometimes life is less complicated if you just eat the chocolate!)

Insight
Sex on the brain
Seven different chemical states are associated with the seven stages from mutual attraction to final afterglow. Five of these seven states are associated with chemicals in your brain which can help different types of thinking. Which of these stages you should prolong (if you can!), depends on what types of thinking you want to do afterwards – but that's probably not what you'll be thinking about.

MANOPAUSE AND MID-LIFE CRISIS – WHAT CRISIS?

Menopause among 50+ women has received much coverage elsewhere, but manopause, the equivalent phenomenon for 50+ men, has not received the same attention until now. According to Dr Ian Banks of Men's Health Forum, the manopause is better known as andropause. Too low a level of testosterone in manopausal men can cause low libido, erectile dysfunction, low mood and irritability – all four of which can lower performance on thinking tasks, given that sex is good for your brain and depression is not (Chapter 1). Psychologically, the resulting gain in weight round the belly and the loss of hair on the pate is sometimes overcompensated for by buying a car with a bigger bonnet, and clothes that are too tight, and by chasing younger women in order to prove…

An alternative to big cars, and making a complete fool of yourself, is to ask your GP to check your available testosterone level – your total might be fine, but too much may be gummed up by sex hormone-binding globulin (SHBG). If your available testosterone is low, consider testosterone replacement therapy (TRT). The main risk is exacerbating a pre-existing prostate cancer – but this can be checked out before you start your course of TRT. The 3G cocktail (Chapter 2) is reported to have favourable effects on libido.

Sun is bad for you – and other myths

The 50+ have always known that they think and feel better after a bit of sun, whatever the doom-mongers say about wrinkles and skin cancer. The 50+ were right! The shrinkage of telomeres, at the ends of parts of your DNA, is a marker for your biological age and, in a study of 2,160 women aged up to 79, Professor Speltor, at Kings College London, reported in November 2007 that your shrinkage is less (i.e. your body is biologically younger) after you sunbathe. The sun appears to make your body younger – no wonder you feel better. Vitamin D produces the same effect and sunshine aids the production of vitamin D in your skin – accounting for about 90 per cent of the vitamin D we need (15 minutes a day, three days a week is all you need). No wonder we feel older in the winter and 'our fancy' returns in the spring. Vitamin D also protects against brain diseases like multiple sclerosis.

The 50+ are well represented among those who buy homes in the sun, but they still need to apply their sun creams after 10 minutes or so to avoid the 'leather look', and to minimize the risk of skin cancer.

10 THINGS TO REMEMBER

1 Eat the kinds of foods your brain needs, when it needs them.

2 Minimize the damage caused by alcohol, tea, coffee, cannabis, cola, ticks and dieting, and avoid 'oxytoxic' foods that increase the risk of brain diseases like Alzheimer's.

3 Use sleep, exercise, smart drugs, dark chocolate and sex to rejuvenate your brain.

4 Mental performance is affected by the sequence in which you eat foods.

5 You can improve mental performance by 'grazing'.

6 Yo-yo weight-loss diets can damage your brain and your thinking. Ditch them. Fitness is more important than fatness. Protect your brain by eating low-oxytoxic foods and high ORAC foods.

7 Physical exercise and how you sit can enhance thinking performance.

8 Dehydration impairs mental activity. Drinking alcohol makes things worse.

9 There is a short boost from caffeine but the effect of theobromine in dark chocolate is more sustained with less fatiguing side effects.

10 Performance on IQ tests can be improved by changing sleeping habits.

Suggested further reading

Craven, K., 'We've got the bug', *The Independent* (15 May 2007, pp. 12–13).

Dharma, D., 'Brain Longevity', *The Lancet* 43 (2004), pp. 324–36.

Frost, A., 'Coffee is good for us' in *The American Journal of Clinical Nutrition*, 83 (2006).

Holford, P., *Optimum Nutrition for the Mind* (London: Piatkus, 2003).

Jarski, R., *Wrinklies' Wit and Wisdom* (London: Prion, 2005).

Svilaas, A., 'Intakes of Antioxidants in Coffee, Wine and Vegetables are Correlated with Plasma Carotenoids in Humans', *The Journal of Nutrition*, 134 (Mar 2004), pp. 562–8

Thomas, G., *Think Yourself Fit* (London: Cassell Illustrated, 2003).

UK Mental Health Foundation 'Feeding Minds': www.mentalhealth.org.uk/feedingminds/

5

....

Making more money

In this chapter you will learn:
- *about your enhanced powers of critical, creative and reflective thinking at 50+*
- *how to exploit the enhanced development of the frontal lobes of the 50+ brain to think logically, solve problems and make decisions*
- *how to use superior 50+ thinking skills to earn a better living working for someone else, or to make more money working for yourself.*

We know the science.
We have predicted the threat.
It's time for action.

Governor A. Schwarzenegger, Jan 2007

Introduction

At 50+ your country needs you! Or, at least, its economy does. Professor Hart of the UK Small Business Research Centre has discovered that new business start-ups by the 50+ generation are adding £24 billion to the national economy. He adds that when economic regeneration is powered by the 50+, it is more likely to succeed in boosting local economies. In the UK, in 2007 alone, according to research by Yellow Pages, the 50+ generation accounted for 16 per cent of new business start-ups.

None of this is surprising when you look at the thinking skill set and mindset that is needed to succeed at work, or in business, and when you see how all its components improve strongly with age, as long as you don't retire and as long as you stay fit and healthy.

Research on men in Boston, USA, has shown that you are more likely to stay fit and healthy, and keep 'ahead at work', if you don't retire. If you follow the low-oxytoxic diet and physical and mental exercise regime suggested in Chapter 4, the chances are that at 50+ you are currently less than halfway through your potential working life. So stop smoking, drink one coffee and eat no more than one quarter bar of dark chocolate a day! Stay ahead at work, earn a better living and live a better life. Death is not what it used to be, so aim to die on the job! Work till you drop – you deserve that better death.

Because 'work' in today's knowledge economy usually means brainwork, staying 'ahead at work' today means thinking ahead. Fortunately, the older you get, the better you become at thinking ahead. Applied thinking requires critical, creative and reflective thinking, and all three improve with age.

Applied thinking

Applied thinking involves the use of critical, creative and reflective thinking.

A mnemonic for the key roles played by critical, creative and reflective thinking in applied thinking could be 'seeing eye to eye':

We are always seeking to get from one word whose initial is **I** to another word whose initial is **I**, via another whose initial is **I**, i.e.

Applied thinking	=	Critical thinking	+	Creative thinking	+	Reflective thinking
Which is getting from...		Information		Information		Information
Via...		Inference		Inspiration		Insight
to...		Implication		Implementation		Intention

Figure 5.1 The process of applied thinking.

When thinking critically at work, or profiting from experience, or for checklists of key actions to take to improve your creative thinking, consult Appendices A–F and read *Train Your Brain* (Horne and Wootton, 2010).

Insight
From assessment to action – applied thinking
Applied thinking is the use of critical, creative and reflective thinking to convert information into useful knowledge on which effective actions can be based. You can improve your critical, creative and reflective thinking by using checklists of questions to ask: there are ten useful questions each about believability, reasonableness, clarity of thought and practicality; ten ways to question what you read; and ten ways to pick holes in other peoples' arguments.

APPLIED THINKING – TEN QUESTIONS TO ASK...

Concerning the believability of Information:

1 Which words or phrases are ambiguous or imprecise?
2 What assumptions are not admitted?
3 What assumptions are admitted?
4 Why is this being said or written?
5 What statistics are offered?
6 Are the statistics skewed?
7 What is omitted?
8 Who might construe this information differently?
9 What concepts underpin the collection, or analysis, of this information?
10 Is their use valid?

Concerning the reasonableness of Inferences:

1 What internal contradictions can we see?
2 What counter-examples can we think of?
3 What opinions are being offered as facts?
4 How authoritative, or biased, are the sources?
5 What evidence is offered?
6 What conflicting evidence is offered?
7 What flaws are there in their reasoning?
8 Have counter-arguments been considered?
9 Is their evaluation fair and their rebuttal convincing?
10 Does the conclusion overstretch the evidence available?

Concerning the practicality of Implications:

1 If the implied action were taken, would it so change the situation that it would invalidate the assumptions on which the argument for action is based?
2 How controllable is the behaviour of the actors in the situation?
3 Are the skills present which will be needed to take the implied action?

4 Are all the consequences beneficial? Judged by what criteria?

5 Are there unwanted side effects?

6 Does the implied action confer the greatest benefit to the greatest number?

7 Does the implied action waste the fewest resources?

8 Does the implied action do least harm?

9 Thinking about resources, how feasible is the implied action?

10 What risks are associated with the implied action? What is the probability of the risk and the extent of the consequence? Is the worst case acceptable, and by what criteria is acceptability judged?

At 50+ you can go on getting better

Aristotle said: 'You are what you habitually do'. If you change what you habitually do, you will change. If, at 50+, you habitually ask questions like the ones that follow, you have already become a great thinker. If you continue to add such questions to your conversational repertoire (Chapter 6), you will continue to become even clearer in your thinking.

TEN QUESTIONS CLEAR THINKERS OFTEN ASK

1 Could you elaborate a little?

2 Can you give me an example?

3 How could we check that out?

4 How are those two things connected?

5 How does that follow on from what you said earlier?

6 Why do you think that is important or significant?

7 How can that information help us to make progress?

8 Can you think of a different way to explain that to me?

9 Can you be more precise? How much, how many, how often?

10 What do you think X would say in reply to that (where X can, for example, belong to another race, culture, gender or socio-economic group)?

YOUR INTELLECTUAL VIRTUES AT 50+

When we hear people like you, at 50+, habitually asking questions like the ones above, we envy your persistence, integrity, empathy, courage and humility. We envy your confidence to think for yourself. These are intellectual virtues. These are the intellectual virtues that help you, at 50+, to reduce hypocrisy, indifference, cowardice, arrogance, injustice and conformity in the world. One way your more developed virtues and habits of mind show themselves is in the way in which you question what other people have written.

TEN WAYS TO QUESTION WHAT YOU READ

1 Why do I think the author wrote this?
2 What question is the author trying to answer?
3 Are there any clues to the author's intentions?
4 What kind of information is being brought forward here?
5 Why am I expected to believe that this information is true?
6 What assumptions are being made explicitly, and also implicitly?
7 What principle, general truth or conclusion does the author want me to accept?
8 Are all the inferences reasonable and supported by valid reasons or examples?
9 If I accept these conclusions, what actions are implied that I, or others, should take?
10 What would be the consequence for others if these actions were taken?

TEN RULES FOR APPLIED THINKING AT 50+

1 Ask yourself what assumptions you are making.
2 Articulate as clearly as possible the criteria you are using to make judgments.
3 Remember to own what you feel, as well as what you think.
4 Treat initial reactions, your own and other people's, only as tentative positions.
5 Enquire whether other people share your perceptions.
6 Empathize with the feelings and thoughts of other people.
7 Decide whether you have enough justifiably believable information to support a tentative conclusion. (Could more information be gathered easily? What kind of information is needed? Is there a reliable source that is readily available? What credibility would the source have and why?)
8 Recognize that all interpretations, including your own, are subjective.
9 Admit the limitations of your information, or of the time spent gathering or checking it.
10 Contextualize your conclusions. Don't claim universal truths or principles.

Ten ways to spot flaws in the arguments of younger people

1 Check whether the arguments offered contradict what has been said elsewhere.
2 Check whether evidence offered is out of date, unreliable, uncorroborated.
3 Check whether correlations are being offered as though they were causes.
4 Are assertions being offered as facts?
5 Does the argument contain non sequiturs?
6 Ask whether there are possibilities that are not being considered. (There are usually more than two possibilities.)
7 Ask: 'On what does this all hinge? What is the crucial point of the argument? On what does it turn?'
8 Ask: 'What is the *sine qua non*? What is it that would invalidate a key conclusion, if it were shown to be untrue?'
9 Judge the parts of the argument you regard as pivotal to the soundness of the assumptions on which it rests.
10 How strong is the reasoning that leads from these assumptions to the conclusions you are being invited to accept – dubious, weak, telling or compelling?

Thinking rules at work

Thinkers can't retire

Louis Armstrong said that musicians cannot retire as long as they have music in their heads. In the same way, thinkers cannot retire as long as they have thoughts in their heads. In the twenty-first century, thinking is work, so you cannot retire from work while you still have thoughts in your head.

So, don't retire, simply earn a better living at work. At 50+, some of the rules at work have changed. The basis on which most businesses – and even charities and publicly funded and provided services – now compete has changed since the 50+ first started work. In Western economies, the basis of competition has moved from brawn to brains. Even the machines have microchips to 'mind' them. Even in the so-called 'knowledge' economies, the knowledge of employees is no longer a sufficient basis for the comparative advantage of one organization over another. Databases are too quickly changed, updated and redistributed to all who are willing to pay for them to remain a source of competitive advantage. Knowledge is now perishable.

It is how well employees can think about what they know that gives one organization an advantage over another and, in all the different ways that it is important to be able to think at work, your 50+ brain is so much better than younger brains.

Insight
The brain-based economy – thinking rules at work
There are 16 thinking rules you should read, so that you continue to justify a salary which may be higher than younger workers. The 16 thinking rules cover getting up in the morning, breakfast routines, thinking on your feet, the use of technology, lunch, talking, writing, morale raising, dress codes, planning, gossip, leadership and relationships. Like any rules, they are for the guidance of the wise and only for the strict obedience of fools.

These basic rules can help your 50+ brain to continue to get better by the day, until well into your eighties:

Rule 1   Wake to increasingly bright light, artificial if necessary, and current affairs radio if you can stand it. If not, pre-selected music that has a strong rhythm.

Rule 2   Eat breakfast – fruit and/or non-dairy protein (eggs or fish). Keep grains such as bread, toast and cereals until the evening and then choose wholegrains. Drink plenty of water from the moment you get out of bed. Load up like a camel. Drink one cup of high quality black coffee. Never add refined or granulated sugar to anything – especially in the morning. Eat sitting down without distraction and with full awareness of taste, texture and chewing. (See Chapter 4.)

Rule 3   As you go through your morning routine, keep swapping hands so that, for example, you do some things with your left hand that you normally do with your right, and vice versa. Do two or three eye exercises and put your head in your hands. (See Chapter 4.)

Rule 4   To get to work, prefer running and cycling over walking, walking over driving and public over private transport, park and ride over ride, shared car over single usage. Carry a refillable water bottle and keep sipping before you get thirsty. When you arrive, favour stairs over lifts or escalators. If you have a choice, choose an office on a higher floor.

Rule 5   Think (and talk) on your feet. Sit as little as possible. Moving about and talking both aid brainwork and help you to remember what has been discussed and decided. Use a whiteboard to log discussions and take down the key points at the end, preferably as a visual map. Do your thinking aloud, on your feet, and away from your computer. Do not work near fax machines or photocopiers or printers, and use fresh air (not air conditioning) for ventilation.

Rule 6   Lunch, if you need it, follows breakfast rule 2, but add in salads and/or vegetables to your fresh fruit as additional sources of complex carbohydrates. Add a teaspoon of olive oil, nut oil or hemp seed oil for your dressing. If you are a grazer, graze. Favour nibbling plain nuts, not salted, and not peanuts. Fresh fruit is better than dried fruit because the sugar content is less concentrated and has a slower release, and the juice helps to keep up your hydration. Take a walk in the park – 20 minutes – whatever the weather (well almost!). If you are going to stay after 5 p.m., take another walk at break time. It will re-oxygenate your neurons and moderate excessive levels of cortisol in your brain.

Rule 7   Talk, think, write – then talk some more. Then walk the talk. Under-promise and over-deliver. Try to show that you are enjoying it. Even if you have to force yourself to smile, your brain chemistry will change to follow suit. That change in your brain chemistry will help you to think well, which will put a genuine smile on your face and, in turn, on the faces of other people around you. This will lift general levels of morale, mood and optimism, which will, in turn, favour improved performance (Chapter 1).

Rule 8   Dress the part – whatever signals success, confidence and competence in your organization. Think of people that you think are on the top of their game. How do they dress? Is there the odd thing you could copy and still feel it was not too false for you? Grooming is never amiss. Have the best haircut you can afford and just before you need it! Stay on top of tooth stains, dry lips, clean cut nails and deodorant. After your midday walk, do a few eye stretches and a hand rub (Chapter 4), and you will hit the afternoon ground running, while all around you struggle with their mental work.

Rule 9   Have a plan – a private plan discussed with a few confidantes: a long-term plan for what you want out of your work, and a short-term plan for what you want to get done this week. When random things happen (which they will) that do not fit with your plan, reel in the slack and hold firm until the next random wind, or tide, turns in your favour.

Rule 10   Do not gossip, whine, whinge, bitch, take sides or play politics and do not spend more time than you have to with people who do. They will take up valuable working space in your brain and preoccupy your thoughts, distract your concentration and lower the mental energy you want for your own work. Defend people who are sniped at by others. Be loyal. Compliment others whenever you can do so sincerely. You can usually find something about them, or their work, that you genuinely like. Ask questions. Show genuine curiosity and interest in other people's work and projects.

Rule 11   Listen, say 'please' and 'thank you', and don't swear or use religious names in vain. If there are ethics or laws peculiar to the sector you are in, be sure you know what they are. Don't lie. Keep adding to your contact/network list, and keep cycling through it to refresh the connections every few months. Adapt your approach for each person. Everyone is different.

Rule 12   At 50+, your predictive thinking is much more accurate
           than a younger person's. So think and lead. Act as if you
           have already taken that step ahead. Wear the demeanour,
           and talk up the talk associated with the next step.

Rule 13   By all means feel angry – it will fuel your mental energy,
           whereas sadness will sap it. But do not lose your temper.
           At 50+ you will be less patient and more easily provoked.
           Squeeze every last ounce of breath from your body and
           allow fresh breath to rush in to fill the vacuum. Do this
           three times and your temper will expire with your breath.
           Do not make gratuitous personal remarks. Avoid sniping
           and cynicism. Cynicism is corrosive. It will corrode you, as
           well as your workplace and thinking space.

Rule 14   Cultivate, nurture and develop close relationships with
           people at work (Chapter 6).

Rule 15   Read *The Rules of Work* by Richard Templar.

Rule 16   If you're not in management, at 50+ you probably should
           be (if you can stand it!). At 50+, you have the attributes
           needed for successful management, much more so than
           younger people. At 50+, you know how to spark emotional
           engagement in people; how to not take meetings too
           seriously; how to spot dead wood and freeloaders and
           have them transferred; how to let younger people make
           mistakes and help them learn from them; how to accept
           your limitations (though you have fewer at 50+ than when
           you were younger); how to encourage others; how to
           spot good people; how to take the rap from time to time –
           especially to shield younger staff (they will love you for this
           rare management attribute); how to get your people good
           kit; how to pour oil on friction; how to celebrate a success
           every week; how to respect individual differences; how to
           listen to the ideas of younger people; how to not always
           need the last word on everything; how to be positive; how
           to protect creative people from necessary control systems;
           how to risk saying 'yes'; how to ask young people for

solutions as well as problems; how to work early and hard as an example; how to enjoy yourself at work; how to use your superior predictive and creative thinking to be proactive about change; how to use superior reflective thinking to learn from mistakes – yours and those of younger people; how to use your superior planning skills to have a plan B as well as a plan A; how to increase the chances that you will get lucky (chance favours your reduced fear of failure at 50+); how to recognize excessive stress; how to know when to let go of an idea or a person; how to visualize success; how to go home before it's time and to have a good home to go to; how to keep learning from your superior experience at 50+; how to concentrate on doing a few out of the many things that you can do better at 50+.

You can apply for a better job now you're 50+

In all psychometric tests, you are likely to out-perform a younger person. Likewise, if an assessment centre includes tests of group work, leadership, problem solving, prediction or creativity, at 50+ you will normally out-perform a younger person. However, at 50+, one of the few things you might be less good at, compared with a younger person, is thinking fast on your feet. This can be a problem in selection tests and selection interviews. Your counter-measure, at 50+, is better preparation. You need to leave the panel in no doubt that you are looking forward to meeting their customers and clients; to meeting and working with some new people; to feeling you are contributing to improving their profits or the service they provide and contributing to their growth and reputation.

> **Insight**
> **Think about a better job**
> It pays to give some prior thought to the 12 questions most frequently asked at interviews. There are different possible answers for you to think about and try out loud, to see which best suit your own thinking. This helps you to make up your own mind. A person who has half a mind and knows it, will always out-perform someone who hasn't and doesn't.

Prepare and rehearse the following questions – remember to do it out loud:

A. Why do you want this job?

The panel will want to be sure that at 50+ you still have 'fire in your belly' – that you really want the job. Think now. Which of the following reasons might you have? Practise giving that reason – out loud.

- ▶ It fits in with my life and career plan, in that…
- ▶ It will enable me to help people by…
- ▶ I will be better off financially because…
- ▶ There will be more opportunity to work on my own and I will enjoy this greater autonomy and responsibility because…
- ▶ I will enjoy the chance to travel because…
- ▶ I will enjoy the chance to learn about…
- ▶ I will enjoy the greater scope for creativity in…
- ▶ It is important to me to have work that I am proud to talk about to others, that I can feel is socially useful, like…
- ▶ It seems that there will be more opportunities for working as part of a team and that is important to me because…
- ▶ It sounds like it will be busy and stimulating, with plenty of variety. I like it when you never know what you might be faced with – when every day brings something new to solve or learn about.
- ▶ I like the fact that I will have to learn new skills, such as….
- ▶ I am attracted by the opportunity of further training in…
- ▶ It will be good to make use of my experience in persuading, negotiation, problem solving…
- ▶ It will be good to put new ideas on… into practice.
- ▶ It will be good to make use of my experience in…
- ▶ I like the thought of going home every day feeling satisfied that I have made a practical contribution to…
- ▶ It will be good to get back to…
- ▶ I much prefer to be in a job where my pay will be directly related to my performance – that way I know I will be well rewarded.
- ▶ I can see that there will be lots of opportunities for extra responsibility and that there are clear promotion routes.

B. How do you see yourself developing, if you come to us?

Emphasize that the immediate tasks described seem challenging and that your first action will be to tackle these to create a firm foundation for the future.

C. Why did you leave your previous job?

Do not be negative about the employer you left. No panel will want to recruit disloyalty. Emphasize the new challenges and learning opportunities of the new job and the improved financial reward. If you do not mention this, the panel will suspect you are not being frank with them.

D. What is wrong with your present job?

It has become too easy, no longer a challenge. You feel under-stretched and ready for something more challenging and more financially rewarding.

E. What have you tried to do to make your present job more demanding?

Refer to proactive proposals you have made and changes you have initiated: 'It's just that scope for this is limited by...'. Or, you hadn't been planning to leave: 'It's just that the opportunity provided by this job seems so much more appealing because...'.

F. Can you give an example of how you handle criticism?

Stress that you haven't had a lot of practice! Explain that it would depend partly on whether or not you felt the criticism was justified and how it was delivered. Cite an example of how you have benefited from criticism.

G. Give an example of how you reacted to not getting your own way.

Explain that you consulted widely and then put your reasons and some other options in writing for management to think about before asking for a meeting to discuss your concerns. Describe your feelings and your reasons for finally accepting that your ideas could not be implemented for the time being.

H. How would you rate your present manager?

Emphasize what you like about her/him and how she/he could perhaps build on her/his strengths to become even better.

I. Ideally, what would you like to be paid?

My current salary is... and by next year it will be... Obviously I am expecting to improve on this. One of the things that has attracted me to your position is the extra responsibility, and clearly I am expecting this extra responsibility to be rewarded as I show that I am capable.

I know that you would not offer me the job if you didn't think I could do it well, so I am expecting an offer of at least...

J. Do you think you are under-paid in your present job?
The present pay is fair for the present job – it's just that you have outgrown it as you have gained expertise and experience and demonstrated that you can do more.

K. Where do you expect to be in three years' time?
Emphasize how you expect to be applying the new learning and experience you will have gained.

L. Do you have any questions for us?
Yes, you do! You must, if you are serious about the job. However, do not dwell on:

- ▶ the salary
- ▶ the holiday entitlement
- ▶ sharing an office
- ▶ the need to arrive late, or leave early, because of...

You can sort out such matters after you get the job offer. Rehearse asking the following questions, and ask at least two, but no more than six, of them:

- ▶ How has the vacancy come about? (Is there anything I should know?)
- ▶ What do you do to encourage internal promotion?
- ▶ What will be my immediate priority on starting?
- ▶ Where would you see me in five years' time?
- ▶ How does the organization hope to change in the next five years?
- ▶ Do you have any reservations about my ability to do this job?
- ▶ When can I expect to hear from you?

The primary purpose of your questions is to convey further information about yourself that will increase your chance of being offered the job. Banish negative thinking about your prospects (Chapter 1). Be prepared to display several forms of your 50+ intelligence (Chapter 2). Visualize yourself enjoying the interview and being offered the job. Feel the good feelings of achievement you will feel doing the job well. Form close relationships with people you meet during the selection process, including the other candidates (Chapter 6).

Making better decisions at 50+

Managers are professional decision makers. They are expected to get more decisions right than wrong – which, at 50+, you generally do. They are expected to get most of the big ones right. Fortunately, at 50+, you are very good at making up your mind. You are very well equipped for decision making.

What should I eat? What should I wear? Who shall I talk to? Should I re-marry? Shall I apply? Having these kinds of choices to make is important confirmation to you that you are free – that you have freedom as an individual and that you are a member of a free society.

You are rarely freer to choose than when you're 50+. Parental pressures may be fading, financial demands may be lessening, and some responsibilities may have flown the nest. At the same time, your knowledge, life skills, experience and thinking powers are burgeoning.

While you are able to make better decisions at 50+, the decisions may take you longer to make. You just need to start thinking about them sooner (your superior predictive thinking will help you to anticipate the need for decisions) and you will tend to think about them for longer (this results in more thoughtful, better-thought-out decisions). For example, at 50+ it will take you longer to absorb and hold in your short-term memory any new information relevant to the decision that you need to take, but your enhanced visual thinking means that you can use cognitive mapping and systems thinking to help you.

At 50+, you have a great deal of life-acquired knowledge and experience to review, to see if it can usefully bear on the current decision you need to take. At 50+, you also now know that opportunities of a lifetime need to be taken during the lifetime of the opportunities.

At work, you will be paid more for your preparedness to take decisions and for keeping your head when younger people all around you are losing theirs! If you are a manager, you are not expected to get all of your decisions right, but you are expected to decide and not to dither. At 50+, when you do get the occasional decision wrong, you will be more philosophical than a younger person – you will be less disabled by regret or guilt. You will be more able than a younger person to move on to take the next decision. You are more likely to get the big ones right, and that's why employers will pay you more.

THE MAKE-UP OF YOUR MIND

Can neuroscience help you to make up your mind? Decisions are made up of a number of mental processes, such as information processing, new memory formation, logic, visual thinking, prediction, emotion and empathetic thinking. Nearly all of these mental processes are very much better developed in the 50+ brain than they are in younger brains. The exception is new memory formation, which is slower, but Chapter 2 gives you the mental moves you can make to ameliorate this.

Insight
Making better decisions

You make much better decisions as you get older. It just takes longer. Because the opportunity of a lifetime may need to be taken during the lifetime of the opportunity, you can use predictive thinking to start sooner, and other thinking skills to conclude more quickly. Neuroscience suggests eight do's and don'ts that can help you to make up your mind. Consider each suggestion, then decide for yourself.

DOS AND DON'TS OF DECISION MAKING

1 Do imagine...

Use your visual thinking to picture what things will look like after your decision is implemented. Looking at that picture in your mind's eye, how do you feel (Chapter 1)? According to Professor Gilbert of Harvard, younger people routinely overestimate, or underestimate, the strength of the feelings they will experience – either positively (too optimistic) or negatively (too pessimistic). The 'forecasts' of the 50+ are consistently more realistic, often based on similar situations of which they have had direct experience.

The 50+ are less constrained by anxieties arising from fear of loss. Professor Kahneman, of Princeton University, reported in *Psychological Science* (vol. 7), that the 'price' of loss aversion in the general population was about 1:2, i.e. people will only risk losing at the level of one, if they stand to gain at the level of two. Because they are more likely to have had more experiences of 'it was not as bad as I feared', the 50+ are less loss averse, and so can contemplate a wider range of options in coming to their better decisions. At 50+, you are better at remembering different ways of seeing the world so that it can continue to be an acceptable place for you to inhabit. You know better than most that the worst may never happen. Even if the worst does happen, you know, based on your experience, that you will survive.

2 The 50+ have guts as well as instincts

So trust your instincts! In the same edition of *Psychological Science*, mentioned previously, Janine Willis of Princeton reported that 50+ subjects were able to decide on another person's likely trustworthiness, competence, aggressiveness or long-term likeability within one-tenth of a second. Given ten times longer, i.e. around one second, they retained confidence in their first decision. This helps the 50+ to compensate for their slower speed of new information processing.

According to Professor Dijksterhuis, of Amsterdam University, writing in *Science* (vol. 311), rather than allowing information overload to impair their decision making, the 50+ default to a well-honed and well-informed gut instinct. The gut instincts of the 50+ are better guarded against the ever-present danger of emotional override that was investigated by Joseph Arvai and reported to the Advances of Science conference in San Francisco in February 2007. Arvai found that when most people are confronted with decisions about what to do about terrorism or violent crime, they generally allowed their emotional reactions to bypass any rational review of the information relevant to their decision.

3 Feel the fear (but not the anger) – before you do it anyway!

Arvai's finding on the dangers of emotional override does not mean that all information needs to be factored into decisions – only that you should not allow emotions to bypass due consideration of as much relevant information as time allows. At the moment of decision, brain scans show that your limbic system – the centre of your emotional thinking – is always active. Damasio found that damage to the limbic system produces chronic indecision, even about what to eat or drink, or even whether to get out of bed. This does not mean that the impact of all emotions is helpful. Anger, for instance, rarely is. Fessler found, for example, that men (not women) made poorer gambling decisions when they were angry.

4 Self-serving bias

It is good to know that your brain is generally on your side – often protecting you from unknown risks by making you anxious about unfamiliar actions for which you do not yet have well rehearsed or learned neuron traces in place. (Often these can be safely rehearsed or put in place by simply visualizing in advance the hoped for successful actions – see Chapter 4, the body rotation exercise.)

One disadvantage of having a self-serving brain is that it tends to introduce bias when you try to weigh up information in decision making. Your brain is predisposed to notice, attend to, give weight to, or favour consideration of information that fits in with preconceived ideas or familiar views. This may be another reason why 'thoughtful conversations' (Chapter 6) are such an aid to accuracy and clarity of thought, as well as to the longer-term creation of increased cognitive capacity. What your 'thoughtful companion' is able to do is to act as a devil's advocate, or to ask questions which are not constrained by your own brain's desire to confirm its own wisdom. De Bono has suggested that you can bypass your brain's self-serving bias by orchestrating an internal dialogue between different aspects of yourself, and explicitly calling up pessimistic black-hat thinking.

5 Oh, that sinking feeling

The 50+ brain is more able than a younger brain to make use of 'that sinking feeling' – to decide to ditch things, or to drop the subject, or to walk away and move on. At 50+, when 'you get that feeling that you've been here before', you are better able to say, 'I've been here before, let's quit ahead, or quit now, before it gets worse'. Younger brains might persist long after they should have aborted the mission. Younger brains are often victims of what Arks and Blomer called 'the sunk cost syndrome' under which, if you've spent a lot of money on a meal, you are inclined to finish it even if you are full already and don't even like it. (Then you really will get that sinking feeling!) Even though you have sunk, or invested, a lot of money in that meal, you really should just leave it! It's the same with that expensive suit you'll never wear again – donate it to charity.

6 Look both ways, before you...

The 50+ are more inclined to do this, and so avoid the 'framing effect' of which Ray Dolan, from University College London, wrote in

Science (vol. 313), in 2006. The framing effect was discovered using an NMR scanner to note the involvement of the amygdala in decision making. People tend to decide between otherwise identical plans in favour of those that are framed in terms of their positive outcomes, and decide against otherwise identical plans that are framed in terms of their negative outcomes, e.g. their cost. This framing effect is neutralized when people are asked to look at the plans both ways. The 50+ are more likely to look at things both ways.

7 Everyone agrees...
The 50+ are much less likely to decide 'X', just because everybody thinks 'X'. The young have a stronger need to conform to peer or social pressure, or to defer to authority or 'expert' opinion.

8 Shortlisting your long list before you decide
In a seminal work on decision making in 1976, Herb Simm distinguished between 'maximizers' and 'satisficers'. 'Maximizers' are people who need to consider all possible options before they can decide. 'Satisficers' are people who decide quickly in favour of the first option that meets their threshold criteria. The 50+ have generally learned to be good 'satisficers' in decision making. That is why they are successful at selecting 'soulmates' or 'life partners' or 'thoughtful companions' (Chapter 6). The 50+ are more 'Quakerly' in their decision making, seeking decisions that are 'good enough' or 'serviceable'. Schwartz found that 'satisficers' are subsequently less dissatisfied with the outcomes of their decisions. 'Maximizers' were far more likely than the 50+ to feel anxious, depressed or frustrated by the results of their decision making.

Bullshit baffles brains

BUSINESS JARGON

At 50+, it is important not to let bullshit baffle your brain at work. Business bullshit can be an elegant, colourful, light-hearted language that bonds the cognoscenti into 'in' groups that have fun and compete successfully. But sometimes, business bullshit covers up a lack of brain power, and it can be used to bluff or intimidate outsiders. Don't be bluffed or intimidated.

If you don't know what some of these mean, have a look on the internet. Alternatively, ask work colleagues if they understand some of the terms – many probably won't. You will probably discover that you are much more managerially 'literate' than your younger colleagues.

Empower	Framework	Driven	On message
Tick the boxes	Brainstorm	Best practice	Synergy
Quality	Ducks in a row	Offline	Flight path
Skill set	Mindset	Basket case	Disconnect
Customer-facing	Trajectory	Suits	Can do
Dissing	Joined-up thinking	Game plan	Bottom line
Empire building	Give me the numbers	The deal	Back to basics
Win–win	Process	Looking good	Close of play
Takes no prisoners	Level playing field	Lessons	The extra mile
Mushroom manager	Seagull	Handbags out	Cherry pick
Fast track	At the end	Wannabe	Low-hanging fruit
Strategic	Feedback	Workaholic	Seeking alignment
Comfort zone	Stakeholder	Focus	Touch base
Pocket science	Don't make waves	Don't rock the boat	Survivor
Template	Benchmark	Barrier to	Free rider
Grasp the nettle	Big picture	Ball park	Blue-sky thinking
Gravitas	Grown up	Outside the box	Go for it
Off the wall	Customer-focused	Halo effect	Hidden agenda
No sweat	Hearts and minds	Proactive	Move the goal
Lean	Knowledge worker	Post-its	Lick and promise
Lifeblood	Holding nerve	Jumping through hoops	Keep it simple
Manage expectations	Key learning points	Lifeblood	No surprises
Ramp it up	Pull-out stops	Long haul	Manage upwards
Hit the ground running	Wake up – smell the coffee	T over A	The elephant in the room
No pressure	Cool	On a roll	Within our gift
Working breakfast	Power nap	Prioritize	Silo management
Deliverables	Profile	Back to back	Park it

Free time	Off the radar	Robust plan	Sink or swim
Feed back	Huddle	Talking shop	Squeaky clean
Straight	With the bark on	Verbal diarrhoea	Window
Bite the bullet	Work ethic	To task	Bring to the table
Fall on sword	Go nuclear	The nuclear option	Work–life balance
Work smarter	Don't do difficult	Keep your powder dry	Lock, stock, barrel
Do easy	You can if you think you can	Loose cannon	Learning curve
Likely landmines?	Long-terms aims	Short-term gains	Scratch where it itches
You scratch my back…	On-side	Mission critical	TQM
RD	On-track	In play	Coalface
On a charge	Pre-emptive	Stir pudding	Sharp end
Dancing round handbags	Blitz	Scattergun approach	Take flak
Dove tail	Seamless	Do you read me?	Explore options
Get act together	Get wagons in a circle	Wait for the cavalry	Walking wounded
Weapons grade	Bite the bullet	20–20 hindsight	Save bacon
Scenario	A bridge too far	Rising tide	At the end of the day
A shambles	Shit hits the fan	Shit or bust	Plate spinning
Balls in the air	Between a rock and…	Sign off	A big ask
Blood bath	Stick to knitting	Sub-optimal	Soft landing
Catch 22	Drill down	Systematic	Dive deep
Get granular	TLC	In the pipeline	Enough on a plate
Fence mending	Flaky	Bear with me	Manage expectations
Fluid	From day one	Genie out of the bottle	Teflon management
Big picture	Hobson's choice	Competitive advantage	Continuous improvement
Off the scale	Knock on	Last chance saloon	Ground rules
Less is more	Let's not go there	Future facing	First principles
Lose the plot	Name and shame	Nesting	White noise

Hardware	Helicopter vision	Nightmare	Blue sky
Non core	Leading edge	Lateral thinking	Quick fix
Re-engineering	No-win situation	Mission statement	Head count
Read riot act	Rearranging deckchairs	Out of the loop	Proposition
Heads roll	Orchestrate	Push the envelope	Reinvent ourselves
To target	Step change	Results driven	USP
Magic bullet	Holistic	Flesh out	Squaring the circle
Value added	On the same wavelength	Scoping it	Differentiation
Brand	Badge	Wow factor	Segmentation
Band width	Iconic	Off-brand/ off-message	To land
Door opener	Feel-good factor	Paradigm	Vehicle
Game plan	Viral	Impacting	Mega
A must	Ramp it up	Heavyweight	Mood music
Must have	Niche monster	Ratchet up	Heroes – show me the
Simply the best	Champions	All systems go	Road map
The Peter Principle	Check in/check out	Fine tune	Get into gear
Free loader	Core competence	Knowledge worker	Green light
Mentor	Open-door policy	On autopilot	Flat structure
Reinvent the wheel	A steer	Tailspin	Bread and butter
Succession planning	Away day	Up to speed	Let go
A bung	Down-size	Right-size	Step up
Class act	To come of age	Cover all bases	The boy done good
Hyper	A jobsworth	A curved ball	Movers and shakers
Dream team	Early bath	Even keel	Scapegoat
Nerdy	Key player	Spin	Own goal
The game plan	In two minds	Dead men walking	Drive
A lightweight	Take to next level	Sticky wicket	Bottom line
Lifestyle choice	Plain sailing	Hardball	Top level

Sea change	One game at a time	80/20 rule	The numbers
Swings and roundabouts	World class	Bean counter	Massage figures
Tweak	Upside	To wash its face	Personal development
Creative accounting	Front-end loaded	The city	Double whammy
Bang for bucks	Built on sand	Apples with apples	OD/ID/PD
Critical path	Cost effective	A red line	Levers
Seed corn	Slippery slope	Line in sand	Done deal
Drivers	Slush fund	Bridge the gap	To nail
In the black/red	Playing the percentages	Got legs	Connectivity
Touchy feely	Up the ante	Access	Fuzzy logic
Cut and paste	Down time	Firewalling	State of the art
Hand holding	Multitask	Portal	B2B
User	Word of mouth	AKA	Swot
Dinky	ROI	Smart	Proof of pudding
TQM	Cooking with gas	Jerry built	Smoke and mirrors
Pigs might fly	Rule of thumb	Run it by	Pear-shaped
Blue in the face	Whistling in the dark	Salmon run	A square peg

Beware of 50+ business consultants

Would-be client: 'What do you charge?'

50+ consultant: 'To initiate consultation, £1,000 for three questions.'

Would-be client: 'Isn't £1,000 for three questions a bit steep?'

50+ consultant: 'Yes, and what is your third question?'

TEXT MESSAGING

Many people today use mobile phone text messaging to communicate with their friends, peers and, increasingly, work colleagues or opposite numbers in customer/supplier organizations. The following selection will give you an idea of what these messages are communicating (source: Ellis Wootton, 13 years old!):

GR8	Great	121	One to one
BBFN	Bye bye for now	2D4	To die for
KIT	Keep in touch	2nite	Tonight
THNQ	Thank you	4get	Forget
NTHING	Anything	4give	Forgive
RUOK?	Are you OK?	BRB	Be right back
R	Are	COZ	Because
8	Ate	G2G	Got to go
B	Be	H8	Hate
B4	Before	Jk	Just kidding
BCNU	Be seeing you	Np	No problem
QT	Cutie	Nutha	Another
D8	Date	Nm	Not much
DNR	Dinner	OMG	Oh my god
EZ	Easy	PLZ	Please
XLNT	Excellent	PPL	People
F8	Fate	Tb	Text back
4	For	2DAY	Today
FYI	For your information	2MORO	Tomorrow
L8	Late	WAN2	Want to
L8R	Later	WOT	What
Lol	Lots of love/laughs	Y	Why
M8	Mate	U	You
PLS	Please	U+me	You and me
PCM	Please call me	Ur	Your
Q	Queue/cue	UR	You are
R8	Rate	VG	Very good
C	See/sea	W8n	Waiting
CU L8R	See you later	Wan2	Want to
SPK	Speak	T	Tea
THX	Thanks	2	To/too

Making money by minding your own business

Being young and in business was greatly overrated. Every failure was devastating. Later on, I realized that you always get another go if you want to.

Attributed to Mary Quant by Felix Dennis

In 2007, 16 per cent of successful new UK businesses were started by people aged 50+. This is not surprising because the mindset – or set of thinking skills – which you need to run a business successfully is highly developed in the 50+ brain. Luck helps, but thinking reduces the need for it. Luck favours the prepared mind, just as chance favours the brave. (Watch *Dead Poets Society* or almost anything else with Robin Williams in it.)

Why run your own business? To make money, rather than just earn a good living. Then you can give the money away, if you want to. But also, perhaps, to have more free time – i.e. time that you are free to spend how you choose, perhaps on writing books, sponsoring artists, volunteering to work with disadvantaged groups, hanging out with friends, or phoning relatives. When you run your own business, your time is your own. When you are earning a good living, your time belongs to others. Money is like sex. Thoughts about sex and money can preoccupy your brain, for example not having enough, not getting enough, how to get to more. The beauty of having enough is that it frees you to think about other things and other people.

HOW MUCH MONEY IS ENOUGH?

Arbitrarily, between £15 million and £40 million is enough money. Alternatively, enough for whatever you need to spend it on, or more than you can give away in a lifetime. So make a start. No task takes longer than a task one does not start. Listen to your wealth-wanting drum and ignore some conventional wisdom. Conventional wisdom, unlike 50+ wisdom, is replete with reasons for not doing things. There are the odd nuggets in conventional wisdom – but they are hard to separate from the fool's gold. Think things out for yourself from first principles. At 50+, you are well equipped to do so.

MINDING YOUR OWN BUSINESS – THE BEST CURE FOR RETIREMENT

In the twenty-first century, wealth comes from the mind and the imagination.

Steve Forbes – a billionaire

Setting up your own business will be such a welcome learning curve. Anyone not busy learning is busy dying. Running your own business may well fend off Alzheimer's. As a minimum, it should prevent the hardening of your neural arteries. Nobody can retire you from your own business. You can work till you drop and so die a good death.

At 50+, you have less to lose, less to fear and less to prove than a younger person – all are major advantages when you start your own business. It will be hard – but no worse for that. It will sometimes get hairy and scary – but it will often be fun.

After a few failures, you will eventually have a small success – and one small success will breed another. All that is needed is applied thinking, and at 50+ you are better prepared for the steps that prevent others. At 50+, you are prepared to take the steps from knowing to doing. In your own business, you are not prevented from taking the steps from knowing to doing – as so often you are when you try to earn a good living from someone else.

Insight
Mind your own business (and make money)

Starting your own business can be a good cure for retirement – a good use of that pension lump sum. Neuroscience can help you to reduce the risk by thinking ahead. Ten things worth thinking about before you mind your own business are: the way teamwork doesn't work; the fear of failure; the need for luck; a 'good enough' idea is good enough; checking assumptions; making predictions; digging holes deeper; profit sharing; partnerships; and thinking twice, before cutting once.

TEAM WORKING ISN'T WORKING

Employers are often fond of teams, groups and meetings. These are purpose-designed to make thinking difficult, and therefore action is often absent or ill-advised. Fear of failure and avoidance of blame stalk most meetings. Only knowing and thinking and doing gets it done.

> Knowing and thinking,
> Is not enough.
> Only knowing and doing
> Is real applied thinking.
> Only knowing and doing,
> Gets it done.

Terry Horne, 2007, after Felix Dennis

THE FEAR OF FAILURE

Let's do it (or at least let's agree to forget it, and thereby create headspace for our next thought). As Dylan said: 'When you got nothing – you got nothing to lose.'

Does your business idea risk utter destitution? At 50+, that is unlikely. Public embarrassment is likely to be your worst-case scenario. At 50+, you are more philosophical about being embarrassed than you were when you were younger. Nevertheless, it is a real fear. It will still wake you up in a cold sweat at 4 a.m. It can still be a nightmare. But it is only a nightmare. At 50+, you have the thinking skills to harness fear. Harnessed fears can fuel your mental energy. The fear of failure prevents many bright young people from becoming your competitors. This is good for you, because there is only room for just so many people to make £15–40 million. At 50+, your fear is a gift – something you can overcome as your potential competitors cringe.

BOLDNESS NOT BRAVERY

The more I prepared, the luckier I got.

Gary Player – golf champion

At 50+, you will hesitate – that is prudence, born of experience. As Goethe knew well, until one is committed there is always hesitance – the chance to draw back. But once you are committed 'providence moves all'. All sorts of things appear to help. Events seem to stream from decisions once taken – all manner of helpful and chance meetings conspire to carry you forward on the tide which you have taken. You have set out on your own and that feels so good after years of being a corporate team player. Team spirit is what comforts good losers. It shackles people to desks for a good living wage. In many professions, like teaching, there will be other rewards – but in commercial organizations, working in groups or teams will compromise your thinking and compensate you in only very small ways for your loss of individuality and your lack of personal fortune.

Fortune, it is said, favours the brave, but at 50+ you know that good fortune is a combination of preparation, preparedness and opportunity. Goethe asked only for a degree of boldness – not even bravery. Boldness can, of course, lead to failures and to losing some battles, but at 50+ you care less about what people will think. At 50+, you know that if opportunities are taken, they need not be taken perfectly. In fact, they do not necessarily need to be taken very well! As long as your execution is good enough, i.e. better than that of a potential competitor, your tide can still lead you on to fortune.

Exercise – see yourself rich?

Expel all the breath from your body and allow the air to rush in and fill your body. Repeat this three times. Close your eyes and picture yourself living your life according to its possibilities. Picture yourself and hear yourself phoning through a large donation to a charity. Picture the difference in the world before and after your donation. Watch yourself spending the rest of the day. Who are you with? What are you doing? What are you talking about? If you can picture it, you can do it!

YOU DON'T NEED GREAT IDEAS

For the 50+, ideas are not a problem. At 50+, creativity is well served by the breadth of knowledge and possibilities and potential creative associations that can only come with living long enough to collect them. But, in 'The Hollow Men', T. S. Eliot warned, 'between the idea/and the reality/between the motion and the act/falls the shadow'.

At 50+, you are less afraid of shadows. Shadows can be illuminated by clear thinking. The question is only whether the light is worth the candle. The 50+ are quicker to dispel dross. Time is more precious and they more readily cut to the chase. Pick one serious idea and keep going. Don't give in.

Never give in.
Never give in.
Never, never
Never give in.
In nothing great
Never give in.
To nothing,
Save conscience,
And good sense.

after Winston Churchill

Five common errors in minding a business

...the history of all human ideas is a history of irresponsible dreams, of obstinacy, and of error.

Karl Popper

1 INVALID PREMISE OR ASSUMPTION

Critical thinking starts with justifiably believable information. This involves taking so-called 'facts' and assessing the credibility of their sources and the validity of any underlying assumptions. At 50+, you are better equipped to check things for sense, because you have more of it. You are better able to judge sources, because you have more experience on which to base your evaluations.

2 OVER-OPTIMISTIC PREDICTIONS

Running out of cash (not profit or orders) is by far the most common cause of business failures. In fact, the more orders you have, and potentially the more profit you expect, the more likely you are to run out of cash and to wind up bankrupt and out of business. In the USA it can be a badge of honour for a budding business person; in Europe it is more embarrassing.

Numerical thinking is the essence of good business. You must hone your ability (and propensity) to estimate and quantify your visual and verbal thinking (See Chapters 6, 8 and 10 in *Train Your Brain*, Horne and Wootton, 2010). Even if lack of cash planning does not doom your business, it may result in your having to sell equity (or shares) in your business to others in return for a cash injection. Any loss of ownership (even one share!) threatens one of your primary reasons for being in business, which is to make lots of money for yourself (to give away again, or whatever). The implementation of all new business ideas must be on the basis of a positive cash flow – or they (and your wealthy ambitions) are doomed. Cash, not profit, is the lifeblood of any business. If your numerical thinking is weak, the situation is not terminal, but you will need to employ the services of someone for whom they are strong.

3 DIGGING THE SAME HOLE DEEPER

When your business idea is in a hole, it is hard to know when to stop digging – when to give up, abort, abandon and start digging somewhere else altogether. How do you decide when to abort? The sooner the better – it is never too soon to fail. Success is the ability to move seamlessly from one failure to the next, looking back without regret and forward with hope. Take your learning with you and there will be a better outcome next time. There is no shame in trying and failing – it is only a matter of timing. An idea before its time may fail – what might have worked last year may not work this year. An idea that failed last year may now be an idea whose time has come.

Cut the cord, before a failing-to-succeed-now idea pulls you under. That way, you may live to breathe life back into the idea when the winds and tides of fortune are more propitious.

Errors on the surface flow
For pearls dive later
And below

After John Dryden

4 BASING BIG ACTIONS ON LITTLE THOUGHT

A good tailor measures twice and cuts once. A good business person thinks twice before acting at all. At 50+ you are better equipped to think creatively of a big idea, and better able to think critically about whether it checks for sense against your experience, of which you have much. Use your visual, predictive and superior numerical thinking to plan actions based on your big idea. Plan the first small step in great detail. Take the first small step and evaluate all the new information that this will always flush out. Re-think if necessary. Re-plan if necessary. Think big and act small and then think big again.

5 NOT SHARING THE PROFITS

You will need to find, nurture, encourage and trust the most able people you can persuade to join you – even if it means paying them more than you pay yourself out of the business. You will make your money when you sell the business. Pay good people out of the business (but not out of the proceeds of selling it – you risked your money for that, the return is yours). You started your business to make money, remember. Take it for yourself and then give it away – don't share it with employees. Incentivize their performance out of the business, not out of the sale. They are earning a good living out of your business. If they want to make money, let them start their own business. Maybe you can help them into their business. Don't let them help themselves to yours.

Do you have a head for business?

Are you an entrepreneur? What are the characteristics of entrepreneurs?

PERSISTENCE

Persistence is not to be confused with stubbornness. Stubborn people persist in the face of plentiful evidence that they should not.

The phrase 'never give in' was useful to Churchill in the context of the Second World War – but 'never' is a dangerous word. Sometimes it is better to surrender a position, an idea, your shares, and move on. Live to succeed another day. Start digging somewhere else. Acknowledging a mistake and making a new plan is not a sign of weakness, it is a sign of good thinking.

DIVERSIFICATION

No matter how good your 50+ idea, and no matter how successfully your well-thought-out plans are bearing fruit, 50+ entrepreneurs know that time will pass and fruits will perish. 50+ entrepreneurs start diversifying almost as soon as their first idea has taken root, let alone borne fruit. Partly driven by 50+ creativity, partly by their 50+ experience that nothing lasts forever, they begin to spread their risk, to license, to franchise, to diversify. Try to keep your diversification closely related to your business, so that you can capitalize on cross-promotion, economies of scale and other synergies.

LEARNING

50+ entrepreneurs are incurably nosey; they learn from their experience and from that of other people. The 50+ have learned what questions to ask and how to listen to the answers without interrupting or arguing (Chapter 6). Courtesy helps the 50+ to learn more easily and to make more money more quickly – especially in the USA. Do not agree to listen to someone for less than 20 minutes – it is rarely possible to 'dive for the pearls' in less than 20 minutes. Likewise, it is hard to concentrate and do justice to what someone is saying for much more than 20 minutes. So there you have it: 20-minute meetings, interviews, presentations, visits – whatever – 20 minutes.

BETTING LUCKY IN BUSINESS

▶ Do not describe or characterize yourself as unlucky or people will not invest in you, personally or in your business.
▶ Thank your lucky stars for lucky breaks you have had.
▶ Do not make plans that need luck for them to succeed.
▶ Accept and take advantage of the lucky breaks that you will get.
▶ Do not be distracted by looking at greener grass.
▶ Just do it. You will probably get away with it. If you don't, apologize.

▶ State fair terms and stick to them.

▶ Don't barter, it makes you seem dishonest from the outset.

▶ Your second thoughts are probably your best. Stick to them.

▶ Do not let your goals or hopes drift upwards out of greed – you are likely to confuse the other side and, if you fail to agree, you will both lose out.

▶ Do your homework on the likely best hopes and goals of others and their likely walk-away position. Do the same for yourself. If there is overlap, you can agree. If there's not, you can't, so don't negotiate. Then it's down to power. If you cannot increase your power, back off. Settle for the best you can and move on.

▶ Adjourn frequently to take advice, but don't let advisors take the decisions. It is you who must live with the consequences. Think the consequences through visually and empathetically.

▶ Be courteous and, if possible, humorous, if not, then self-deprecating. Creative thinking is usually required to find mutually beneficial win–win solutions and this is helped by good humour (Chapter 1).

▶ Once you've agreed, honour your agreement. Do not try to squirm or renege afterwards. If you don't agree, adjourn and return another day. But once you agree, that's it. Honour it and don't weasel. If the other side try it on, don't retaliate. Your word is your word, whether given to a good person or to a knave.

Felix Dennis holds up philosopher Francis Bacon (1561–1626) as a model:

> *If you would negotiate with any man (or woman), you must think about their nature, so to lead them; their goals, so to persuade them; their weaknesses, so as to awe them; or those who have power over them, so to control them. With cunning persons, interpret them, but do not believe what they say. Say as little as possible in return. Do not aim to reap all at one sitting. Ripen your fruits by degrees.*

Insight

Do you have a head for business?

Do you have the mindset of thinking skills commonly found in entrepreneurs? You will need persistence; the drive to broaden your knowledge base, and your product and customer base; insatiable curiosity; the ability to learn from every success and failure, and from every person at every level. You will need to learn how not to depend on luck – luck favours the prepared mind.

THE JOYS OF OWNERSHIP

In Chapter 1, we discovered that making lots of money brought 'yacht envy', not happiness. However, the more realistic pursuit of BLISS involves an S for Satisfaction, of which a key element is possession – the ability to say 'this is mine'. This is one of the reasons that running one's own business is so deeply satisfying, quite apart from the autonomy, independence, status, power and physical possessions that you buy if you make a lot of money. The fact that you own the business is intrinsically satisfying. Being an owner-manager feels completely different from being an employee-manager. All the more important, then, that you fight tooth and nail to retain your ownership or equity. To become very rich you must own most, preferably all, the shares in your business. You may need to become as possessive about your own business as Gollum was about his 'precious' ring in *The Lord of the Rings* (J. R. R. Tolkien). According to Felix Dennis, ownership is not just the most important thing – it is the only thing. Only when you are the owner can you afford to be reasonable.

The Virgin brain and The Body Shop brain

Think about Richard Branson and Anita Roddick. If you took away all their money, it would not be long before they were each of them rich again. This is because you haven't taken away their ability to think and that's what made them rich. (Paul McKenna – friend of Richard Branson and Anita Roddick, 1942–2007.)

THE PERILS OF PARTNERSHIP

The relative shares of the partners need to reflect who is putting in the capital and who is doing how much work in the venture. Choose partners who are brilliant at what you're not good at – even if they constantly show you in a bad light by comparison. A partnership is not like a marriage, in which you may be prepared to die for your partner and let them share all. In your own business, the making of money comes first. If you are fortunate in your partners, friendship or even affection may follow, but the needs of the business to make money comes first. Bad partners can take hours of precious time to convince to do something, or not to do something. The perils of partnership can easily outweigh the advantages, if you make a bad choice of partner.

GOING PUBLIC

Unless it is your final cut and run with the money, don't go public if you can afford to stay private. You will lose many of the joys and freedoms for which you set up your own business in the first place. Your actions and even your private life and conversations will become constrained, quite properly, by a whole raft of regulations designed to protect the public.

Insight
Thinking about employing someone else?
Do not employ anyone to take your place: the farmer's eye fattens the cattle. Reserve the right to attend management meetings, and do so regularly. Ensure that all important personnel decisions and bank transactions above an agreed figure require your countersignature. Sign off all new products, markets and brochures, and every press release. Set out clear financial targets, and then encourage others to suggest how they might best be achieved.

TEN LESSONS ON EMPLOYING OTHERS IN YOUR BUSINESS

1 Whatever title you retain, or take, be sure that it empowers you to attend all management meetings, and try to do so at least once a month.
2 In your absence, your chief executive should stand in for you and be responsible for ensuring that you receive prompt verbatim minutes.
3 Do not allow anyone to be appointed, or removed, from the senior management team, including any directors, without your agreement.
4 Do not allow anyone to relocate any office.
5 Do not allow anyone to dispose of any asset.
6 Insist on approving any changes to the product or marketing plan.
7 Insist on approving any written information about the company, its policies, products or services.
8 Insist on signing off bank transactions above a significant threshold.
9 Insist on approving all press releases.
10 Make clear the target figures for growth and return on assets, but allow others to suggest how best these might be achieved.

1 Allow money to be the measure of how well the business is doing. Publish the financial scores. (Ring-fence money for investment. Separate it from money for costs.)
2 If you get a good offer, sell out while the going is good.
3 Look after your suppliers as well as you look after your customers.
4 Minimize secrecy.
5 Advertise regularly for new staff – whether you need them now or not. Interview them yourself. Applicants are an excellent source of market intelligence.
6 Actively seek to train and promote junior staff.
7 Back up managers who make decisions – even if they make some mistakes. If they make too many, sack them.
8 Favour one-on-one meetings over group meetings. Manage individuals. Use a conversational management style.
9 Share profits with employees and decide on bonus payment personally.
10 Reduce overheads by 10 per cent at the end of each year.

The neurochemistry of making money

When you want something, your brain releases dopamine into your blood. This creates a craving – the 'must have' feeling. When you get the thing you crave, your brain releases serotonin – a 'feel good' chemical. It can be addictive. If doing deals and making money becomes your main source of serotonin, you will never have enough. You will be 'driven', but never satisfied. Money cannot fill a psychological black hole, for example to feel 'safe'. The fear produces adrenaline which drives the pursuit or the chase. The serotonin of success soothes, but not for long!

Critical thinking at work – a wealth warning

Now that you know how to use applied thinking, at work to earn a high salary, or to make a lot of money by working for yourself, it may be worth thinking about the tensions between a healthy mind and a wealthy bank balance.

According to the philosopher Francis Bacon, even when wealth is not a direct impediment to virtue, wealth is an encumbrance on your journey through life. You are unlikely to give it up, because you will think it too valuable. Yet harbouring it will inhibit spontaneous ease of travel. You will need often to watch over your wealth, constantly needing to check it and to conceal it from the envious eyes of others. In these ways, wealth can be a burden not a blessing.

The process by which you acquired your wealth may develop habits of mind of which you are not proud. Becoming wealthy in your life may preoccupy your mind, and the minds of others, with thoughts of what will happen to your wealth when you die. This can impoverish the quality of relationships while you are still alive. The pressure on you to share out your wealth before you die might become very tiresome. Your best hope is that, having had all the fun, learning, stimulation and sense of achievement of using your 50+ thinking power to acquire wealth by keeping your head at work, you will have thereby acquired the wisdom to give it all away, wisely!

10 THINGS TO REMEMBER

1 At 50+ you have enhanced powers of critical, creative and reflective thinking.

2 Furthermore, you can exploit the enhanced development of the frontal lobes of the 50+ brain to think logically, solve problems, make decisions and make plans.

3 At 50+ you can use your superior thinking skills to earn a better living working for someone else, or to make more money working for yourself.

4 Applied thinking is aimed at change. It can make the world a better place.

5 Applied thinking is supported by critical, creative and reflective thinking, all of which develop more powerfully as you get older.

6 Critical thinking empowers the 50+. The 50+ are less impressed, and less easily oppressed, by power or celebrity than younger people.

7 Critical thinking is not negative. Its intention is to support the person whose ideas are the subject of the critical thinking.

8 Applied thinking develops in its wake the courage, intellectual independence and social self-reliance that are more commonly found in people who are 50+.

9 The superior applied thinking of the 50+ generation rests on their superior critical, creative and reflective thinking. This argues against their early retirement and in favour of their earning a better living at work or, importantly, generating wealth in our economy by minding their own businesses.

10 In a knowledge economy, where competitive advantage goes to those who can think well about what they know, older people do not need to be a burden to be cared for by a younger generation.

On the contrary, the 50+ generation can earn the wealth not only to look after themselves, but also to fund the longer periods of education now needed by the young. If the 50+ continue to work until they are 80+, they will never be the burden they sometimes fear to be.

Suggested further reading

Baggini, J. and Stangroom, J., *Do You Think What You Think You Think?* (London: Granta Books, 2006).

Dennis, F., *How To Get Rich* (London: Ebury Press, 2006).

Edmonds, E., *Bullshit Bingo* (London: South Bank, 2005).

Horne, T. and Doherty, A., *Managing Public Services – Implementing Changes: A Thoughtful Approach to the Practice of Management* (London: Routledge, 2003).

McKenna, P., *I Can Make You Rich* (London: Bantam, 2007).

Middleton, J., *Upgrade Your Brain* (Oxford: Infinite Ideas, 2006).

Templar, R., *The Rules of Work* (Pearson Education, 2007).

Thompson, A., *Critical Reasoning* (London: Routledge, 1999).

Wootton, S. and Horne, T., *Strategic Thinking* (London: Kogan Page, 2000).

6

Lust, love, sex and intimacy at 50+

In this chapter you will learn:
- *to exploit your superior verbal intelligence at 50+*
- *to use internal dialogues to augment your thinking power*
- *to use thoughtful conversations to develop intimate relationships as well as your brain*
- *about the neurochemistry of friendship, love and sex.*

Logic is little more than knowledge of a language with which to talk about it.

Charles Lamb, 1801

Introduction

Before you begin reading this chapter, look back at Figure 0.3 on page xxiv.

Neuroscience points strongly to the effectiveness of oral rather than written work as the better way to connect up your brain and extend its cognitive capacity. An important resource is conversation. Thoughtful conversations have an added bonus. Thoughtful conversations develop closer, more intimate relationships. Close personal relationships are a rich source of BLISS (Chapter 1), further adding to your ability to think well and clearly express what you think, both orally and in writing. Talking better, thinking better, writing better, and acting more effectively become a virtuous circle, leading to increased cognitive capacity (Chapter 2), and increased success at work (Chapter 5), adding further to your state of BLISS (Chapter 1).

Given the centrality of talking in your education, personal development and successful living, it is useful to be able to feel comfortable in social situations, because these provide rich and varied opportunities for you to practise thinking aloud.

Verbal intelligence is the ability to ask yourself questions that help you to think well and then to answer them! Both operations involve remembering, selecting, using and then connecting words together. These operations make up an 'internal dialogue' – a thoughtful conversation that you have with yourself inside your head.

Whatever other thinking modes you also use (see Appendices A–F), you are limited by the ability of your internal and external dialogue to communicate to yourself and others the results of your thinking. That may be why psychologists since the 1900s have measured vocabulary, verbal reasoning and verbal IQ. Early psychologists realized that verbal intelligence was closely correlated with success in the world of business and in other professions where it was important for you to think clearly and to clearly communicate your thinking to others.

Good thoughts – spoken or written in the right words – have the power to persuade, inspire or seduce, or just to influence events. At 50+, you have more words and more word power, and therefore more thinking power than when you were younger.

The neuroscience of wordplay

Most of the verbal action takes place on the left side of the brain, which is the side that is active when you are cheerful or optimistic. Perhaps that's why having a chat cheers you up (Chapter 1). Broca's area of the brain handles grammar and speech; Wernicke's area of the brain handles sound and meaning (see the diagrams on page 179.) These areas of the brain are on the opposite side of the area that handles visual images. That is why you stand a better chance of getting and keeping the whole-brain attention of an audience if you can use words to tell a 'graphic story', i.e. a story that conjures up a 'big picture' in the mind of the listener. The linguistic left of the brain functions better when levels of oestrogen are higher. Levels of oestrogen are generally higher in typical female brains. Typical female brains display a superior command and use of language to typical male brains (See Appendix G).

Seeing the funny side at 50+

Robert Ornstan discovered that, while normal verbal thinking (internal dialogue) takes place substantially on the left side of your brain (if you're right-handed), wordplay (as in puns, jokes, humour, double entendre) is more likely to involve the right side of your brain. People who have a stroke in the right side of their brain often lose their sense of humour.

Insight
Conversation trains your brain

It is worth learning how to hold a thoughtful conversation. A thoughtful conversation provides an excellent mental workout because it connects lots of neural pathways in your brain. This is why paired learning is such an effective way of developing both the capacity of your brain and your skill in using it.

Conversation and brain training

Levelt discovered that you use three distinct areas of your brain when you talk to someone else. You connect lots of neural pathways, even before you get to the content of what you want to say. As you search for the next word you need in your spoken sentence, your brain accesses the smell, colour and sounds that are associated with the word you are seeking, thereby calling up even more neural connections. That is why a word can be on the tip of your tongue before you finally say it.

In the meantime, your brain will be finding back-up synonyms and holding them in reserve, in case you cannot find the exact word that's on the tip of your tongue. All this happens, word by word, throughout your conversation. Small wonder thoughtful conversations are such a good mental workout. Small wonder paired learning is the learning method of choice if you want to develop the capacity of your brain, as well as your skill in using it.

Your brain can generally find, and provide sounds for, between 120 and 180 words a minute, i.e. up to 10,000 words an hour. It is a myth that this slows down when you get older. True, the older you get, the more possible words you have to choose from, but this can be worked around. Having more words at 50+ is an asset for verbal thinking, and for any thinking tasks that involve creative and reflective thinking (Appendices E and F).

READING IS IMPORTANT, BUT...

Reading can play an important part in training your brain. Reading is a useful source of new information, which your brain must struggle to map, connect, crosscheck, and then integrate with information already dispersed in your memory. But reading is not as good at developing your brain as talking and listening. Thoughtful conversations about old and new information involve more of your brain than just reading, and so conversations increase your general cognitive capacity, as well as helping you to consolidate new information in your memory.

At the moment in the UK, under the government's literacy scheme, valuable brain development time is lost teaching children to read too many words. The government literacy scheme requires children to read 158 prescribed words by the age of seven. In 2005, Jonathan Solity, from Warwick University, analysed over 900,000 words used in adults' and children's books. Solity discovered that only 100 words were needed to read most books in English. (The extra 50 per cent of time needed to learn the extra 58 words added only about 2 per cent to a reader's understanding. This time could be better spent developing a love of reading, by giving children a wider range of stories and topics.)

Don't be boring at 50+

A gossip talks about others.
A bore talks about himself.
A conversationalist listens,
To you.

Anon

Insight
Employers test for literacy

To ensure literacy standards are maintained, employers are increasingly making use of psychometric tests in the recruitment process. Your performance on these tests can be improved by following the general advice on preparing for them, and by practising the eight types of literacy questions typically asked.

Tests of verbal thinking, verbal IQ and verbal reasoning

In 2007, The National Association of Graduate Recruiters in the UK reported that it had failed to fill one-third of its vacancies for graduates, because of a lack of suitable applicants. Facing a general decline in literacy standards, and a decline in the ability of even graduates to think clearly and to express clearly what they think, employers have been forced to employ recruitment consultants to pre-screen graduate applicants by using psychometric tests. In future years, they will need to seek more people of 50+ to make good their shortfall!

The advice for what to do on the day of a verbal thinking test is the same as in Chapter 2 (on IQ tests). The specific brain training you need for verbal thinking tests is to practise answering the following eight types of question that are used in psychometric tests of verbal reasoning and verbal IQ:

1 find the synonyms
2 find the antonyms
3 double meanings
4 double uses
5 missing word pairs
6 mistaken use of words
7 verbal analogies
8 redundant words.

If you need to brush up on any of these types of questions, read *Train Your Brain* (Horne and Wootton, 2010).

The neuroscience of word games

....

Insight
Neuroscience of word games
At least six different areas of your brain are engaged by the word game itself, to which may be added another six if the game involves retrieval from memory, to which may be added another half-dozen if you play with, or against, a partner. Try alphabetics, passwords, association games, word pairs, proverbs, dictionary games and party games like charades or adverbs.
....

CROSSWORDS AND ALPHABETICS

Alphabetic puzzles are English crosswords in which you use all 26 letters of the English alphabet, but use each letter only once.

Example 1

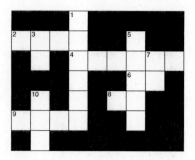

ACROSS

  2. A receptacle for cereal

  4. Something you can get from an accident

  6. Abr. advertisement

  8. Master of ceremonies

  9. You might wear under your shirt

DOWN

  1. To promise

  3. Pulls a plough

  5. Noise a duck makes

  7. Road abr.

10. Turkish hat

Hint: If you list the alphabet and cross out each letter as you use it, this process of elimination helps to reduce the final few words to anagrams.

ANSWER

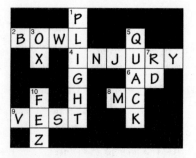

Although they appear simple, alphabetics are good for developing spare cognitive capacity because they use many parts of your brain simultaneously.

For example:

Word games can also develop 'fluency' or 'speed'. For example:

▶ Try to write down as many mammals as you can in one minute.
▶ Now try to write down all the words you can that begin with 'B'.

PASSWORD AND ASSOCIATION GAMES

In password-type games, which are played two against two, you try to get your partner to guess what word you have in mind by giving, as one-word clues, words of associated meaning. If I had the word 'pickle' in mind, I might, in succession give words like 'onion', 'vinegar', 'fix', 'acetone', 'jam', 'mess', 'ploughman's', 'predicament'. If my partner guesses the word I have in mind, i.e. 'pickle', after only one clue, we score 10. Thereafter we can only score 10 minus the number of clues I have to give before my partner guesses the word I have in mind. For this game, Broca's area of the brain is important and so is the angular gyrus:

The angular gyrus is the area where the left temporal, parietal and occipital lobes meet. In harder versions of these games, the word to convey is supplied by your opponents, perhaps along with three or more forbidden clues. In our example of 'pickle', you might have been forbidden to give as clues 'onion, 'vinegar' and 'preserve'. N.B. Any form or part of the word in mind is always 'forbidden' or 'taboo', as is the use of proper names or trade names, in any of the various password games.

The games are called 'password', because your partner can always say 'pass' – meaning, 'I'm not sure yet, give me another clue'. A good fun variant is when you play in groups and all groups have the same word in mind. Members of each group take it in turns to give their partner a 'clue', in the hearing of everyone. This opens up the possibility of laying 'trails' of association to put the other players off the scent, while still using words that you believe your partner will eventually associate with your word.

Another game to try in a larger group, for example in a minibus or on a long coach or train journey, is the 'association game'.

The association game

One person starts with a word. The next must follow, without hesitation, with an associated word. The first person to stumble breaks the round and starts a new round with a new word. Any player can challenge any association offered by another player. If the explanation is not satisfactory, the successful challenger starts a new round. If someone uses a word that has already been used earlier in the game, they can be challenged for repetition. This game develops quick thinking, creativity, imagination, concentration and memory.

PAIRED WORDS OR PROVERBS

Both sides of the brain are involved in these types of games. They involve dividing words into pairs, or groups, using some given rules. It involves what psychologists sometimes call 'divergent' – as opposed to 'convergent' – thinking. 'Divergent' thinking is good brain training for creativity and imagination, i.e. very good for creative, visual, spatial and symbolic thinking. This form of brain training helps with the production and interpretation of metaphors, similes, symbols, parables, poetry, and figurative and creative writing.

In more complex versions, definitions are made up of rare or unfamiliar words picked from a dictionary and opponents have to guess which are 'true' and which are 'false', or which 'words' pair with which definitions. The trick is to make the definition you invent sound plausible. One example is the 'dictionary game'.

The dictionary game

You need a dictionary, preferably two, and writing materials. Create two teams. Each member of the team chooses an obscure word and writes its meaning on a piece of paper. The dictionaries are then put away. Team members then write out false definitions

for each word (but not for the one they chose themselves). Teams take it in turn to read out a word and a set of possible meanings, including the correct one. If a nominated member of the opposite team spots which is the correct definition and guesses right first time, they score 10 points. If the team confer, they can still score 6 points provided they guess correctly the second time. A third guess that is correct scores 2. Anyone whose false definition is selected scores 4.

Different people group and match words using very different organizing principles, schema, frameworks or associations. The trick is to get to know how your partner's mind works – to tune into your partner's way of thinking. Matching by function normally takes place on the left side of your brain, and visual or metaphorical matching on the right side of your brain. Puns, double meanings and most sexual innuendoes come from the right side of your brain. A 'Carry On' film is a right-brain workout!

Recent research has refined Broca's original view that 'we speak with our left brain'. About 95 per cent of right-handed men are left-brain dominant for syntax (sentence structure) and semantics (meaning). Sally Shaywitz has used NMR scanning to show that women are not so strongly lateralized for language and talking as men are. In a study with two matched groups of around 20 men and 20 women, all 20 men revealed blood flow in the left frontal lobe while talking, but all the women showed equal blood flows in their left and right hemispheres. We can begin to see why 50+ women do so well in a 'knowledge or thinking economy', once freed from societal prejudice. Stereotypical female brains have more areas involved when they talk than do stereotypical male brains. Left-handers and ambidextrous people generally have more active language areas in their brains.

PET scans show that getting people to explain how 'squirrels invest' or why 'beginners are green', takes place on the right side of the brain of right-handed people. During the dictionary game, the right side generates possible options, which the left side evaluates and selects. The right side adds intonation and gestures and physical expression, which are usually illegal in most word games, but 'de rigueur' in charades or the 'adverb game'.

The adverb game

This is good with children, or as an icebreaker at adult parties. Person A and person B leave the room. A gives B a mystery adverb – a word that describes how something is done, for example 'quickly', 'thoughtfully', 'confusingly', 'seductively'. A and B return to the room and B's task is to get the audience to guess the mystery adverb. The person who first guesses becomes A in the next round and gives another person B a new mystery adverb. The audience guesses the adverb by taking turns to ask B to carry out various actions in a way that would be described by the mystery adverb, for example 'Open an envelope this way'. Person B would then have to demonstrate how they would open an envelope quickly or thoughtfully or seductively... The audience can be divided into competing teams who take turns to demand an action and to guess the mystery adverb.

Both Howard Gardner and Ellen Winner have reported that people with right-brain stroke damage (or who have severe lateral dominance) do not respond to 'hints' or indirect requests ('gosh, that meal was good but it's created a lot of washing up' equals 'will you please help me wash up these dishes'). The critical, creative and reflective thinking which supports applied thinking proceed via Inferences, Insight or Inspirations, and these involve the right-hand side of the right-hander's brain. This underlines the crucial role of brain training in securing whole-brain development. Most government educational regimes strongly favour literal left-brain development. However, laughter, health, mood, thinking and BLISS all need you to involve your whole brain – left and right. The world needs the thinking power of more creative, more optimistic, less unhappy people. (According to the World Health Organization, suicide and self-harm have now become the world's major health threat.)

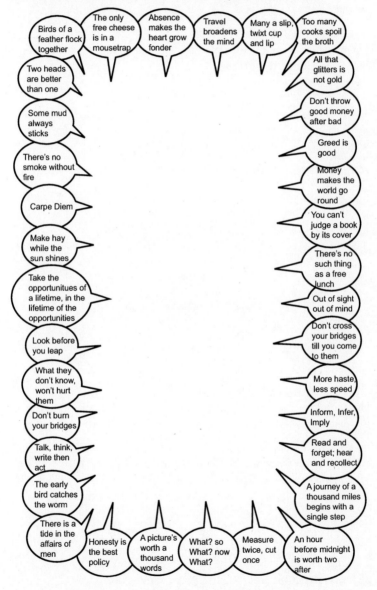

At 50+, your right brain can hold the many contradictory ideas and images generated during a joke, or an emerging humorous situation; your left brain finally 'gets' a joke or 'sees the funny side' of an otherwise depressing situation. Take a look at the proverbs on page 183.

Try pairing the ones that mean the same by drawing dotted lines between them. Then find pairs that appear to contradict each other and join them with solid lines.

WORD WHEELS

On a brain scanner, word wheels have been shown to activate similar areas to literal crosswords (cryptic crosswords 'electrify' many more brain circuits).

In word wheels, the words don't just interact, they overlap. For example:

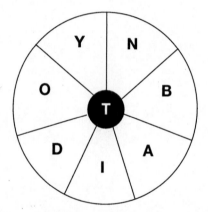

Using the given letters no more than once, make as many words as possible of four or more letters, always including the central letter. How many did you find? We found 25 (see bottom of the page).

At first glance, the word wheel above seems to be filled with random letters, but on closer inspection the collections can be divided into English words. If you talk aloud about the letters and the possible

(Answers: adit, anti, antibody, atony, bait, bandit, baton, bint, biota, boat, botany, dainty, dirt, doit, into, iota, oaty, obit, obtain, tidy, tiny, toad, toady, today.)

words you can make, your brain scan will show more activity, in more regions of the brain, leading to greater residual cognitive development. In healthy brains, word wheels activate your Broca's area; your Wernicke's area; a part of your left frontal lobe that hears the melody in your speech or singing; a corresponding part of the right frontal lobe that hears the pitch and the rhythm of your speech – so you can see, hear, understand why it is important to think aloud. Counting round the circle involves the part of the brain associated with calculation and the angular gyrus is active as you read and re-read the letters.

The verbal superiority of the 50+ brain

David Selacter's work on memory underscores the need of the 50+ to do brain training in order to unleash and exploit their superior potential as verbal thinkers. Selacter illustrates:

> *I cannot remember what I ate for dinner a year ago, because I have had dinners since then and it would take a while to review them all before deciding which was the one I ate a year ago. The 50+ have had many more than 364 dinners!*

The superior, more extensive vocabulary of the 50+ requires longer to review before selecting the most apt word (and all its associated sounds, shapes, meanings, intonations, pitch, tunes and rhymes) – no wonder learning and reciting poetry and drama are so good for a child's brain development.

The role played by verbal superiority in the overall superiority of the 50+ brain is better understood as we turn to the central role of internal dialogue.

Thinking as internal dialogue

> *To think is to talk, if only to yourself!*

Simon Wootton, 2003

Up to and including the 1980s, references to intra-personal conversations were rare. Since the 1990s, the idea of thinking as an internal dialogue has been widely discussed. Key among the implications of this idea is the importance of vocabulary and hence of brain training exercises, puzzles and games that develop your vocabulary. Clearly you cannot think – as an internal dialogue – about things for which you have no vocabulary. Neither can you manipulate mental concepts for which you have no labels. Learning to talk clearly will aid clear thinking, and clear thinking will aid clear writing. In the worlds of business and social policy, government and the caring professions, this will enable effective action to be taken. Because of the superiority of the 50+ vocabulary, the role of the 50+ in the management of business and public services will become pre-eminent as we become a brain-based economy.

INTERNAL DIALOGUE – PHYSICAL FITNESS AND PSYCHOLOGICAL WELL-BEING

Since the 1990s, doctors and sports scientists have shown a lot of interest in the mind–body connection, especially in the survival rates for major surgery and cancer and in the times taken to recover from sports.

Internal dialogues appear to co-ordinate and connect the work of different parts of the brain, such as the sensory cortex and the motor control functions. Internal dialogues, the conversations you have with yourself, determine how you view your own body, the importance you attach to it, the respect with which you treat it, and whether or not you allow other people to abuse it.

THINKING ALOUD

John Steiner observed that people often introduce their internal dialogues into conversations with other people. They 'fly kites' or 'float ideas'. Consciously, or unconsciously, these people are seeking reactions: 'Will it fly? Or will it sink like a lead balloon?' While it is clear that thinking aloud, with or without others present, exercises much of the brain, it is less clear that all thought necessarily involves the use of language. With or without language, the brain can manipulate more complex symbols than words. Images, metaphors, schema and symbols, as in systems thinking for example, can all be used to aid complex thinking. Caruthers has recently decided that normal spoken and written language is definitely involved in thinking processes such as believing, desiring and reasoning. Words join images and sounds as symbols which can be manipulated during the thinking process.

'Keep your head, when all about you are losing theirs' (Rudyard Kipling, 1910)

Since the 50+ vocabulary is more sophisticated, the 50+ can talk about more complex things more precisely. If you learn to talk more fluently, you will be able to think more quickly. You will be able to think faster under pressure and to talk more calmly under duress. You will be able to 'keep your head, when all about you are losing theirs'.

Insight
Thoughtful conversations

Thoughtful conversations simultaneously improve the quality of your present thinking and develop your subsequent ability to think quickly and accurately. There are at least 15 things you can do to make your conversations more thoughtful, and at least 30 different thought-provoking questions which you can use to help your companion to respond more thoughtfully.

How to have a 'thoughtful conversation'

▶ Convey non-verbally that you are listening to and taking seriously the other person.

▶ Look out for things that puzzle you, rather than for things with which to disagree.

▶ Respect the other person, even if you disagree with them.

▶ Give good reasons for any opinions you express.

▶ Ask for clarification of what is puzzling you.

▶ Ask others for reasons and examples.

▶ Avoid intimidating language like, 'It's obvious that...' or, 'Nobody in their right mind...'.

▶ Use ideas as temporary 'sky hooks' to hoist up the level of the discussion.

▶ Stay open to the possibility that you may be wrong, or misinformed.

▶ Remain tenacious in your desire to get to the bottom of things.

▶ Avoid disguising statements as questions.

▶ Connect what you say to what has been said earlier.

▶ Realize that people need help to understand how proposed future actions flow from current opinions and how these, in turn, are based on other information.

▶ Delay, for as long as possible, coming to firm conclusions about what is being discussed. (When there is time – and there nearly always is – float ideas tentatively. Agree to come back to the matter in ten minutes, or later that day, or that week.)

▶ Remain tolerant of the opinions of other people. (People do not like to enter 'thoughtful conversations' expecting to be judged by someone older and wiser.) Try not to interrupt their train of thought, however woolly you find it. As a minimum let them finish their sentences. A conversation is not a competition.

30 USEFUL THINGS TO SAY IN THOUGHTFUL CONVERSATIONS

1 My concern is…
2 Why do you say that?
3 What do you mean by that?
4 How would that affect… ?
5 What can we agree on?
6 How is this different from… ?
7 How is… consistent with… ?
8 What leads you to think that?
9 How are you able to prove that?
10 How can you be sure about that?
11 I'm sorry, I didn't quite follow that.
12 Can you explain the relevance of… ?
13 What assumptions are we making here?
14 OK, so where does that take us to next?
15 Can you just take me through that again?
16 Have you considered the possibility that… ?
17 Do you have any evidence to support that?
18 So am I correct that what you are saying is… ?
19 We appear to have two or three quite separate ideas here.
20 Is it possible to check any of these things out? If so, how?
21 Can we just agree again what we know to be the case?
22 While I can accept…, what does not seem to follow is…
23 How is that connected with what you just said about… ?
24 When you said ABC, you seemed… (label the emotion).
25 You seem to be very certain of that. Can you help me to understand why?
26 You seem to be starting from quite different assumptions. What are they?

27 Can you give me a concrete example of how it might work out in practice?

28 You might be right, but I don't quite follow how you got there. Please explain.

29 What would have to happen before you reconsidered your point of view?

30 I have lost the thread. How does that connect with what you were just saying?

Think like a man

Should you choose a man or a woman as a 'thinking companion'?

One of the best ways to improve your verbal thinking, and to expand your overall cognitive capacity, is by choosing carefully those with whom you have 'thoughtful conversations'. Favour constructive, challenging, tentative, non-judgemental 'thoughtful' companions, who are interested in exploring ideas as well as facts. At 50+, it is especially important to avoid cynics and people who complain all the time. They will drain your spirit as well as your energy. At 50+, avoid people who only want to preach arguments they have already rehearsed. When choosing your 'thoughtful companion' or 'critical friend', should you choose a man or a woman?

The answer is that it all depends on what sort of brain you have, and what sort of brain your potential partner has. While typical male brains (TMBs) do think differently from typical female brains (TFBs), very few men are 100 per cent TMB and very few women are 100 per cent TFB. (You can get an indication of the male–female balance in your brain by answering the questions in Appendix G.)

FEMALE INTUITION STILL GOING STRONG AT 50+

Roger Gorski found more activity in the corpus callosum in women. This is the bundle of nerves that connects the left- to the right-hand side of the brain. This means that even when talking, which is a predominantly left-brain activity, women may still be accessing right-brain associative play on the meaning of the words said or heard. This is what may give their conversations a more intuitive or 'off the wall' feel. Furthermore, neuroanatomist Sandra Wikelson, who has performed several hundred autopsies since 1977, reports that the corpus callosum in women does not shrink with age.

Building close relationships – intimacy and a 'meeting of minds'

When conversations between two people are thoughtful, not only does the thinking benefit, so does the relationship. Research by Steven Duck and Anne Giradot, replicated in 2003 by Doherty and Horne, found that relationships between work colleagues, friends or sexual partners became closer, the greater the extent of the disclosure between them. When the disclosure moved from information to thoughtful opinion, the relationship intensified. When empathetic thinking and shared 'visions' of the future were added, intimacy often resulted. Humour and creative thinking (and maybe dark chocolate) sometimes completed the route to bed! The 50+ are more creative than younger people, so all you need to do is buy the dark chocolate and keep your sense of humour!

In a virtuous circle, creative thinking profits from relationships that are secure, and creative thinkers have been found to be more sexually attractive.

> **Insight**
> **Building close relationships – an intimate meeting of minds**
> Having thoughtful conversations with another person improves both your thinking and your relationship with that person. Sharing information and opinions intensifies the relationship, and empathetic thinking can lead to intimacy. There are many ways to make thoughtful relationships closer.

MAKING THOUGHTFUL RELATIONSHIPS CLOSER

▶ Make disclosures related to your partner, and to the present time and place.
▶ Keep disclosures in balance with your partner, not under- or over-disclosing.
▶ Add opinions to the information you disclose.
▶ Add feelings to the opinions you disclose.
▶ Begin more sentences with 'I… (notice, think, feel)'.
▶ Build trust by aligning your actions with your opinions.
▶ Try to match any intimate self-disclosures made by your partner.
▶ Avoid having 'secrets' and things that 'you just don't talk about'.
▶ Are you sufficiently self-aware and honest to match the openness of your partner?

(taken from Horne and Doherty, 2003)

Don't argue!

At 50+, you have less patience and are less inclined to 'tolerate fools gladly'. Latent envy of youth (usually misplaced) can fuel uncharacteristic aggression towards younger people who have made the mistake of being adversarial. Resist your reputation to 'take no prisoners'! This is important. But for some 50+ people, it can be difficult. Some younger people are so competitive that nearly every discussion becomes an argument and an argument that they must win. At 50+ you will normally win the arguments but you may be losing friends. At 50+ having friends is more important than winning arguments. It is easier to pick arguments than find new friends.

Winning the argument at 50+

In order to prevent arguments, I prefer to do all the talking myself.
Oscar Wilde

According to Roger Drake, in a face-to-face argument, you are more likely to win if you move slightly to your right. This moves your opponent's eyes to their left, thereby activating the right side of their brain, which is less confrontational and more open to novelty and change. Also, you are more likely to change another person's mind if you whisper into their left ear, and thereby talk to their right brain.

Check out how argumentative you are. Consider the following 20 statements and write your score in the unshaded boxes.

Score: rarely true = 2, occasionally true = 3, often true = 4, always true = 5

	Y	X
I try to avoid arguments if at all possible.		
In the middle of an argument, I feel excited.		
I generally come out best in an argument.		
A good argument clears the air.		

(Contd)

	Y	X
Only afterwards can I think of what I should have said.	■	
An argument is an intellectual challenge.		■
I don't like people who are argumentative.	■	
I don't like to just let things go.		■
It takes skill to avoid getting into an argument.	■	
I will always stand up for myself and defend my corner.		■
I feel sick if I sense an argument brewing.	■	
There's nothing like the cut and thrust of debate.		■
Arguments leave me shaking and upset.	■	
It's nice to make a point and have a counter-argument.		■
Arguments create problems and never settle things.	■	
Each time arguments happen, I say 'never again'.	■	
I feel very energetic and fired up when I argue.		■
I avoid arguments at all cost.	■	
Arguments are good mental exercise.		■
If I argue, people won't like me.	■	

Your score is Total Y minus Total X.

= Score

HOW DID YOU DO?

People who can make good use of verbal thinking in thoughtful conversations, or who make good 'critical friends', generally score between 2 and 6. The 50+ are usually too 'nice' or too 'polite' to argue and hence have low scores. Sometimes low scorers are from Asian cultures in which any kind of confrontation is to be avoided. The 50+ who score above 6 are often too argumentative, too competitive, too abrasive or too adversarial. In general, the 50+ are more likely to have the confidence to concede; they know that life's too short to sweat over small stuff. They are more inclined to keep their powder dry for important matters of principle.

> **Insight**
> **Stop arguing, start thinking; stop talking, start listening**
> At 50+, winning arguments will be easier but there may be a cost. More relationships break down over the way people argue, rather than what they argue about. About 50 per cent of these breakdowns are avoidable. It seems to matter where you stand (physically) in relation to the person with whom you argue.

SO, I'M TOO COMPETITIVE, TOO ADVERSARIAL, TOO ARGUMENTATIVE, SO WHAT!

If you win arguments and lose friends you will be the loser. Having close friendships is strongly correlated with good health, creative thinking and real-world achievement. The connection between friendship and physical health is not well understood. Perhaps it is a by-product of reduced cortisol, and of increased endorphin and serotonin when friends talk to each other. Both of these changes in the chemicals in your brain are associated with enhancements in your immune system.

Close friendships are a safe haven from which creative excursions can be made, and creative thinking is strongly correlated with success in professions like science, engineering, medicine and management, as well as in the more obvious areas of art, advertising, marketing, media and journalism.

Clearly there is more to forming close thoughtful relationships than balancing excessive compliance and excessive argumentativeness. For example, everyone would prefer partners (and neighbours and work colleagues) who are reasonable – and you are much more likely to be reasonable if you can reason.

It's *how* you row that matters!

In a 2006 YouGov survey of couples, where one or both partners were thinking of splitting up, the number one reason for dissatisfaction with the relationship was disagreements over money. But the second reason, way ahead of disagreements over sex, children, alcohol, coming home late, the in-laws etc., was dislike of the way the other person argued. People disliked the *way* their partners argued, more than *what* they argued about. Linda Waite, who has been tracking

(Contd)

crumbling relationships since 2000, says about half of slow-rumbling, grumbling, crumbling relationships eventually break down altogether. Yet half improve and describe their relationships as 'now happy'. So you can learn to argue better – the prognosis is not good if you don't!

The neurochemistry of love, lust, attachment and sex

When we are talking about love here, we are talking about romantic love. Romantic love, lust and attachment each have separate neurochemical systems. Each can react without the other. However, lust, followed by love and then attachment is a common sequence. Lust is a temporary urge for sexual gratification. Romantic love is a sense of elation in the presence of, or at the thought of, one particular person. Attachment is a sense of peace and security conducive to having children.

> **Insight**
> **Sexual chemistry**
> Romantic love, lust and attachment are each associated with a different chemical reaction in the brain, so each feeling has a different effect on the way you think.

Writers on youth and age, love and sex

I never enjoyed youth so much as I do now that I am 50+. (after George Santayana)

But enjoyment and love are not the same thing. Love as a young person is as nothing compared to the love of an old man for his wife. (after William Durant)

The yearning for love and romance persists – it outlasts even the capacity for sex. (after Joseph Heller)

THE NEUROCHEMISTRY OF ONE-NIGHT STANDS

Lust is associated with increased testosterone in the brain. In 50+ men, this occurs daily in the morning and is more noticeable in

194

autumn. In pre-menopausal women, it occurs monthly at the time of ovulation. But testosterone levels can be stimulated at other times. Testosterone levels can be stimulated in 50+ men by the sight of a cleavage, the flash of leg, by pornography or by an offer of sex. In women, testosterone is stimulated by affection, words, deeds or humour. It is stimulated in both sexes by danger, novelty and dark chocolate. You should be aware of the risk that what you might think of as 'lust only' sex can easily precipitate romantic love and the desire for attachment.

Myths about male and female orgasm

In 2005, Professor Holstep in the Netherlands investigated what happens in your brain when you have an orgasm. He got couples to make love while their brains were scanned using a PET scanner. (Laboratory conditions had to be improved before some partners could rise to the occasion! Lights were lowered and socks issued to those who got cold feet.)

Contrary to myths that the parts of the brain involved in verbal and emotional thinking needed to stay engaged for women to have good sex, female brains (as well as male brains) experienced major neurological shutdown as orgasm approached. The orgasms released endorphins – endorphins help creative thinking and reduce depression and anxiety, thereby enhancing speed and accuracy of thinking.

INTERCOURSE – VERBAL AND PHYSICAL

It may be no coincidence that the word for physical and verbal communication is the same – i.e. intercourse.

She: 'How can I stop him thinking all the time?'

Friend: 'Castration?'

Physical communication patterns in bed mirror verbal communication patterns elsewhere. For example, sulking will turn up as withholding sex, controlling will turn up as dominating sex, anger will turn up as punitive or humiliating sex, teasing as… teasing sex, and so on. Think about it.

On carrying a baby at 50+

Fearing genocide, the inhabitants of a Muslim village fled during the night. To escape they would need to cross a cold high mountain. They took a little-known path. The path was very steep and very high and very cold. The mothers carried their babies. The fathers helped the older children and the older people struggled on alone. Eventually, some of the older people began to sit down by the edge of the path, exhausted by the cold and the lack of oxygen.

The older people said: 'We are exhausted. We have become a burden. We are slowing everyone down. We will all be caught. Leave us here. You can carry on more quickly without us.'

The mothers said: 'We too need to rest. With every step our babies are becoming heavier and heavier to carry.' And so, the mothers gave, to each older person, a baby to carry. The mothers said to the older people: 'Look, instead of just sitting down and dying in the cold, please carry our babies as far as you can, before you sit down to die. Your bodies will at least keep our babies warm and you will give us respite to regain our strength so that we can reach the summit tomorrow.'

The older people clasped the babies tight against their chests, and started walking. And you know, the older people never stopped! They climbed all the way over the mountains, still carrying the babies. The babies had given them reason and reason had given them strength.

A story told to Fakhrun and Danya by Abbu, when Danya was two years old. It is based on a true story originally told by Ruby Lee.

Social situations at 50+

HOW COMFORTABLE ARE YOU IN SOCIAL SITUATIONS?

Either before, during, or after a social interaction (perhaps with someone you would have liked to get to know a little better), how often did you have thoughts similar to those below? Write your score in the unshaded box.

In social situations I have thoughts similar to...		Score 1–4
Score: 1 = I rarely had thoughts similar to this. 2 = I sometimes had thoughts similar to this. 3 = I often had thoughts similar to this. 4 = I very often had thoughts similar to this.	**A**	**B**
1 I'll throw caution to the wind – in for a penny, in for a pound.		
2 I wish I could just avoid the whole situation.		
3 We could get on really well.		
4 We probably have a lot in common.		
5 Come on, what's the worst that could happen?		
6 I must make a good impression or I'll let myself down and feel terrible afterwards.		
7 I don't have to put myself through this.		
8 This is going to be awkward, but I can handle it.		
9 What is there to lose? It's worth a try.		
10 I'll probably come across as really stupid.		
11 If I blow this, I'll never be able to fail again.		
12 This will be a good opportunity to...		
13 I'm just not good in these situations, something always goes wrong.		
14 I'll try breaking the ice by asking/talking about...		
15 These kinds of situations scare me to death.		
16 I'm afraid they will think I'm...		
17 I'm beginning to feel more relaxed now.		
18 I'll panic if I can't think what to say.		
19 I will feel really awkward if...		
20 Whatever, I'll handle it somehow.		
Total As:		
Total Bs:		

How did you get on?

What did you get for your A and B totals?

Total A measures how **positive** you feel about social situations.

Compare your score with typical scores for men and women:

Male A score	Female A score	Percentage scoring this high
27+	30+	15%
25+	28+	30%
23+	26+	50%
21+	24+	70%
20+	23+	85%

Total B measures how **negative** you feel about social situations.

Compare your score with typical scores for men and women:

Male B score	Female B score	Percentage scoring this high
27+	22+	15%
25+	21+	30%
22+	18+	50%
20+	17+	70%
17+	15+	85%

So, what does your score mean?

A high B score means that you probably agree with whoever said: 'Better to remain silent and look a fool, than to open my mouth and remove all doubt!' People with high B scores are nervous about social situations and you make yourself even more nervous through self-defeating internal dialogue.

A high A score, on the other hand, shows that you do not have excessive social anxiety (a little is good, it revs you up ready for the social fray!). You see yourself as quite socially adept. Even if you sometimes don't get the reaction you would like, it is no big deal to you. You are more likely to think: 'Nothing ventured, nothing gained.'

Men and women also seem to behave differently when they have high B or low A scores. 50+ women are more inclined to carry on regardless – tolerating their discomfort and anxiety, and making the (often enormous) social effort. Shy 50+ men, on the other hand, are more likely to become, or remain, isolated and develop low BLISS scores, and lead less successful lives. If, at 50+, you are in the bottom 15 per cent for A and the top 15 per cent for B, you are likely to prefer staying at home, maybe watching television or having a drink alone. This is not very satisfactory for you, or for a society that is in urgent need of the superior brain power of your 50+ brain. The good news is that this is not irreversible and you can change things.

Now, what to do about your score?
Look at the statements that you are making that contribute to high B or low A scores and stop making them, especially to yourself in your internal dialogue. If you rehearse them, and myelinate them, they might become self-fulfilling. Take the following five steps:

Step 1   For two weeks, smile, give eye contact and say 'hello' to any stranger who smiles back. This can be at work or at a class, or at the checkout. You may get the odd quizzical look, but research evidence suggests that people will usually smile back.

Step 2   For the next two weeks, practise adding small talk to the initial smile, eye contact and 'hello'. Waiting in a queue, or a line, is a good time to practise. Try a comment about the weather, some new feature in the shop, the price of things, a local sports result, a programme on television last night, or an item on the news. If you are served by the same person more than once on successive weeks, try 'How have you been keeping?' You will be surprised that people often seem glad to reply in some detail – about a trip or an illness in their family. This can then be followed up the next week – 'How was your trip?' 'Is your mother recovering OK?'

Step 3   Set yourself a target of finding one good or complimentary thing to say to at least one person each day. This can be quite a daunting target to start with, especially as evening approaches and you still haven't met your quota! You may have to ring someone or go and buy something such as milk at the local shop. Soon it will feel more natural and you can raise your target. People tend to like people who like them – show them that you like something about them – if only their hair colour or cut. Comment if they have a new tan – did they get it on a trip? It is natural to take interest in when and where, and where else they have enjoyed...

Step 4   Make the first move with invitations. Ask a co-worker what they usually do for lunch. It may seem OK to ask if you can tag along or to recommend somewhere different they might want to come and try...? If you and your neighbour are in the garden on a sunny day, invite them round for a cold drink, or to give advice on a sickly plant. Talking about a good film on television last night may lead to a new film release that looks good and would they like to come along and see it? Not everyone will say 'yes', not everyone will like you, just as you don't like everyone you meet. That's why you have to keep going to find the odd person you do like and who does like you.

Step 5   Now you have got neuron traces in your brain that are familiar with smiling, giving eye contact, saying 'hello', starting small talk, showing interest, making suggestions and accepting 'no' and sometimes 'yes' – it is time to move into a circle or group where there is high chance that there is someone with something in common with you, or even a shared love (or pet hate). Try joining an assertiveness class, or a language class, or a book club, or a hillwalking club, or an art or craft class. Why not volunteer to work in a charity shop? Bookshops readily reveal people's interests and can prompt conversation and joint endeavour. Prepare a few sentences that you could say at your class or group or to a particular individual. Write them down or record them. Rehearse them and forget about them. Later that day or evening, you will find it easier to speak up. Nobody will notice how nervous you were, and someone may later take you up on what you said. Never assume that anyone making the effort to speak to you is doing so without good reason. They may like you, or find you interesting, attractive even. If you are 50+, who can blame them? You are likely to be one of the most interesting people in the room and if you did have a high negative B score on social anxiety, you are probably sensitive and unthreatening – just the sort of person a person like you would want to get to know.

(The test design with norms and percentiles, was originally published by Carol Glass in Cognitive Therapy and Research.)

The nuns are at it again

I want a few friends at the end. With my vast store of aged wisdom, it seems a pity not to speak it all, so keep me from the recital of endless detail and give me wings to get to the point. Oh, and seal my lips on my aches and pains – they are increasing as I get older and my love of rehearsing them is getting sweeter as the years pass. I dare not ask for grace enough to enjoy the tales of other people's pains, but help me at least to listen with more patience.

I do not wish to be a saint – for they are hard to live with – but a sour and cynical old person is the crowning work of the devil. Give me the ability to see good things in unexpected people and give me, please, the grace to tell them so.

From a seventeenth-century nun's prayer

INTIMACY AND TRUST – CAN YOU GET CLOSE TO OTHERS OR LET OTHERS GET CLOSE TO YOU?

Having made the acquaintance of others, some of whom you may now be meeting quite regularly under circumstances of mutual interest and congeniality, your brain and thinking will already be benefiting from the opportunities you now have to think aloud, to have thoughtful conversations. If you were able to use the opportunities provided by these thoughtful conversations to develop a closer, more intimate and trusting relationship with one or two of your acquaintances, your brain would benefit even more. Discussions based on deeply held beliefs might become possible and this would involve the many parts of your brain connected to your amygdala, as well as the parts of your cerebral cortex dealing with words and logic and perhaps imagination. The sharing of important past events will cause your hypothalamus to activate 17 or more additional areas of your brain associated with your long-term memory. The question is, can you do it? Can you tolerate closeness and intimacy? Can you sufficiently trust another person?

> **Insight**
> **Can you let others up close and personal?**
> When you can tolerate closeness and intimacy, i.e. when you learn to trust, your conversations will involve more parts of your brain. For example, when relating childhood experiences, the many other areas of your brain dealing with long-term memory will be used.

Do you agree or disagree with the following statements?

Thinking about the following statements I would give a score of...	
1 = strongly disagree, 2 = mildly disagree, 3 = mildly agree, 4 = strongly agree	Score 1–4
1 Closeness can lead to good feelings and bad feelings.	
2 The desire for closeness with someone usually follows feeling attracted to them.	
3 I can usually see another person's point of view.	
4 When I can be open and close to another person, I feel good.	
5 When another person is attracted to me, I usually want to get closer to them.	
6 Generally, I find it equally easy to get close to men or women.	
7 I feel close to others when I can discuss my sex life with them.	
8 The closer I feel to someone, the more accepting I am of them as they are.	
9 It is important to me to have some close relationships in my life.	

10 Close relationships have usually brought me great satisfaction.	
11 I can reveal my deepest feelings to people I trust.	
12 Being able to express how I feel makes me feel close to someone.	
13 I like it when other people tell me how they are feeling.	
14 I like feelings of closeness to others.	
15 I like to share my feelings with other people.	
16 I do not react negatively to demands from people close to me.	
17 I am not worried about being dominated in a close relationship.	
18 Sex and intimacy are not the same thing.	
19 I am open and not normally secretive.	
20 I am not worried about rejection in trying to get close to someone.	
21 I do not resist closeness or intimacy.	
22 I do not always need to be in control all the time.	
23 I find it easy to have more than one close relationship in my life.	
24 I can become close to people with whom I initially have little in common.	
25 I am not worried that I might lose my individuality in a close relationship.	
26 I am not worried about maintaining my personal space.	
27 I feel a strong need to share my thoughts and feelings with someone else.	
28 When people become close they always listen well to each other.	
29 I am not afraid to talk about sex and my sexual feelings.	
30 I am not worried about being too trusting of other people.	
Capacity for closeness, trust and intimacy score:	

How did you get on?
What was your total score for capacity for closeness and how does it compare with other people's?

The percentage of people who score	is
75+	85%
80+	70%
86+	50%
90+	30%
100+	15%

So, what does your score mean?
According to Dr Treadwell, on whose work (reported in the *Journal of Personality Assessment*) our test is based, the lower your score, the greater you are at risk of alienation, loneliness and impaired health as well as impaired thinking. But very high scores are not entirely unproblematic. Many of the 50+ will remember having insufferable 'encounters' with people who were members of 'encounter' groups and 'sensitivity training' groups in the 1970s. The graduates of such groups often graduated with a missionary zeal to find and convert others to the joys of 'authentic' close relationships. Their indiscriminate openness was often unwanted. That said, you should hope for a score that allows you readily to be close to your spouse or long-term partners or old friends. You deserve to have at least one person who 'calls you friend', who believes in you, gives you hope and who you need too. Even so, over-disclosure or unreciprocated levels of disclosure, can actually threaten a relationship if the level of disclosure becomes too burdensome for one partner, or if one partner lacks sufficient self-knowledge or self-awareness to be able to reciprocate.

Now, what to do about your score
If your score was less than 70, ask yourself whether you close down all your relationships, because, according to Horne and Doherty (2003), 'closeness in a relationship – at work, or at play, is a function of the extent of and depth of the disclosure'. If you feel lonely or isolated or just 'grey and empty', it may, in part, be due to a lack of closeness, particularly if it usually falls short of emotional disclosure.

If your score was 105+, you might be overwhelming some people with your intensity.

If your score differs from that of an existing (or potential) partner by more than, say, 20 points, that might highlight some imbalance ahead. Both reserved, or both intense, may work, but very disparate positions portend a great deal of frustration, about feeling 'over-disclosed', 'making all the running', and about 'carrying the whole emotional burden of the relationship'.

HOW SATISFACTORY IS YOUR 50+ RELATIONSHIP?

We have looked at how you can get into (or back into) a relationship at 50+, and the importance of balanced disclosure, closeness, intimacy and trust, not only for the health and survival of the relationship, but also as a supportive framework for the kinds of thoughtful conversations that develop the cognitive capacity of your brain. Is your brain getting this kind of nurturing in your present close relationship(s)? How satisfactory is your 50+ relationship with partner X? Please answer the following questions about your relationship with X and ring the score beneath the word that most closely fits your answer.

1	How many major problems are there in your relationship with X?			
Possible replies	Very many	Some	Few	Very few
Score	1	2	3	4

2	How much do you love your partner?			
Possible replies	Not a lot	Somewhat	Quite a lot	Very much
Score	1	2	3	4

3	Does your relationship with X still live up to your original hopes?			
Possible replies	Hardly	Partly	Mostly	Completely
Score	1	2	3	4

4	How often do you think: 'I wish I had never got into this relationship?			
Possible replies	Nearly all the time	Often	Sometimes	Almost never
Score	1	2	3	4

5	How good is your relationship with X compared to most?			
Possible replies	Poor	Bearable	OK	Excellent
Score	1	2	3	4

6	In general, how satisfied are you with your present relationship?			
Possible replies	Not satisfied	It's tolerable	It's good	Extremely satisfied
Score	1	2	3	4

7	How well is partner X meeting your needs?			
Possible replies	Not well at all	Not well enough	Well	Extremely well
Score	1	2	3	4

Your total score for your relationship with X:

How did you do?

What is your total score for your close relationship with X at 50+ and how does it compare with the way other people rate their close relationships?

The percentage of people who score	is
18+	85%
21+	70%
23+	50%

The percentage of people who score	is
26+	30%
28	15%

(Source: The design, norming and percentile scoring for this test were based on original work by Susan Hendrick, reported in the Journal of Marriage and Family.)

So, what does your score mean?

We have to note that Susan Hendrick worked largely with married couples and the scores she normed correlated with much more detailed inventories of satisfaction with married life. At 50+, one of your close relationships is likely to be with someone to whom you are married. Hendricks' scale does pretty well at predicting which co-habiting couples will still be together one year ahead.

You might find your score a bit unnerving. You have to remember that at 50+, you are probably more resigned to, or more realistic about, your relationship than younger people who may still have idealized views of themselves and their partners. By definition, the norms are for couples who are together and prepared to talk about their relationships. They will therefore be skewed towards a more favourable view – so don't be too alarmed if most of them appear to be reporting that they are more satisfied with their close relationships than you are with yours. Most people will be reluctant to admit to themselves, let alone an interviewer, that they have had to accept second or third best for their close relationship. So, at 50+, you need to take the scores of younger people with a pinch of salt – they may have inflated the averages with which you are now comparing yourself. It may be more instructive to get your partner to complete the test. Long-term couples tend to give similar (high or low) ratings for their relationships. If you are reluctant, or afraid, to have such a discussion with your partner, it does not bode well for the ability of your relationship to nurture your brain and your verbal thinking power!

Such a reluctance to engage in verbal intercourse may mirror, or contribute to, a reluctance to engage in sexual intercourse. This chicken and egg situation can be very difficult to sort out at 50+, when there can be other physical or hormonal reasons for a decline in satisfaction with the physical side of a relationship. Since it is a two-way street, one can 'affect' the other. It may surprise you to know that, at 50+, there is not a strong correspondence between frequency of sex and satisfaction with the relationship, though total absence is sometimes an indicator that all might not be well. Neither is frequency of arguments negatively correlated with satisfaction (what seems to matter more than how often you argue, is *how* you argue). However, what does correlate with satisfaction is frequency of sex minus frequency of arguments, i.e. if you are going to argue, having sex is an important way to make up and repair damage to self-esteem or confidence in the relationship. Awareness of the pattern may be helpful, lest you or your partner end up picking fights when you would be better off picking your moment for a cuddle that could lead to some sexual satisfaction, the chemistry of which is good for your brain as well as your relationship.

A good sex life at 50+ is not only good for your brain, it is becoming more widely expected. When the 50+ were young, it was rare to see 50+ stars in films enjoying sex. Now it is commonplace. Granny sex is mainstream, and 50+ stars like Helen Mirren, Harrison Ford and Meryl Streep are regarded as very sexy and sexual without extensive artifice. Many male stars go on into their late seventies. This can create expectations and pressures on your 50+ relationship. Hundreds of books have been written on how you can improve! But most of them focus, mistakenly, on physical techniques. They point out, rightly, the aphrodisiac power of novelty, and advise you to try new settings, new outfits and surprising homecomings. These techniques will rejuvenate your sex life for a while but, by definition, the novelty will wear off! A more enduring solution is to work on the quality of your verbal intercourse.

Verbal intercourse not only improves your capacity for internal dialogue when you think, it mirrors and rehearses the talk for your sexual intercourse later. At 50+, men, especially, report an increased desire to have sex for different reasons from when they were young and enslaved to their testosterone. At 50+, men want to express love and affection through sex and to feel the reassurance of having that reciprocated. At 50+, it is more about love than lust. At 50+, the key to improving your sex life is to spend more time talking to each other and doing things together. Try making deliberate and specific attempts regularly to revitalize any feelings of love, respect and admiration for your partner as they arise. There will probably be many genuine opportunities each day. Make it a goal to seize at least one. So how much do you know about sex at 50+?

Sex at 50+

I still have two abiding passions – model railways and women. Now that I am 89, I am finally getting a bit too old for model railways!

Pierre Monteaux, orchestral conductor, aged 89

The quality of your thinking about some aspects of your sex life may be limited by the quality of the information on which that thinking is based. At 50+, you are likely to know more about sex than a younger person – and will probably have had more (sex, that is). But your knowledge may not be up to date in terms of social attitudes or well informed by recent science. It might be as well to check out what you do know about sex, now that you are 50+.

Tick your best answer for the 20 questions in the following sex check test and then check to see if you were right. If you do well, fine. Follow up on the ones you got wrong. If you do badly, fine. Get a book and discuss what you discover with your partner.

SEX CHECK TEST

1	Bisexuality: studies have shown that...	
A	It does not exist	
B	It is commonplace	
C	Bisexuals are homosexuals in denial	

2	Dressing up: studies have shown that dressing up for sex...	
A	Indicates mental disorder	
B	Is intended to degrade, belittle or humiliate	
C	Is normal and commonplace	

3	Menopause: studies have shown that a woman's sexual behaviour after menopause is determined by...	
A	Her residual levels of oestrogen	
B	The attitude of her partner during menopause	
C	Her attitude towards sex before menopause	

4	Effects of age: studies have shown that as men get older...	
A	The urgency of their sex drive slows down	
B	They require more physical stimulation by their partner	
C	They take longer to recover between orgasms	
D	All of the above	

5	Testosterone: studies have shown that male testosterone	
A	Declines from age 40	
B	Disappears in mid 50s	
C	Remains high until late 90s	

6	Pornography: people who use pornography...	
A	Become confused about fantasy and reality	
B	Show a temporary increase and interest in sexual activity	
C	Develop deviant or coercive interests in sex	
D	Come to regard their partners as sex objects	

7	Sex therapy: the most effective therapies are based on...	
A	Thinking, i.e. cognitive therapies	
B	Psychoanalysis	
C	The use of surrogate partners	
D	Medication	

8	Getting it up: erectile dysfunction is not caused by...	
A	Age-related arthritis	
B	Slipped discs	
C	Diabetes	
D	Alcohol	

9	Most common male sex problem: studies found it to be...	
A	Premature ejaculation	
B	Erectile dysfunction	
C	Low desire or interest	

10	Menopause: studies have found that female menopause causes...	
A	Hot flushes and sweating	
B	Painful dryness of the vagina	
C	Insomnia, irritability, lack of concentration, impaired thinking	
D	All of the above	

11	Age and fertility: the most common cause of infertility is...	
A	Age-lowered sperm count in the male partner	
B	Age-lowered oestrogen levels in the female partner	
C	Increased toxins in the environment	
D	A removable blockage in the fallopian tube	

12	A baby at 50+?: studies have shown that you will maximize your chances of conceiving your child if you have sex	
A	5 to 10 days after the first day of the menstrual cycle	
B	5 to 10 days before the first day of the menstrual cycle	
C	3 days before and 3 days after the menstrual cycle	
D	5 days before and 5 days after the day the egg is released	

13	Female orgasm: studies have shown the best sexual position is...	
A	Man on top	
B	Woman on top	
C	Rear entry	
D	Side by side (spoons)	

14	**Age, gender and masturbation: studies have found that...**	
A	Both women and men masturbate, and sometimes when they are together	
B	Masturbation continues throughout life to death	
C	Many people masturbate and have regular sex with a partner	
D	All of the above	

15	**Sex vs. love: studies have found that...**	
A	Male love is diminished by frequent sex	
B	Male satisfaction with sex is not enhanced by love	
C	That for a man, sex does not need to involve love	

16	**Female ejaculation: studies have found that...**	
A	Between 10% and 40% of women ejaculate liquid on orgasm	
B	The vagina sweats during intercourse, producing a clear liquid	
C	The clear liquid is a sign of a urinary tract infection	

17	**The clitoris: studies have found that...**	
A	The clitoris can become erect during love play and intercourse	
B	The clitoris is often concealed prior to erection	
C	The sole purpose of the clitoris is to provide pleasure	
D	All of the above	

18	**Contraception: the risk of conception is lowest using...**	
A	A cervical cap	
B	A sponge	
C	An intrauterine device (IUD)	
D	Oral contraception	

19	Risky contraception: studies have shown that there is the greatest risk of conception when using...	
A	A cervical cap	
B	A diaphragm	
C	A condom	
D	An intrauterine device (IUD)	

20	Age and risk to babies: studies have found the biggest contributor to birth defects in Western countries is...	
A	Malnutrition	
B	Age of parents	
C	Cigarette smoke	
D	Cocaine	
E	Alcohol (even one unit)	
F	Sexual activity during pregnancy	

Answers

Score 1 for a correct answer.

Question	Answer
1	B
2	C
3	C
4	D
5	A
6	B
7	A
8	A
9	C
10	D
11	D

Question	Answer
12	D
13	B
14	D
15	C
16	A
17	D
18	D
19	D
20	E
	Total score

How did you get on?

How many of the 20 sex check questions did you and/or your partner answer correctly? Follow up on any areas of doubt. Keep talking. It's the talking that develops your brain. The by-product is better sex and with better sex come brain chemicals that enhance your thinking skills and your thinking power.

A sex warning – don't say we didn't warn you!

What is undoubtedly good for your brain, might not be so good for your body. Graham and Lynne Jones (in *I Love Sex*) report that sex had been a suspected cause of acne, thrush, cervical cancer, blindness, body odour, whooping cough, gout, sore throat, loss of teeth, tennis elbow, Achilles heel and housemaid's knee.

Some of these might be due more to 'how' than to 'how often'!

'Guessing the truth'

When she was a mother
It was the role that she loved best.
A fullness and fulfilment rose
To fill her heart and breast.
And that's the truth – we guessed.
She could not put her arms around
Their innocence and youth,
To keep them safe
From her own death
And that must be the truth.
For there is no more hostelling,
She's walking all alone.
And they now fly throughout the world,
Her little ones have flown.
Yet wind still blows across this hill,
A sound she loved to hear,
And she would love it still,

> If she were here
> And still, upon this hill.
> For when she was a mother,
> It was the role that she loved best.
> And that's the truth.
> We guessed.
>
> An unhappy and happy conjunction of Pam Ayres, Ann Murray, Simon Wootton
> and the thoughts of Carolyn Horne at 50+, Terry Horne 2008.

In Chapter 6 we have been concerned about the capacity for thoughtful relationships because relationships affect your general health and your predominant mood, and both of these affect the ambient chemistry of your brain. The chemicals present in your brain determine your ability to think well, and to resist degenerative disease. Also, close, intimate relationships are a vehicle for thoughtful conversations.

Thoughtful conversations help you to develop spare cognitive capacity. If your brain has spare cognitive capacity, you may be able to continue to think well, even if you do develop a degenerative brain disease like Alzheimer's. Thoughtful conversations rehearse your ability to express clearly what the world now needs – the clear thinking of its most powerful brains – the brains of the 50+.

10 THINGS TO REMEMBER

1 You can exploit the superior verbal intelligence that you have at 50+.

2 You can use superior internal dialogue to augment your thinking power.

3 At 50+, you can use thoughtful conversation to develop intimate relationships as well as continuing to develop your brain.

4 It is helpful to understand the neurochemistry of friendship, love and sex.

5 Verbal thinking and overall IQ are governed by internal dialogue.

6 Your vocabulary and fluency are better than when you were young.

7 The 50+ have more extensive, more precise vocabulary than young adults.

8 Embedding your verbal thinking into conversations with another person not only improves your ability to think for yourself, it also develops intimacy between you and the person you are talking to.

9 It is brain 'chemistry' that matters, in lust, love, attachment and sex.

10 You can deepen your relationships, and achieve closeness and intimacy, through thoughtful conversation and the 'meeting of minds'. You can learn to make your conversations more thoughtful.

Suggested further reading

Bragdon, A. and Gamon, D., *Learn Faster and Remember More* (Geddes and Grosset, 2005).

Bryon, M., *How to Pass Graduate Psychometric Tests* (London: Kogan Page, 2001).

Bryon, M., *How to Pass Civil Service Tests* (London: Kogan Page, 2003).

Carter, P., *IQ and Psychometric Tests* (London: Kogan Page, 2005).

Cox, E. and Rathvon, H., *Mensa Cryptic Crosswords* (New York: Stirling, 2007).

Fisher, H., *Why We Love: The Brain Chemistry of Love* (New York: Henry Holt, 2004).

Gamon, D., *Building Mental Muscle* (Geddes and Grosset, 2005).

Horne, T. and Doherty, A., *Managing Public Services – Implementing Changes: A Thoughtful Approach to the Practice of Management* (London: Routledge, 2003).

Howard, P. J., *The Owner's Manual for the Brain: Everyday Applications from Mind and Brain Research* (3rd edn, Austin, Texas: Bard Press, 2006).

Tolley, H. and Thomas, K., *How to Pass Verbal Reasoning Tests* (London: Kogan Page, 2006).

Final thoughts

The 50+ brain – only joking

Age only matters when one is concerned about ageing. Now that I am finally old, I might just as well be 20.

Pablo Picasso, aged 80+

Old myths die hard and myths about the old die harder.

You have only to review the 'humour' section of your local bookshop to see how cliché-ridden is the image of old age: 'So you're 50!', 'So you're 60!', 'A Jubilee of over 60s Jokes', 'Old Wreck Jokes' and so on. People who would think twice, or even three times, before making remarks about people based on gender or race, appear to have no compunction about making gratuitous remarks at the expense of the 50+, who are routinely mocked, trivialized, patronized or simply ignored. Unjust and unjustified remarks undermine the self-image and self-confidence of the 50+ and this, in turn, can lower mental performance (Chapter 1). In this way, the gratuitous remarks can become self-fulfilling.

Yet such remarks are neither justified nor substantiated by our study of the ten components of applied thinking. With the exception of only one aspect, of only one of the ten components of applied thinking, we have found older brains to be superior to younger brains. Instead of mocking, society would be better harnessing the burgeoning brain power of the 50+ to aid its economic development.

In the UK, the 60+ already represent over 20 per cent of the population, rising rapidly to 30 per cent by 2030, but 60+ people appear in less than 8 per cent of media advertisements. Western media perpetuate insidious, belittling remarks like 'on the wrong side of 50', 'even though he is in his sixties he still...', '56 and still going strong'. The likely cumulative effect of such remarks is self-evident. Yet such belittling remarks about the 50+ are not universal. Travelling in Asian and African countries, such remarks are not evident.

This is not to be unrealistic about the limitations and cracks that appear with age. The Japanese treatment of old objects might provide a helpful metaphor: 'where possible, fill in cracks with gold'! To the Japanese, something that has age, experience and history is to be valued and enhanced, even when it has suffered some damage and the cracks are beginning to show. Given that one day we will all be old, to allow ageist remarks and jokes to go unchallenged is like Western turkeys voting for Christmas!

Perhaps, in the former Age of Brawn, or even in the more recent Age of Machine Minding, we were deeply afraid of becoming physically frail. Perhaps the sight of an elderly person reminded us of the inevitability of our own ageing, and maybe this made us anxious. One way to dispel anxiety is to joke or poke fun. But in the Age of the Brain, neuroscience equates age with increased thinking skill and increasing brain power. We no longer feel quite so anxious about getting old. We no longer need to manage our anxieties by poking fun at the elderly.

That is great news for our millennium babies, because they are expected to live to 120+. What would have been the point of them living an extra 30 years, if those 30 years were to be filled with derision and discrimination? There is far more to life than just staying alive.

So power up your 50+ brain and shine the light of your 50+ thinking skills on the problems that face us. Do not wait for great visions from great leaders. These are few. Put your faith in the light of your own thinking. Maintain the power of your 50+ brain and keep your thinking skills switched on. No darkness can ever extinguish light.

10 THINGS TO REMEMBER

1 The image of old age is full of stereotypes that are now out of date.

2 Patronizing remarks about older people are out of date.

3 Discrimination on the basis of age is just as unacceptable as other forms of discrimination.

4 Of the ten components of applied thinking, nine improve with age and the tenth can be improved by brain training.

5 Society needs to harness the burgeoning brain power of the 50+ to aid economic development.

6 In the UK, the 60+ already represent over 20 per cent of the population.

7 Perhaps, in the former Age of Brawn, or even in the more recent Age of Machine Minding, we were understandably afraid of becoming physically frail. In the Age of the Brain, neuroscience equates age with increased thinking skill and increasing brain power.

8 That is great news for our millennium babies, because they are expected to live to 120+. There is far more to life than just staying alive.

9 Increased thinking skill and increasing brain power will ensure that millennium babies are economically productive, and will not feel they are a burden. They will live full and varied lives, and will not feel lonely in the twenty-first century.

10 We now need the 50+ to shine the light of their superior thinking powers on some complex problems that are the unintended consequences of some good science, but poor thinking in the twentieth century. Credit crises, climate change, terrorism, nuclear proliferation and the disaffection of young people – these are complex problems and we are unwise to put our faith in great leaders to solve them, for leaders are easily corrupted by power. Complex problems require clear thinking, clearly expressed – these are the strengths of the 50+ brain.

Appendices

Appendix A: The hierarchy of applied thinking skills

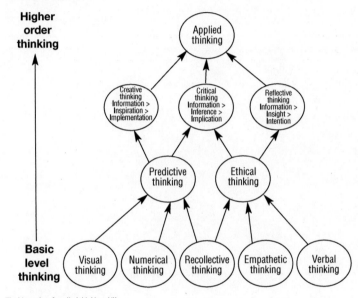

The hierarchy of applied thinking skills.
(from Train Your Brain, Horne and Wootton, 2010).

Appendix B: The model of applied thinking (the nine Is)

Process / Types of thinking	Inform *from*	Infer *via*	Imply *to*
Critical thinking	Information	Inferences	Implications
Creative thinking	Incubation	Inspiration	Implementation
Reflecting thinking	Incidents	Insights	Intentions

(Based on Train Your Brain, *Horne and Wootton, 2010).*

Appendix C: The process of applied thinking

The process of applied thinking.
(*from* Train Your Brain, *Horne and Wootton, 2010*).

Appendix D: Unpacking critical thinking

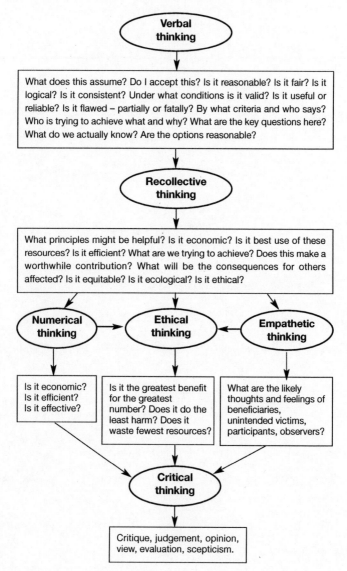

Verbal thinking

What does this assume? Do I accept this? Is it reasonable? Is it fair? Is it logical? Is it consistent? Under what conditions is it valid? Is it useful or reliable? Is it flawed – partially or fatally? By what criteria and who says? Who is trying to achieve what and why? What are the key questions here? What do we actually know? Are the options reasonable?

Recollective thinking

What principles might be helpful? Is it economic? Is it best use of these resources? Is it efficient? What are we trying to achieve? Does this make a worthwhile contribution? What will be the consequences for others affected? Is it equitable? Is it ecological? Is it ethical?

Numerical thinking → **Ethical thinking** ← **Empathetic thinking**

Is it economic? Is it efficient? Is it effective?

Is it the greatest benefit for the greatest number? Does it do the least harm? Does it waste fewest resources?

What are the likely thoughts and feelings of beneficiaries, unintended victims, participants, observers?

Critical thinking

Critique, judgement, opinion, view, evaluation, scepticism.

(from Train Your Brain, *Horne and Wootton, 2010).*

Appendix E: Unpacking creative thinking

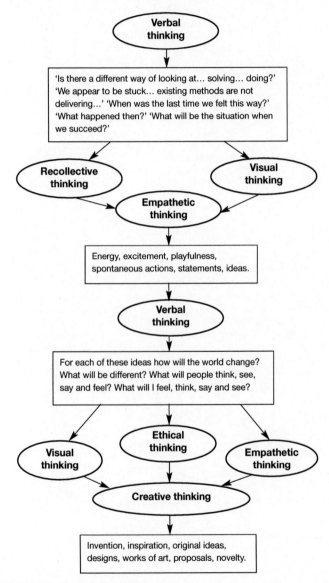

(from Train Your Brain, Horne and Wootton, 2010).

Appendix F: Unpacking reflective thinking

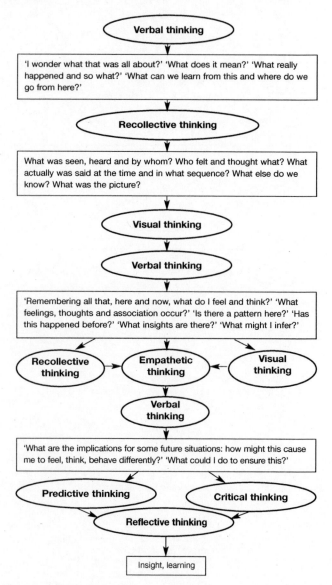

Verbal thinking

'I wonder what that was all about?' 'What does it mean?' 'What really happened and so what?' 'What can we learn from this and where do we go from here?'

Recollective thinking

What was seen, heard and by whom? Who felt and thought what? What actually was said at the time and in what sequence? What else do we know? What was the picture?

Visual thinking

Verbal thinking

'Remembering all that, here and now, what do I feel and think?' 'What feelings, thoughts and association occur?' 'Is there a pattern here?' 'Has this happened before?' 'What insights are there?' 'What might I infer?'

Recollective thinking   **Empathetic thinking**   **Visual thinking**

Verbal thinking

'What are the implications for some future situations: how might this cause me to feel, think, behave differently?' 'What could I do to ensure this?'

Predictive thinking   **Critical thinking**

Reflective thinking

Insight, learning

(from Train Your Brain, *Horne and Wootton, 2010).*

Appendix G: Do you think like a man (TMB) or do you think like a woman (TFB)?

Men score		Women score
	1 At the end of a hard day you prefer to:	
3	▷ talk to someone about your day	4
2	▷ listen to other people talking	2
0	▷ not talk at all	0
2	▷ None of the above	2
	2 Thinking about your spelling and writing:	
3	▷ You find both easy	4
2	▷ One is okay but not the other	2
0	▷ Both are weak	0
2	▷ None of the above	2
	3 In arguments you are most upset by:	
3	▷ a lack of response, silence or sulks	4
2	▷ a refusal to agree with you	2
0	▷ being contradicted or questioned	0
2	▷ None of the above	2
	4 On the question of routines, you prefer to do things:	
3	▷ whenever you feel like it	4
2	▷ according to a general but flexible plan	2
0	▷ about the same time every day	0
2	▷ None of the above	2
	5 When shopping you tend to:	
3	▷ buy special offers, frequently on impulse	4
2	▷ sometimes buy, sometimes don't	2
0	▷ purchase only what you went for	0
2	▷ None of the above	2
	6 You prefer to read:	
3	▷ fiction	4
2	▷ newspapers or general magazines	2
0	▷ specialist magazines or non-fictional information	0
2	▷ None of the above	2

(Contd)

Men score	7	You prefer to work:	Women score
3		▷ with a group of people you like	4
2		▷ on your own task but in the company of others	2
0		▷ in solitude	0
2		▷ None of the above	2

Men score	8	A friend has a personal problem:	Women score
3		▷ You can generally understand and sympathize	4
2		▷ You can usually explain why it's not so bad after all	2
0		▷ You usually give advice or suggestions on how to solve the problem	0
2		▷ None of the above	2

Men score	9	Today you meet more than seven new people. Tomorrow:	Women score
3		▷ you can picture at least seven of the new faces	4
2		▷ you could put some names to some faces	2
0		▷ you could remember names but not many faces	0
2		▷ None of the above	2

Men score	10	You cannot find your keys:	Women score
3		▷ You do something else until they turn up	4
2		▷ You try to do something else, but you're distracted by the loss	2
0		▷ You keep retracing your movements until you find them	0
2		▷ None of the above	2

Men score	11	When predicting what is going to happen:	Women score
3		▷ you use your intuition	4
2		▷ you rely on gut feelings to interpret relevant information	2
0		▷ you use trends based on historical statistics or other data	0
2		▷ None of the above	2

Men score	12	When you have heard a song:	Women score
3		▷ you can sing some of the words next time you hear the tune	4
2		▷ you can remember the tune but not the words	2

Men score			Women score
0		▷ you can vaguely remember the tune	0
2		▷ None of the above	2
Men score	**13**	You are listening to the radio or TV and the phone rings. Do you:	**Women score**
3		▷ just take the call and talk	4
2		▷ turn down the radio/TV and talk	2
0		▷ turn off the radio/TV, tell others to be quiet and talk	0
2		▷ None of the above	2
Men score	**14**	You need to reverse a vehicle into a tight spot to park it. Would you:	**Women score**
3		▷ look for another parking spot	4
2		▷ attempt to park, preferably with assistance	2
0		▷ just try to reverse in	0
2		▷ None of the above	2
Men score	**15**	In a place you are visiting for the first time:	**Women score**
3		▷ you would not know which way was north	4
2		▷ you could have a good guess which way was north	2
0		▷ you would know which way was north	0
2		▷ None of the above	2
Men score	**16**	A child's mechanical toy won't work:	**Women score**
3		▷ You can sympathize with the child and discuss how they feel about it	4
2		▷ You can find somebody else to fix it	2
0		▷ You will usually try to fix it	0
2		▷ None of the above	2
Men score	**17**	After a good film you prefer:	**Women score**
3		▷ to picture the scenes in your own mind	4
2		▷ to describe it to someone else	2
0		▷ to relate ideas or themes or lines from the film	0
2		▷ None of the above	2
Men score	**18**	When explaining or defining something:	**Women score**
3		▷ you often use a pencil, pen, paper or gestures	4
2		▷ you rely on verbal and non-verbal communication only	2

(Contd)

Men score			Women score
0	▷	you could define it clearly without repeating yourself	0
2	▷	None of the above	2
Men score	**19**	Asked to read a map:	**Women score**
3	▷	you would prefer some help	4
2	▷	you would have to turn it to face the way you were going	2
0	▷	you find it straightforward	0
2	▷	None of the above	2
Men score	**20**	When thinking about your forthcoming day:	**Women score**
3	▷	you often write a list	4
2	▷	you think about what you want to achieve that day	2
0	▷	you run through places and activities in your mind	0
2	▷	None of the above	2

If you are a man, add up your score under the men score column.

If you are a woman, add up your score under the women score column.

Most men we have tested scored less than 44.

Most women we have tested scored more than 40.

People with lower scores tended to use typically male brain (TMB) thinking skills. People with low scores were more likely to rely on logic, deduction, analysis and disciplined organization. The closer they were to zero, the more likely it was that they were good at making detailed plans. They tended to be less easily swayed by emotions and more objective when making decisions.

People with high scores tended to make more use of the thinking skills more frequently used by women. People with a higher score were more likely to be creative or artistic. They made greater use of intuition or gut feelings. They could think inductively, recognize patterns and identify and solve problems on the basis of less information. Men who scored closer to zero had great difficulties when in relationships, especially with women who scored nearer 80 and vice versa.

Mid range scores indicated people who had the ability, under many circumstances, to think either like a typically male brained (TMB) man, or like a typically female brained (TFB) woman. Such people seemed to perform well when working in groups, or when working as managers, especially where there were multi-factor problems to be solved and where novel solutions were needed.

Since we began our research in 1982, knowledge about the structure and working of the brain has exploded. This has helped us to infer that brain differences might account for the differences in the thinking and behaviour that we encountered. In turn, this has allowed us to examine some implications for the way we might behave more effectively when talking to, relating to, working with, or working for people of the opposite sex.

Appendix H: Oxytoxic indices

Baking

Crumble	28
Marzipan	30
Wholemeal pastry	32
Shortcrust pastry	35
Flaky pastry	38

Beans and lentils

Baked beans in tomato sauce	5
Broad beans	5
Cannellini beans	5
Chilli beans	5
Marrowfat peas	5
Tofu	5
Lentils	6
Mung beans	6
Red kidney beans	6
Aduki beans	8
Black-eyed peas	8
Chickpeas	8
Couscous	8
Cracked wheat	8

Biscuits

Orbit sugar free gum	10
Bubble gum	17
Ryvita	22
Jelly babies	22
Matzo	22
Jaffa cakes	26
Fig rolls	26
Heinz stem ginger	26
Wagon wheels	28
Carr's Water	29
Nice	30
Cream crackers	30
Ginger nuts	31
Cracker wheats	31
Rich Tea	32
Jammy Dodgers	32
Smarties	32
Custard creams	33
Croutons	33
Ritz	33
Cadbury choc chip	33
Chocolate digestives	33
Gypsy Creams	33
Club	33
Hobnobs	33
Shortbread	34
Dinky wafers	35
Milky Bar Buttons	36
Penguin	36
Cheddars	36
TUC	36
Cadbury Fingers	36
Yo-Yo Mint	36
Boasters	37
Cadbury Snack	37

Bread and cakes

Rye bread	10
Wholemeal roll	10
Soda scone	10
Pikelet/crumpet	13
Wholemeal bread	14
White roll	19
Swiss roll	19
Chapatis	20
Hot cross buns	20
Naan	22
Garlic bread	24
Jam tart	24
Chocolate roll	24
Treacle tart	24
Victoria sponge	24
Tortilla	25
Danish pastry	25
Cadbury gateau	25
Mince pie	25
Scotch pancake	25
Carrot cake	25
Almond slice	26
Chocolate chip	26
Lemon slice	26
Crunchy Bar cake	26
Frozen éclair	27
Iced cakes	27
Lemon curd tart	27
Brownies	28
Bakewell slice	30
Croissant	30
Battenburg	30
Éclair cake	32
Caramel shortcake	32
Flapjack	33
Fried bread	35
Milky Way cake	35

Breakfast cereals and bars

Porridge (water)	2
Porridge (milk)	6
All Bran	19
Muesli	19
Weetabix	22
Bran Flakes	22
Alpen (no sugar)	24
Fruit and Fibre	24
Nutrigrain	24
Cornflakes	25
Nutflakes	26
Alpen cereal	28
Coco Pops bar	30
Jordan's Maple Bran	30
Harvest Crunch	31
Rice Krispies bar	32
Tracker bars	36

Burgers, chips, fries and sauces

Cider vinegar	1
Tabasco	1
Coleman's mint sauce	1
Wine vinegar	1
Soy	3
Ross chip shop chips	5
Heinz tomato ketchup	7
Balsamic vinegar	7
Horseradish sauce	7
McCain's oven chips	8
HP Sauce	8
Dijon mustard	8
Veggie burger	9
Coleman's mustard	12
McCain's hashbrowns	13
McCain's microchips	14
Croquet potatoes	14
Baxter's mint sauce	19

Frozen chips	20	Gruyere	26
Meat burger	21	Cathedral City	27
Lea and Perrin's	22	Cracker Barrel	27
Tartare sauce	34	Shropshire Blue	27
BBQ sauce	40	Parmesan	27
		Stilton, blue	27

Butter/Margarine

Boursin 28

		Cambozola	28
Olivio spread 20%	18	Double Gloucester	28
Olivio olive oil	35	Mascarpone	28
Vitalite	40	Sage Derby	29
Flora	41		
Clover	43	**Chutney/pickles**	
Willow	47	Sauerkraut	1
Stork	48	Piccalli, Heinz	6
Lurpak	50	Tomato pickle, Heinz	7
Olivio spread 50%	50	Branston	10
		Mango, Burgess	19

Cheeses

Cook-in sauces/marinades

Cottage, low fat	5	Ross, casserole	1
Ricotta	9	Sharwood's, soy	1
Philadelphia, light	11	Dolmio, chicken and	2
Philadelphia, full	17	vegetable	
Feta	17	Dolmio, herb and red wine	2
Mozzarella	17	Homepride, Indian tomato	2
Cheddar, half fat	18	Ragu, basil and oregano	2
Camembert	19	El Paso, fajita	3
Gorgonzola	20	Homepride, balti	3
Heinz, reduced	20	Homepride, red wine	3
Processed slices	20	Homepride, tarragon	3
Stilton, white	23	Knorr, wine and onion	3
Goat's, soft	23	Uncle Ben's, blackbean	3
Roquefort	23	Lea and Perrin, chilli	4
Jarlsberg	24	El Paso, burrito	5
Danish blue	24	Homepride, sweet and sour	5
Edam	25	Knorr, Moroccan	5
Gouda	25	Sharwood's, oyster	5
Wensleydale	25	Batchelor's, cheese	25
Red Leicester	26		
Lancashire	26		

Coleman's, korma	30	
Bisto, cheese	33	
Bisto, parsley	33	
Bisto, white	34	
Knorr, fajita	40	
Knorr, five spice	40	
Knorr, Californian chicken	44	
Knorr, creamy ham	45	
Knorr, Jamaican jerky	45	
Knorr, tandoori chicken	46	
Knorr, herb chicken	51	

Crisps and nibbles

Poppadoms	24
Trail mix	29
Golden Rights	30
Twiglets	30
Walkers lite	30
Low-fat crisps	32
Kettle, cheddar	32
Golden Wonder	32
Doritos	33
Yogi peanuts/raisins	33
Quavers	34
El Paso tortilla chips	35
Walkers cheese and onion	36
Peanuts, roasted	40
Popcorn, plain	40

Dairy products

Soya milk	2
Skimmed milk	2
Fat-free yoghurt	3
Provamel rice	3
Fromage frais, fruit	3
St Ivel Shape 0%	3
Muller Light	3
Whole milk	4
Goat's/sheep's milk	4

Greek low-fat yoghurt	4
Plain, whole yoghurt	4
Goat's yoghurt	4
Greek sheep's yoghurt	6
Jersey milk	6
Yoplait drink	6
Muller Fruit Corner	7
Muller Thick and Creamy	7
Greek cow's yoghurt	9
UHT Elmlea single	10
Half cream	11
Sour cream	13
Single cream	13
St Ivel smoothie	13
Nestlé condensed milk	19
UHT Elmlea	23
Crème fraîche	25
Whipping cream	26
Nestlé evaporated milk	28
Double cream	33
Clotted cream, fresh	40

Desserts/Puddings

Tropical Juice Bar, Lyons	2
Jelly (water)	4
Sago, Ambrosia	5
Muller rice	5
Semolina, Ambrosia	5
Muller rice, fat-free	5
Rice, Heinz	5
Tapicoa, Ambrosia	5
Lemon sorbet, Carte D'or	5
Soft scoop, Walls	5
Custard, low-fat	5
Tapioca, semi-skimmed	6
Chocolate ice, Lyons	6
Semolina, semi-skimmed	6
Chocolate mousse, Heinz	6

Cornish ice, Lyons	6	Sour cream dips	24
Sago, semi-skimmed	6	Taramosalata	35
Rice, Ambrosia	6		
Napoli coffee	6	**Dressings**	
Light choc mousse, Cadbury	8	French, Kraft 3%	3
Trifle, Heinz	8	Blue cheese, Heinz	4
Rice pudding	9	1,000 Island, Kraft 5%	5
Cheesecake, Heinz	10	Caesar, Kraft 4%	6
Chocolate mousse, Cadbury	12	Mayonnaise light, Heinz	8
Trifle, Cadbury	18	Salad cream, Heinz	21
Bread pudding	19	1000 Island, Kraft	24
Cheesecake, McVities	20	Blue cheese	29
Christmas pudding	21	Hellmann's Basil	30
Tiramisu, McVities	22	French dressing	32
Sponge, Heinz	22	Baxter's Seafood	35
Bounty ice cream	22	Mayonnaise, Hellmann's	50
Blancmange, B&P	22	Mayonnaise, Heinz	50
Tapioca, Whitworth	23		
Profiteroles	24	**Drinks (alcoholic)**	
Semolina, Whitworths	24	Dry wine	4
Spotted dick, McVities	24	Wine white, sparkling	5
Ice cone mints, Lyons	24	Wine white, medium	5
Sago, Whitworth	24	Lager, Heineken	6
Magnum, Walls	24	Martini brandy	6
Meringue	24	Wine white, sweet	6
Rice, Creamola	25	Beer (500 ml)	9
Galaxy ice cream	25	Lager, bottled	10
Snickers ice cream	25	Sherry, Bristol Cream	10
Trifle, Mr Kiplings	26	Lager, Tennent's	10
Twix ice cream	27	Newcastle Brown Ale	11
Nestlé Smarties ice cream	28	Bacardi Breezer	12
Nestlé Milky Bar ice cream	30	Bacardi Breezer Twist	12
Angel Delight	30	Cider, dry	12
Dream Topping	46	Malt whisky	14
		Brandy	14
Dips/Dressed salads		Teacher's whisky	14
		Vodka	15
Primula, spicy Mexican	21	Cherry brandy	16
Primula, mango curry	22	Baileys	20
Primula, garnishes	23		

Grand Marnier	21
Cognac, Courvoisier	24
Cointreau	24
Strong ales	26
Cider, strong	37

Drinks

Special R, Robinsons	1
Diet cola	1
Fruit Break (no sugar)	1
Dietade	1
Libby R (no sugar)	1
7 Up Diet	1
Dandelion Topdeck	1
Pepsi Max or Diet	1
Tango light	1
Lucozade, low-calorie	1
Tea, PG Tips	1
Lemonade, Corona	1
Ribena Spark low	1
Lipton Tea	2
Cranberry, Britvic	3
All Juice lemonade	3
Citrus Spring	3
Grape Schloer	3
Tonic water, Schweppes	3
Lemonade 250, R Whites	3
Apple and Blackcurrant, Quosh	5
Lemonade 250, Barrs	5
Ovaltine	5
Apple juice, Robinsons	6
Coca Cola 200	7
Tango	7
Nescafé Gold Blend	7
Ginger ale, Britvic	7
Nescafé Decaffeinated	7
Irn-Bru	7
Pepsi 250	7

Nescafé Instant Espresso	7
7 Up 250	8
Horlicks	8
Ribena Spark	8
Bovril, chicken	8
Lucozade	12
Bovril, beef	12
Horlicks, skimmed milk	12
Nestlé Cocoa	20
Coffee syrups, caramel	21
Nesquik, chocolate	25
Nescafé Instant Cappuccino	26
Horlicks chocolate	26
Nesquik, strawberry	26

Eggs/Fish/Seafood

King prawn, Lyons	3
Tuna Italiana, Heinz	4
Prawn stir fry, Ross	4
Prawns, boiled	4
Seafood, Young's	4
Smoked haddock, Ross	5
Shrimps	5
Cod steak in butter, Ross	6
Fish pie	6
Tuna pasta Napolina	6
Cod in cheese, Birds	6
Salmon and Broccoli, Heinz	6
Fish steak with parsley	6
Cod, grilled	6
Eels, jellied	6
Mussels	6
Plaice, steamed	6
Tuna in brine	6
Cod, baked	6
Cod, poached	6
Haddock, smoked	6
Sole, steamed	6

Trout, Young's	6	Cod, fried in batter	16
Fish in tomato, Ross	8	Bacon bun	20
Seafood lasagne, Ross	8	Egg salad sandwich	20
Pilchards	8	Tuna sandwich	22
Swordfish, grilled	9	Pizza Express tortellini	23
Cod and chips, Ross	10	Cheese sandwich	23
Boiled egg	10	Pretzels, low-fat	26
Salmon, canned	10	Burger King Fries	27
Poached egg	10	Wimpy Bacon cheeseburger	30
Salmon, salted	10	Quarter pounder and cheese	31
Fish and Potatoes, Ross	12	Chargrilled chicken crisps	32
Kedgeree	12	Cheese and onion crisps	32
Omelette	12	McDonald's Big Mac	33
Herring, grilled	12	McDonald's Kingsize	37
Sole goujons, baked	12	Jacket skins	38
Sardines	12	McDonald's Big Breakfast	40
Tuna in oil	12	Pizza Hut garlic bread	41
Fried egg	12	Pizza Hut tomato bake	44
Mackerel	12	Pizza Express mushroom	44
Fish fingers, Birds Eye	12	Pizza Hut lasagne	44
Haddock, breaded	13	Pizza Express salad nicoise	48
Cod Crispy Crunch, Heinz	14	Pizza Express American hot	50
Skate in butter	14	Pizza Hut meat feast	64
Kippers	14	Pizza Hut mixed grill	64
Salmon, grilled	14		
Plaice, breaded	14	**Fruit**	
Fish cakes, Ross	16	Raspberries	1
Fish fingers in oil	16	Cranberries	1
Haddock Steak Crispy, Birds Eye	16	Rhubarb	1
Cod in batter, fried	16	Strawberries	1
Cod, breaded	16	Blackcurrants	2
Fish fingers, Ross	16	Melon	2
Prawns Hot, Lyons	18	Pawpaw	2
Omelette with cheese	18	Apricots	2
		Peaches	2
Fast foods/Snacks		Plums	2
		Blackberries	2
Toffee low-fat yoghurt	4	Damsons	2
Skate, fried in batter	11	Grapefruit	2
Chips, fried in oil	16		

Guavas	2	Peanut butter	41
Oranges	2	Hazelnut spread	45
Apples	3	**Meat and poultry**	
Grapefruit, tinned	3	Gammon, boiled	13
Kiwi	3	Beef topside, roast	16
Pineapple	3	Sausages	20
Mandarins, tinned	3	Rabbit, stewed	24
Nectarines	3	Turkey breast, grilled	25
Clementines	3	Pheasant, roast	26
Grapes	4	Bacon, grilled	28
Mango	4	Venison, roast	32
Gooseberries, stewed	5	Duck, roast	33
Prunes	5	Rump steak	33
Bananas	6	Lamb leg, roast	35
Dates	8	Chicken liver, fried	35
Figs	8	Lamb chops, grilled	35
Figs, dried	14	Calf liver, fried	36
Bananas, dried	14	Stewing steak	37
Dates, dried	16	Bacon, fried	40
Apricots, dried	16	Chicken breast, fried	41
Cherries	32	Bacon, microwaved	41
Coconuts	44	Bacon streaky, grilled	46
		Beef rib, roasted	50

Jams and spreads

De Ville spread, Heinz	7	Goose, roast	50
Raspberry spread	8	Large steak	60
Pineapple and ginger	9	**Oils and fats**	
Diet strawberry	10	Suet	35
Blueberry spread	10	Coconut	60
Diet marmalade	11	Palm	60
Diet raspberry jam	11	Vegetable	60
Blackberry jelly	14	White Flora	60
Apricot jam	17	Corn	60
Blueberry jam	17	Sunflower	60
Blackberry jam	17	Wheat germ	60
Honey	18	Olive	60
Nutella	36	Soya	60
Chocolate nut spread	36	Crisp and dry	60
Cashew butter	40	Lard	60

Pasta

Fresh tomato and basil	3
Fresh pesto	3
Heinz spaghetti	3
Heinz spaghetti hoops	4
Heinz ravioli	5
Heinz spaghetti bolognaise	6
Wholemeal spaghetti	7
Fresh spaghetti	9
Fresh lasagne	10
Ravioli	11
Pesto in jar	28

Pizza and pies

Veggie sausage roll	17
Cheese and tomato thin	18
Fray Bentos chicken and mushroom	20
Napolina bases	20
Steak pie	20
Pork and vegetable pie	23
Pork pie	24
Quiche, cheese and egg	24
Sausage rolls	26
Tyne steak and kidney	30
Fray Bentos steak and mushroom	30
Fray Bentos steak and ale	32
Tyne meat and veg	38
McCain's cheese and veg	40
Tyne meat and potato	40
Yorkshire pudding	40
Ross chicken and veg	50
Ross beef and onion	50
Ross giant pastie	50
Ross vegetable pie	50
Fray Bentos steak and kidney	60
Game pie	70

Ready meals

Ross sizzling prawn	2
Tyne vegetable curry	4
Heinz tortellini	4
Heinz vegetable hot pot	5
Tyne chicken stew	5
Heinz chicken tikka	5
Ross vegetable bake	5
Heinz chilli pots	5
Tyne beef casserole	6
Tyne cheese and potato	6
Heinz bolognaise	6
Findus spicy lasagne	6
Tyne beef curry	6
Ross Caribbean chicken	6
Ross paella	6
Heinz chicken korma	7
Tyne stew	7
Tyne chilli con carne	7
Birds vegetable rice	7
Findus chicken curry	8
Uncle Ben's wholegrain rice	9
Egg fried rice	14
Birds spicy chicken	16
El Paso burrito	19
Birds glazed chicken (0% fat)	22
Birds roast pork	22
Dolmio five cheese tortellini	22
Heinz beef lasagne	22
Birds roast lamb	24
Birds chicken curry	31
Birds chicken and rice	32
Birds chilli chicken	32
Samosa, vegetable	32
Birds spaghetti bolognaise	35
Birds beef curry	35
Birds roast turkey	36

Birds chicken tandoori	37
Birds mustard chicken	40
Samosa, meat	40
Heinz chicken mexicano	67

Snacks

Knorr cheese & ham snackpot	6
Chicken & prawn snackpot	6
Knorr tikka masala pasta break	6
C&B spicy tomato snackpot	6
C&B curry pasta snackpot	6
Findus chicken & broccoli snackpot	7
Heinz chicken tikka sandwich	12
Chicken & sweetcorn pot noodle	24
Nice and cheesy pot pasta	25
Kraft cheese lunchable	27
Chicken & mushroom pot noodle	29
Batchelors beef supernoodles	30
Batchelors chicken supernoodles	30
Chow mein supernoodles	30
Batchelors curry supernoodles	30
Sausage & tomato pot noodle	30
Sweet & sour supernoodles	30
Batchelors mushroom supernoodles	30
Batchelors balti supernoodles	30
Chow mein pot noodle	31

Soups

Baxter's beef consommé	1
Baxter's French onion	1
Campbell's mushroom	1
Heinz chicken noodle	1
Heinz parsnip and carrot	1
Baxter's carrot and chicken	2
Baxter's cock-a-leekie	2
Baxter's garden soup	2
Heinz lentil soup	2
Baxter's royal game	3
Baxter's highland broth	3
Baxter's spring parsnip	3
Campbell's asparagus	3
Heinz big beef broth	3
Heinz cream of chicken	3
Heinz leek and bacon	3
Heinz thick soups	3
Baxter's cajun	4
Campbell's cream of mushroom	4
Heinz cream of tomato	4
Knorr French mushroom	4
Knorr chicken noodle	20
Knorr French onion	20
Knorr chinese tomato	22
Knorr potato and leek	24
Knorr golden vegetable	26
Knorr carrot and coriander	26
Knorr tomato and red pepper	27
Knorr cream of tomato	29
Crofter's chicken and leek	30
Knorr cream of chicken	37

Sugar and sweets

3 squares dark chocolate (75% cocoa)	4
Meridian maple syrup	18
Tate & Lyle golden syrup	21
Boiled sweets	21
Refreshers	25
Polo mints	26

Tunes	26	Bisto, chicken gravy	26
Cravens limes	26	Whitworth, sage/onion	26
Mint imperials	26	Oxo, lamb/mint	27
Murray mints	26	Knorr, basil	32
Tate & Lyle demerara	27	Perfect garlic	37
Tate & Lyle granulated	27		
After Eights	27	**Toppings**	
Creme Eggs	29	Heinz chicken and mushroom	3
Double Decker	30	Heinz cheese, ham and pepper	6
Milky Way	30	Primula pizza cheese top	30
Mars Bar	30		
Aero	31	**Vegetables**	
Crunchie bar	31	Artichoke, globe	1
Rolo	31	French beans	1
Walnut Whip	32	Cabbage	1
Bounty bar	32	Celeriac	1
Fruit and nut chocolate	32	Fennel	1
Maltesers	33	Leeks	1
Snickers	34	Mushroom, boiled	1
Blue Riband	34	Okra (ladies' fingers)	1
Cadbury Buttons	35	Onions, boiled	1
Galaxy	35	Peppers	1
Yorkie bar	35	Spinach	1
Toblerone	35	Turnip	1
Terry's Chocolate Orange	35	Cherry tomatoes	1
Flake	36	Tomatoes, tinned	1
		Runner beans	1
Stock cubes/Stuffing		Broccoli	1
Tomato purée	5	Spring greens	1
Burgess gravy	5	Celery	1
Paxo, sage/onion stuffing	8	Courgettes	1
Paxo, thyme stuffing	10	Lettuce	1
Bovril	11	Swede	1
Knorr, chicken	15	Carrots	1
Bisto, original	16	Chicory	1
Marmite	16	Cucumber	1
Oxo, vegetable	17	Radish	1
Oxo, beef	21	Beetroot	2
Paxo, golden crumbs	24		

Corn, canned	2	Potatoes, baked	9
Ginger root	2	Cassava	10
Water chestnut	2	Mushroom, fried	10
Cauliflower	2	New potatoes, roasted	10
Kale	2	Avocado	12
Asparagus	2	Sundried tomatoes	14
Mangetout	2	Okra, stir fried	18
Broad beans	3	Aubergine in oil	20
Peas frozen	4	Onions, fried	20
New potatoes, boiled	4	Mushrooms, dried	20
Parsnips	4	Artichoke, Jerusalem	23
Peas	5	Garlic paste	28
Sweet potatoes	5		
Garlic	6	**Vegetarian**	
Potatoes and milk, mashed	7	Rice dream	4
Yam	7	Quorn	6
Corn, boiled	7	Burgers, Linda McCartney	8
Olives in brine	7	Soya milk	12
Peas, mushy	7	Cornish pasty	14

The figures in these tables are a relative index and intended only to inform your own choices. They are based on UK government data published by HMSO (the Composition of Foods Summary). In European countries consumers can check latest manufacturers' labels for up-to-date values of the energy (joules) content of processed foods.

Appendix I: ORAC scores

The US Department of Agriculture compared the ORAC scores of well-known brain foods like spinach, blueberries and broccoli, with dark chocolate. (ORAC scores measure the concentration of flavonoid antioxidants in foods.)

Broccoli	890
Sprouted alfalfa	930
Plums	949
Sprouts	980
Raspberries	1,220
Spinach	1,260
Strawberries	1,540
Kale/Cabbage	1,770
Blackberries	2,036
Blueberries	2,400
Dark chocolate	13,120

Eat 4 oz of fish a week, either as one meal or keep snacking on, for example, a smoked mackerel.

Appendix J: Some brain recipes

1 Brain booster morning drink (Oxytoxic Index – 4 per drink)
Ingredients:

> 2 cups of blanched sliced almonds
> 2 cups of soya milk
> 3 drops of vanilla essence
> 8 peaches (fresh if cheap and in season, if not then tinned in juice not syrup)
> 1 tablespoon of honey (e.g. Manuka)
> 4 tablespoons of low-fat yoghurt (preferably Greek)
> 8 ice cubes

Method: Blend from chilled ingredients and serve cold.

2 Beef up your brain stew (Oxytoxic Index – 6 per portion)
Ingredients:

> *500 g stewing beef, diced (solid white fat removed)*
> *130 g chopped onion*
> *1 tablespoon of olive oil (less if using a non-stick pan)*
> *30 g wholemeal flour*
> *500 ml water or stock*
> *150 g carrots, chopped, plus any other left over root vegetables*
> *½ teaspoon of salt, ½ teaspoon of pepper, 1 teaspoon of turmeric*

Method: Brown and seal the meat and onions. Add the flour and stir for 1 minute. Add water (or stock), vegetables and seasoning and put in the oven for 2 hours at 180°.

3 Cognitive cauliflower cheese (Oxytoxic Index – 6 per portion)
Ingredients:

> *25 g olive oil*
> *1 small cauliflower (700 g)*
> *100 g strong cheese (preferably soft not solid)*
> *100 ml water*
> *20 g wholemeal flour*
> *250 ml skimmed milk*
> *½ level teaspoon of salt*
> *black pepper to taste*

Method: Boil the cauliflower until it will just break into florets. Drain, and save 100 ml of the water. Make a white sauce from the oil, flour, milk and water. Add three-quarters of your cheese to the white sauce and pour over the cauliflower. Top with the remaining cheese and brown under a grill or in a hot oven at 220°.

4 Cerebral casserole (Oxytoxic Index – 3 per portion)
Ingredients:

> *240 g potato plus 120 g each of carrot, onion, swede, parsnip – all diced*
> *90 g tinned sweetcorn*

90 g frozen peas
90 g chopped tomatoes
450 g tinned tomato
1 teaspoon of Marmite

Method: Stir into a casserole dish, cover and cook for 1 hour at 190°.

5 Neuronal fish pie (Oxytoxic Index – 6 per portion)
Ingredients:

200 g cooked white fish, e.g. coley
100 g mashed potato
150 g semi-skimmed milk
15 g olive oil
15 g wholemeal flour
½ level teaspoon of salt

Method: Make a white sauce and mix it with the flaked fish. Put the mashed potato round the edge of the casserole dish and pour in the fish and sauce. Brown in the oven at 200° for 30 minutes.

6 A fresh-ideas fruit salad (Oxytoxic Index – 2 per portion)
Ingredients:

2 tablespoons of lemon juice
1 small apple, cored and cubed
1 medium pear, cored and cubed
1 can/220 g grapefruit segments, in grapefruit juice
1 can/220 g mandarin orange segments, in natural juice

Method: Pour the lemon juice into a bowl, add the apple and pear and swirl to coat. Add the grapefruit and mandarin segments (including all juice), gently stir to mix. Pop in the fridge until ready to serve.

(Thanks to HMSO and Sayaka Mitsuhashi of the Okinawa Centenarian Centre.)

Image credits

Front cover: © Stankevich

Back cover: © Jakub Semeniuk/iStockphoto.com, © Royalty-Free/Corbis, © agencyby/iStockphoto.com, © Andy Cook/iStockphoto.com, © Christopher Ewing/iStockphoto.com, © zebicho – Fotolia.com, © Geoffrey Holman/iStockphoto.com, © Photodisc/Getty Images, © James C. Pruitt/iStockphoto.com, © Mohamed Saber – Fotolia.com

Notes

Notes

Notes

Notes

Notes

Notes

Notes

Notes

Notes